MANIPULATION TROUGH

DARK PSYCHOLOGY

MIND CONTROL TECHNIQUE

BY

Craig Cialdini

instructions contained therein is the total, and absolute obligation of the user addressed.

The author is not obliged, directly or indirectly, to assume civil liability for any restoration, damage, or loss resulting from the data collected here. The respective authors retain all copyrights not kept by the publisher.

The information contained herein is solely and universally available for information purposes. The data is presented without a warranty or promise of any kind.

The trademarks used are without approval, and the patent is issued without the trademark owner's permission or protection.

The logos and labels in this book are the property of the owners themselves and are not associated with this text.

What is body language?

Body language is a non-verbal expression that includes body activity. "Operation" may also be referred to as body language, an entirely non-verbal means of communication. People in the office can share a great deal of knowledge without speaking; by non-verbal contact. Not all of our principles, opinions, feelings, and goals are orally expressed. Any of these are conveyed non-verbally in the current conversation. In Non-verbal communication, our human body communicates our thoughts and actions through conscious and unconscious emotions and postures, followed by gestures, facial expressions, eye contact, and touch. Collectively, this forms a distinct vocabulary of the body within the context of an active conversation. It's called Body Language.

How does the body speak?
Our human body communicates through conscious and unconscious emotions and actions, hand gestures, facial expressions, eye movements, and contact. Any of these bodily motions of the body parts may be used as individual terms and could be understood differently by other human beings within a specific framework of contact.

Importance of body language
Since perceptions of body language vary from people to people and cultures in different countries, it is interesting to learn about them. The body language alone is 55% of the overall speech, while the spoken word is 7%, and the voice tone is 38%.

Importance of body language in public speaking
Why is body language so important? You may tell that having the wrong body language means that your talk will hardly be a victory. You need a lot of talent for other things to make up for poor body language. Examples of poor body language include: turning your back to the crowd, jumping around too often, or standing behind a table. Effective management may harm your speaking, also. Becoming overly loud in your movements, drumming your fingers, or even chewing your nails is poor examples. But even if you're not doing a bad job, improving your body's language can significantly impact. The audience receives your speaking, particularly on the way. It can make a distinction between chatting politely and persuading people. That's why everyone needs to pay attention to that.

What kind of thing to pay close attention to?

Better body language means that you pay attention to various things. For example, you need to know how to walk, where to look, where to stay, and what movements to make.

Looking at the crowd

Are you looking at your audience? Or are you one of those commentators who prefer to gaze at the screen behind you? Are you paying attention to your whole audience and not just a few lucky ones?

Where are you on stage?

As a presenter, you need to know where you're on track. It means you've got to think about where you're going to go in a group debate and whether to (not) move around.

Happy vs. sad

What idea are you going to get through with your body? Are you displaying your happiness? Why are you upset about that? This is focusing on the viewers.

Significance of facial gestures: are you laughing?

Did you know, for example, that smiling makes people more relaxed as a speaker with you? In public speaking, facial expressions are highly significant. The way you smile says a lot about how you feel and your speech. At the same time, you don't want to be laughing at a sad story. Your facial expressions should be in line with your narrative.

Types of body language
What kinds of body language can be differentiated?

The body language is generally separated into two parts.

1. Parts of the body

2. Purpose of creating

So, what styles can be included in each category of people?

Parts of the body included
From head to foot, here are classes for body parts:

- Head-Movement and turning of the head, front to back, right to left, side to side, including tossing the heads.

- The facial gestures-The face has several muscles (anywhere between 54 and 98, depending on who you ask) that move many parts of the face. Every variation of gestures of the following facial elements expresses the state of mind:

- Eyebrows, raised, down, scowling.

- Eyes-Left, right, up, down, grinning, eye tapping.

- Nose-Wrinkle (at the top) and twitching of the nostrils.

- Lips-Smiling, snarling, puckering, licking, opening, closing.

- Tongue-In, back, flipped, tip-up or down, licking the lips.

- Mouth-Open, locked, clinked, lower jaw left, or right.

- Body Posture-The way you position your body and arms and legs in comparison to each other and someone else:

- Body proximity-How far or near to someone.

- The motions of the shoulder-up, down, standing, hunched.

- Positioning of arms-up, down, bent, upright.

- The positioning of legs and knees-straight, bent, placing of weight, knees against a talking partner or pointing somewhere, slipping feet.

- Hand and finger gestures-The way you handle and move your hands and fingers is exceptionally informative in the reading of people.

- Handling and positioning of items (e.g., markers, documents, etc.). -The weird one out of here. Technically not a body part, but objects play a significant role in body language interpretation.

Intentions

Another way to organize the forms of body language is by Intent:

- Voluntary / Intentional motions-usually referred to as "expressions." These are the gestures you were trying to make, like raising a hand, offering a finger, blinking with one eye.

- Repetitive movements-usually referred to as "tells," but "ticks" often fall under this group. Anybody activity you don't have any control overcomes in this range. Although there is theoretically no movement of the muscle, sweating still appears.

Voice tone

Though generally used as body language, the tone of voice and pronunciation is different from the body language.

For the sake of completeness, below are the classes that can be contained in the tone of voice:

- Voice pitch-high, medium voice, intonation.

- Loudness-Everything from yelling to moaning.

- Breathing-Slow, rapid breathing, shaky voice.

Gestures of body language

"It is the expressive movements of a part of the body, particularly of the hands or heads."

- It has a critical impact as a component of oral speech.

- A person's expression conveys much more than he says.

- The wave of a hand to signify goodbye or to attract a person's attention.

- Shaking hands are demonstrating affection.

- Shrugging of the shoulders shows ignorance and unconcern.

- The index finger shows an accusation or claim.

- The thumbs-up symbol shows that you like "Good Luck."

Postures body language

- Means "the body's behavior or position."

- Each action of the body has expressive and protective functions.

- The way we sit, stand, and walk out shows us a lot about ourselves.

- Well, a strong stance shows a positive attitude.

The body language of movements
Expression of the face

- All facial organs on the human face suggest a descriptive facial message.

- Hair, forehead, eyebrows, eyes, chest, jaw, nose, neck, ears, teeth, tongue, etc.

- Facial gestures come spontaneously and are thus beyond the influence of the speaker.

Examples of facial gestures

- The expression reflects love and appreciation.

- The lifted eyebrows express surprises.

- A furrowed brow reflects concern and fear.

- Frown indicates annoyance or mistrust.

Appearance and dressing

- The type of dress we wear and the way we style ourselves to demonstrate our value and mood.

- We've affected how others pose and what they wear.

- Physical appearance plays a significant part in our perception of individuals.

- People's clothing and personal appearance express a lot of details about them.

Eyes contact

- Eye contact has a lot to do with face-to-face conversation.

- Lack of eye contact indicates a loss of confidence and comprehension.

- We look more quickly rather than listening or communicating.

- The eyes are human portals, except that there is no existence.

- The speaker would look in the audience's eyes from right to left and from left to right, building confidence and reducing nervousness.

- Construct the relationship between the speaker and the audience.

Silence

- "Talking is silver, but silence is gold."

- It points out the relationship between the communicators.

- Moments of silence – You don't know how to keep going.

Modulation of speech

- The speaker must make fair use of his voice.

- Someone needs to be a successful speaker; a strong speaker is a must.

- A strong voice is a blessing of God.

- One should take phonetics lessons to develop one's voice.

More examples of body language

Arms folded in front of the chest. This is one of the instances of body language that shows that one is defensive. The body language indicating crossed arms can often indicate dissatisfaction with the views and actions of other people with whom you speak.

Nail-biting

This example of body language suggests that one is lost in thinking, possibly thinking something. You can be in deep focus while your hand is on your cheek, and your brows are furrowed.

Finger taping or playing drums

This behavior reveals that while waiting, one is growing strained or anxious.

Touching your nose

Touching or scratching your nose means indifference, dismissal, or lying about something.

The consequence of rubbing your hands

This may indicate that your hands are cold, which may mean that you're anxious about something, or you're ready to wait.

Attempting to put fingertips together

This is called "steepling" or bringing fingertips together to show power or authority.

Open hands, face upwards

The gesture is a symbol of integrity, loyalty, and innocence. This is how some people show respect and obedience.

Head in your hands

The body language of this expression may be one of frustration, be angry, or be embarrassed because you don't want to expose your face.

Locking the ankles

When you're seated or standing, while your ankles are closed, you express anxiety or nervousness.

Stroking your cheeks or your mustache

This expresses when one is immersed in thought. This behavior is always performed unintentionally as one attempts to come up with a decision.

Pulling the ear

Pulling an ear lobe may mean that you're trying to make a choice, but you're always indecisive about anything.

Picking of Lint

Catching an imagined lint is another example of the body language of displacement movements, which one uses to demonstrate criticism of the actions or views of others. This gesture lets one turn away from the other when performing some meaningless gesture.

Posture of Catapult

This seated version of the "Hand-on-Hip" male poster, with the hands behind the head and the elbows sticking out, is used to threaten or show a relaxed attitude. This provides a false sense of protection before an attempt is made.

Lower head

This means that one of us is hiding something. You may display shyness, embarrassment, or timidity when you lower your head when you are praised. It can also express that you keep a distance from another person, show skepticism, or think about yourself.

Body language tips

The healthy language of the body may be trained. You will do this by rehearsing or preparing in front of your peers. You must be vigilant of the training in front of the Mirror. The rugged use of body language plays a vital role in the conversation. Many of our verbal training courses have an element of body language to them. Here are ten tips for functional body language that we've learned from coaching teams worldwide over the past two decades.

1. Assume a power pose to raise your confidence

Study at Harvard, and Columbia Business Schools demonstrates that merely keeping the body in spacious, "high-powered" positions (leaning back with the hands behind your head and feet up on your desk, or standing with your legs and arms widely open) for as little as two minutes induces higher levels of testosterone. A hormone-related to strength and dominance and lower levels of cortisol, a stress hormone. Try this when you are threatened. However, you want to be confident. In addition to triggering behavioral changes in both males and females, these poses contribute to increased feelings of dominance and enhanced risk perception. The study also showed that people are more frequently affected by how they feel about you than what you think.

2. To maximum benefit, look like you're listening

If you want people to strike up a conversation, don't think about multitasking when chatting. Avoid the temptation to check your text messages, check your watch, or check how the other participants respond. Instead, concentrate on those who speak by rotating the head and body to face them squarely and making eye contact. Bending forward, smiling, and tilting your head are other non-verbal ways that indicate you're involved and paying attention. It's essential to understand people. It's almost as necessary to make sure they know that you're listening.

3. To foster cooperation, eliminate barriers
Physical obstructions are incredibly harmful to cooperative efforts. Take out something that blocks your vision or establishes a bridge between you and the rest of the team. Particularly after a coffee break, be mindful that you can create a shield by keeping your cup and saucer in a way that appears to obstruct your body or pull you hidden from others purposely. A senior executive told me that he could measure the satisfaction of his colleagues from how high they kept their cups of coffee. It was his finding that the most dangerous situations they saw, the higher they kept their coffee. People with their hands held at the waist level felt more relaxed than those with high shoulders.

**4. Shake hands to communicate directly
      with others**
Touch is the most basic and robust non-verbal cue. Touch others on the arm, hand, or shoulder for as little as 1/40 of a second establishes a social connection. Physical touch and warmth are created in the office by a handshaking practice, and this physical interaction provides a permanent and optimistic feeling. Handshake research by the Income Center for Trade Shows found that people are twice as likely to recognize you if you shake hands with them. Researchers also observed that people respond to those they shake hands by being more open and welcoming.

5. Stimulating positive thoughts, smile
A real smile not only improves your sense of well-being; it also shows everyone around you that you are approachable, friendly, and honest. A genuine

expression gently comes out, crisscrosses the eyes, lights up the face, and eventually fades away. Most notably, smiling impacts explicitly how other people react to you. When you smile at others, they're almost always smiling in return. And, since facial gestures evoke similar emotions, the smile you get back really affects the mental state of the person positively.

6. Showing agreement, mirror gestures, and body movements

If customers or company partners unwittingly mimic your body language, it's their way of non-verbally saying that they like or agree with you. If you imitate other people intently, it can be an essential aspect of establishing relationships and developing feelings of mutuality. Mirroring begins by watching a person's face and body movements and then consciously making the body take on identical expressions and postures. Doing this would make the other person feel appreciated and accepted.

7. Using your hands to strengthen your voice

Brain Imaging has shown that a region called the Broca field, which is critical for speech development, is activated not only when we speak, but when we wave our hands. As the action is integrally connected to the voice, behaving when we say it will potentially enhance our thoughts.

8. Watch people's feet to find the facts

When people want to regulate their body language, they rely mostly on facial expressions, body postures, and hand/arm movements. Although the knees and the thighs are left hidden, they are often where the reality can most frequently be found. Under pressure, people also demonstrate nervousness and discomfort by increased foot movements. Feet are going to fidget, move, and wind around each other or the chairs. Feet rolls and twists to alleviate stress, or even kicks off in a miniaturized effort to escape free.

9. Keep your voice low to sound definitive

During a speech or a significant phone call, encourage the voice to calm at its highest pitch through holding the lips close and creating "um hum, hem hum, hem hum" sounds. And if you're a woman, note sure your voice doesn't raise at the end of the sentence as though you were posing a query or requesting permission. Instead, when you express your opinion, use the authoritative arc, where the voice begins on one line, increases in pitch through the phrase, then drops back down at the end.

10. Uncross your arms and legs to strengthen your memory

Body Language Researchers share an interesting finding from one of their studies. When a team of enthusiasts attended a lecture and sat with their arms and legs extended, they recalled 38% better than the community who participated and sat with their arms and legs folded. Uncross your arms and legs to boost your persistence. If you see the crowd showing aggressive body language, change tactics, take a rest, or ask them to move — and don't attempt to force them before their bodies open up.

If you follow these ten essential and useful body language tips, I guarantee that you can maximize your non-verbal effect on the workplace. To develop your leadership skills as a whole, try taking a course in communications.

How body language unveils feelings and ideas?

Body language is an implicit expression of the mental state of an individual. An action or word may be a valuable link to a person's emotion at that moment. For example, a man who is self-conscious about increasing weight may tug at the fold of the skin under his chin; a woman who is mindful of extra pounds on her thighs may loosen her dress; a female who feels nervous or insecure may fold her arms or cross her legs or both. The trick to interpreting body language can understand it. The mental state of a person when listening to what they are saying and mentioning the conditions in which they were you claim it. This helps you to distinguish reality from fantasy and fiction. In current years, humans have obsessed with the spoken word and our desire to be a conversationalist. Many citizens, however, are surprisingly ignorant of this.

Why Females are much more observant

When telling someone's 'perceptive' or 'sensitive' about others, we're unknowingly referring to their capacity to interpret the body language of another person and compare these signs with verbal signals. In other words, when we say that we have a 'hunk' or 'good feeling' that someone has told us a lie, we generally mean that their body language and their spoken words don't match. This is also what speakers call collective consciousness or group awareness. For, e.g., if the crowd is seated back in their chairs with their chins down and their arms crossed over their chest, a 'perceptive' speaker would get a hunch or sense that his speech was not going well.

He would understand that he wanted to take a new path to reach the crowd. Likewise, a speaker who wasn't 'perceptive' would have blundered. Overall, women are much more discerning than men, which has led to what is widely referred to as 'women's intuition.' Women have an inherent capacity to pick up and interpret non-verbal messages and a keen eye for specific information. That's why few husbands can lie to their wives and get away with it, and why, on the other hand, most women can pull the wool over the eyes of a man without considering it. A study by psychologists has found that women are much more attentive to body language than men. They displayed short scenes, with the sound switched off, of a man and a woman talking, and the participants were asked to interpret what was going on by analyzing the faces of the people. Analysis has found that women interpret the condition, precisely 87% of the time, while men are just 42% efficient.

Men in 'nurturing' professions, such as musical forms, acting, and nursing, did about the same thing as women; gay men even scored high. Women's intuition is especially apparent in people who have raised children. For the first few years, the mother depends nearly entirely on the non-verbal contact medium with the kid. This is why women are always more perceptive negotiators than men since they practice early reading of signs.

What the brain scans are revealing
Many people have a brain structure to connect to every man on the planet. Magnetic Resonance Imaging brain scans (MRIs) specifically demonstrate that women have a much better able to interact with and assess people than men do. Women have between 14 and 16 regions of the brain to determine the actions of others over the individual in four to six

areas. This illustrates how a woman will attend a dinner party and easily hear about the friendship of other partners at the table who has argued. It also illustrates why, from a woman's point of view, men don't seem to speak much, and, from a man's point of view, women never want to shut up.

The female brain is designed for multitasking — the average woman will juggle between two and four different subjects simultaneously. She will watch a TV show while chatting on the phone, then listen to a second chat behind her while drinking a cup of coffee. In one discussion, she will speak about multiple subjects and use five-voice tones to shift the issue or highlight points. Unfortunately, only three of these tones can be identified by most persons. As a result, men frequently lose their focus as women attempt to interact with them. Studies suggest that a person who depends on clear visual evidence face to face about the actions of another person is more likely to make more informed decisions about another person than someone who relies solely on their gut feelings. The proof is in the person's body language, and while women can do it consciously or unconsciously, everyone should train themselves to interpret the signs consciously. That's precisely what this book is about.

The Universal Gesture
The shoulder shrug is also a clear example of a common expression used to indicate that a person does not know or understand what you mean. It is multiple gestures with three main parts: open palms to show that nothing is hidden in the hands, hunched shoulders to shield the neck from attack, and raised brow, a standard, promiscuous greeting. Just as verbal language varies from culture to culture, confident body language signs can also vary.

Whereas one gesture may be familiar in a specific culture and may have a simple sense, it may be irrelevant in another culture or may have a different significance.

Three Rules of Successful Reading

What you see and hear in some situations does not generally reflect the actual behaviors that people may have. You need to obey three simple principles to get it right.

Rule1. Read the Cluster Expressions

One of the most significant faults that a beginner can make in body language is interpreting a single gesture in isolation from other movements or situations. For example, scratching your head can mean a variety of things – sweating, confusion, dandruff, fleas, forgetfulness, or deception – depending on the various movements that coincide. As every spoken language, body language includes vocabulary, phrases, and punctuation. The gesture is like a single word, and an available name may have many different meanings. For, e.g., in English, the term 'dressing' has at least ten implications, including the process of putting on clothes, the sauce for food, the stuffing for a chicken, the application for a cut, the fertilizer, and the grooming for a horse. It's when you place a word in a conversation of other words that you can completely understand its meaning. Gestures arrive in 'sentences' called clusters, which inevitably show the collections.

A body language cluster, much like a verbal sentence, has at least three words in it before each word can be clearly described. The 'perceptive' person is the one who can read body language sentences and balance them precisely to the person's verbal

38

corrections. So often look at the clusters of movements for an accurate interpretation. -Each of us has repeated signs that indicate that we're either bored or under pressure. Continual hair touching or twirling is a typical indication of this. However, in contrast to other movements, it is likely to indicate that the individual is insecure or nervous. People stroke their hair or head because that's how their mother comforted them when they were young.

To prove the argument regarding clusters, here is a typical the most Important Appraisal symbol is the hand-to-face gesture, with the index finger pointing up the cheek while the other finger is shielding the mouth and the thumb safeguarding the chin. Further confirmation that this person has severe feelings for what he sees is that the legs are near crossed, and the arm covers the body (defensive) while the head and the chin are down (negative/hostile). This body language 'sentence' means things like, 'I don't like what you're doing,' 'I disagree,' or 'I hold back bad emotions.'

Research indicates that non-verbal signals have about five times as much effect as verbal signals. When the two are incongruous, people, particularly women, rely on non-verbal messages and neglect oral information. If you as the speaker, were to ask the listener mentioned above to give his opinion about what you said, and he responded that he disagreed with you, his body language gestures would be compatible with his verbal statements. That is, they would fit. If he was to say that he agreed with what you said, he would be more inclined to lie because his vocabulary and actions would occur incongruously. If you see a politician standing behind a rostrum speaking proudly but with his arms near crossed over his chest (defensive). And head down (critical/hostile) while reminding his crowd how welcoming and open he is too young people's thoughts; would you be convinced? What if he wanted to reassure you of his warm, loving attitude when giving the lectern short, fast karate chops? Observation of the clusters of gestures and the compatibility of the verbal and body language sources are the keys to a detailed understanding of attitudes by body language.

Law 3. Read Legislation in context
The context in which they occur, all movements should be considered. For example, if someone was seated at the bus terminal with his arms and legs near crossed and head down, and it was a cold winter's day, that would most definitely mean he was freezing, not defensive. If the person used the same expressions when sitting across the table attempting to sell him a concept, product, or service, that may be accurately interpreted as implying that the person was feeling pessimistic or refusing the proposal. Throughout this book, all body language movements will be viewed in context, and, where possible, the clusters of actions will be analyzed. Why it may be simple to misread?

Everyone who has a soft or sloppy handshake — especially a man who is likely to be suspected of being frail. But if anyone has arthritis in their hands, they're more probably to use a gentle handshake to prevent the agony of a firm one. Likewise, artists, singers, surgeons, and others whose work is fragile and require their hands usually tend not to shake hands, although, if they are coerced into it, they can use a 'dead fish' handshake to shield their hands. Someone who wears inappropriate or tight clothes may not be able to use such gestures, which may influence their use of body language. For example, obese people cannot cross their legs. Women wearing short skirts will sit with their legs near crossed for safety, but this will make them look less open and less likely to be invited to dance in the nightclub. These conditions apply to a minority of individuals, but it is essential to recognize the effects that physical limitations or disabilities may have on the mobility of an individual.

Why children are easier to understand?
Older people are challenging to read than younger people, and they have less muscle tone in their mouths. The pace of specific movements, and how clear they appear to others, is often connected to the age of the person. For, e.g., if a five-year-old boy says a lie, he's likely to instinctively cover his mouth with one or both of his hands. The act of shielding the mouth will warn the parent to the falsehood, and this mouth-covering action is likely to occur for the life of the child, typically only differing in the pace at which it is performed. When a teenager says a lie, the hand is taken to the mouth in the same manner as a five-year-old. Except in the simple hand-slapping gesture above the mouth, the fingertips rub softly across it. In adulthood, the initial mouth-covering action becomes much more comfortable. When an adult says a lie, it's as if his brain instructs his hand to shield his mouth to hide the dishonest words, just as he did with the five-year-old and the teenager. But, at the last minute, the hand is drawn away from the mouth, and a nose-touch gesture is made. It's also the adult version of the mouth-covering motion that was used in childhood. This illustrates how, as people grow older, their movements get more involved and less noticeable, and that's why it's sometimes more challenging to understand the actions of a fifty-year-old than those of a five-year-old.

Can you fake body language?

We're asked daily, 'Can you have fake body language? 'The general response to this question is 'no' because of the lack of unity that is likely to exist between the significant movements, the micro-signals of the body, and the spoken words. For e.g., open palms are synonymous with sincerity, but when the faker holds out his hands and smiles at you as he tells a lie, his micro-gestures give him away. His eyes will widen, one eyebrow will raise, or the corner of his mouth will twitch, and these signs counter the open hand expression and the genuine smile. As a consequence, receivers, particularly women, tend not to believe what they hear.

How to Become a Good Reader?

Set aside at least 15 minutes a day to research the body language of other people and become conscious of your movements. A firm reading ground is where people meet and connect. The airport is a mostly right place to experience the full continuum of human expressions. People freely communicate their eagerness, rage, sadness, pleasure, impatience, and many other emotions by body language. Group events, corporate meetings, and gatherings are similarly fantastic. Television also provides a great way to read. Switch the volume off and try to visualize what's going on by seeing the image first. By turning the volume on every few minutes, you'll be able to check how correct your non-verbal readings are, and, before long, you'll be able to see the whole show without any volume and understand what's going on, just as deaf people do.

Learn to interpret body language cues not only make you more consciously aware of how others are trying to control and exploit. It helps you understand that others are sometimes doing the same thing to us, and, most critically, it allows us to be more open to other people's thoughts and emotions. We also observed the rise of a new type of social scientist-the Body Language Watcher. Even as a bird watcher likes to keep birds and their actions, so the Body Language Watcher delights in observing the non-verbal signs and gestures of human beings. He watches them at social events, on the beaches, on tv, in the workplace, or wherever people communicate. He is a relational student who needs to learn about the behaviors of his fellow people so that he can potentially learn more about himself and how he can strengthen his interaction with others.

How to Detect Transparency?

If people try to be vulnerable or honest, they always hold one or both palms out to the other person and say something like, 'I didn't do that! I'm sorry if I offended you,' or 'I told you the truth.' If anyone tries to open up or be honest, they are likely to show any or half of their palms to the other person. As other body language gestures, this is an implicit expression that gives you a 'natural' impression or a hunch that the other person tells. When children lie or try hiding something, they frequently cover their hands behind their backs.

Similarly, a man who wants to cover his whereabouts after a night out with the boys may hide his hands in his pockets, or an arm-crossed pose, explaining to his wife where he was. But hidden palms can give her an innate feeling that she's not telling the truth. A woman who is trying to hide something will try to avoid a topic or chat about a variety of unrelated issues while doing different other activities at the same time. Salespeople are trained to watch the customer's uncovered palms as they give excuses or protests as to why they can't purchase a commodity.

When anyone offers legitimate reasons, they usually reveal their hands. When people are open to justify their reasoning, they use their hands and show their eyes, when someone who isn't telling the truth is likely to give the same verbal explanations, just to hide their hands. Holding their hands in their pockets is a favorite item of men who don't want to take part in a conversation. Initially, the palms were like the vocal cords in body language, so they were more 'talking' than any other body part, and holding them away was like having one's mouth shut.

The Five C of the Body Language

Body language is like a machine. We all know what it is, but most of us never know precisely how it operates. That's because the method of obtaining and transmitting non-verbal messages is always performed without our conscious consideration. Human beings are genetically designed to check for signals of facial and actions and to grasp their significance rapidly. We see a gesture from another, and we immediately judge the purpose of that motion. And we've been doing it for a long, long time. As humans, we learned how to acquire friends and influence people — or avoid those we couldn't be friends with — long before we understood how to use expressions. Our ancestors took survival choices based entirely on the complex pieces of visual knowledge they obtained from others. There is a world of knowledge that you can discover about people by actually watching how they use their bodies to give non-verbal signals. But to interpret these signals exactly, you need to stop the automated decision mechanism and evaluate the experiences. To understand its true significance, body language needs to be learned in context, interpreted in groups, analyzed for continuity with what is spoken, measured for continuity, and screened for cultural factors.

Filter the first experience

Non-verbal cues play a vital role in allowing us to make brief observations. Our ability to do this is one of our fundamental survival instincts. At the same time, our brains are hard-wired to react immediately to such non-verbal stimuli. This mechanism was set up a long time ago when our ancient ancestors faced risks and obstacles that were very different than those we face in today's modern society. Today, life is more complicated, with layers of social constraint and ambiguous interpretations added to the intricacy of our interpersonal relations. This is particularly true in the workplace, where organizational culture adds its complexities — a diverse collection of constraints and behavioral rules. Although first observations cannot always be right, you may enhance the ability to read someone's body language by going through the five C's: context, clusters, correspondence, consistency, and culture.

Context

Imagine this situation: a cool winter evening with light snowfall and a north blowing wind. You see a lady you know she's a co-worker sitting on a bench at a bus station. Her head is down, her eyes are closely closed, and she's slumped, trembling slightly and hugging herself. Now the scene changes: the same woman is in the same physical role. And instead of sitting outside on a bench, she's lying behind her desk in the office next to yours. Her body language is the same: head down, eyes closed, slumped over, shuddering, and hugging herself. The non-verbal signs are the same, but the current environment has changed your interpretation of those signs. She's gone from informing you in a flash, "I'm so cold! "To say," I am in pain. The sense of non-verbal communication varies as the context shifts. As in real estate, location counts. We can't try to grasp the actions of others without understanding the conditions in which the behavior happened. As our example shows, the message sent by that woman's body language shifted drastically based on whether she was seated outdoors in the cold or alone in her office. And certain conditions need more formal actions that may be viewed quite differently in some other environment.

When people communicate, a lot of the context is dictated by their interaction. The same man talking to a customer, a supervisor, or a manager will have a very different body language. Duration of day, assumptions based on previous experiences, and when contact takes place in a private or public setting — all these factors form the context in which body language happens. They need to be taken into account when determining significance. The key is to evaluate if non-verbal conduct is relevant to the context in which it happens. Dave and Diane, for example, have been friends and coworkers for years. As such, they stood next to each other, kept good eye contact, tapped each other on the shoulder, and always laughed during their discussions at the office. No one thought to comment on this before Diane revealed her relationship with another employee in the same organization. Equipped with that detail, the next time a colleague saw Dave and Diane laughing and enjoying each other's business. He said, "Careful now, and she's engaged. The background of the relationship had abruptly altered. Apparently, the non-verbal actions that Dave found acceptable when Diane was "alone" was now regarded as a potential issue.

Clusters

Non-verbal cues are a collection of gestures, postures, and behaviors that emphasize a common point in an expression cluster. A single gesture may have multiple meanings or indicate none at all (sometimes a cigar is just a cigar), but when you pair the single gesture with other non-verbal symbols, the meaning becomes clearer. An individual may cross his arms for a variety of reasons, but when a move is combined with a scowl, a headshake, and his legs turned away from you, you have a composite picture and a justification for inferring that he is resistant to anything you have just suggested. Always note to search for conduct clusters. The cumulative action of an individual is much more revealing than a particular gesture perceived separately. A smart person starts every meeting of workers by taking off his jacket, and he selects a chair in the middle of the conference table (not at the head). These actions alone would send a message of informality, but it is the rest of his movements that push the point home. Whenever anyone talks at the conference, the boss steps in with a look of curiosity on his forehead, smiles in agreement and gives the speaker full eye contact. Symbolically, this cluster of motions sets the tone for just what the discussion needs to be an open sharing of thoughts and questions.

Correspondence

Classic research reveals that the overall effect of a speech is based on 7% of the words used, 38% of the voice tone, and 55% of the facial expressions, hand movements, body posture, and other modes of non-verbal contact. You can't hear a human speak a foreign language and understand 93% of what is being conveyed. Even you can bet that when verbal and non-verbal channels of communication are out of balance, people — especially women — are likely to focus on non-verbal messaging and ignore verbal material. When feelings and actions are in tune, you see that they are substantiated in their body language. Their movements and actions are following what they mean. You may also see incongruity, where movements contradict words: a side-to-side headshake when saying yes or someone frowning and looking at the ground when telling you she's glad.

Consistency

You ought to know the basic actions of a person under comfortable or usually stress-free environments so that you can correlate them with the behaviors and movements that occur when the person is under stress. What's his usual way of looking about, sitting, standing while he's relaxed? How does he react when he addresses a non-threatening issue? Knowing someone's behavioral baseline strengthens the ability to detect major variations. One of the techniques employed by skilled police interrogators to diagnose dishonesty is to pose a set of non-threatening questions when watching how the person acts while there is no need to lie. Then, as more complicated group problems are approached, the officers look for shifts in non-verbal actions that suggest deceit at critical points. We all have trouble attempting to determine the consistency of someone we've just met.

Culture

This non-verbal interaction is informed by our cultural history, which is explored at length. Right now, it's important to realize that when reading body language, you should consider the levels of tension that the person is under. That's because the higher the emotional intensity, the more likely culture-specific expressions would pop up. Besides, body language is influenced by the various subcultures of which we are a participant—taking your pose, for example. Ballet dancers are taught to keep their bodies chest-forward, so you can always see them standing together with their heels and pointed toes (an adjusted first position). The most office staff are round-headed with a slight sag in their chests from hours spent hunched over their keyboards. Military forces also have a shoulder-back, spine-straight pose even after their service tour has finished. People from different parts of the same world can also use their bodies in a somewhat different way.

Take, for example, the rapidly changing pace of a modern New Yorker, and compare it with someone from the South's more relaxing gait. Note the possible variations in body language between a prototypically reserved and formal Young Englander and his more relaxed California counterparts. The more you know about a person's history, activities, and preferences, the more you can understand why those movements or postures are part of his particular repertoire — and why a break from these habits is important. Often people change their postures as they change topics. Remember the five Cs — context, clusters, correspondence, consistency, and culture — as you're reading through the rest of this book.

There is no question that people use non-verbal interactions to show their state of mind. Yet interpreting body language is not only about studying non-verbal signals; it is also about understanding how to get to the true meaning behind those signals.

"Manipulation" means that no matter what strategy you use to persuade others, you're manipulating them. Whenever you persuade someone to do what you're proposing other than what they want to do, you're influencing them. The term manipulation has many different interpretations, some of which can be perceived as disruptive. To impact someone or something is not evil in itself. It can only be harmful if it is meant to hurt someone or create problems. My use of the term deception is to be able to do the following thing:

- To regulate our behaviors, values, and attitudes through self-suggestion and self-hypnosis.

- To be able to manipulate with a degree of intensity to persuade others to come to our way of thought or doing something.

- To be able to place others in a position of benefit where the outcomes are a win/win for all the people concerned and are mutually agreeable.

The idea of using your sense of control to manipulate others is as ancient as our culture, without getting through all the details of Hypnosis, Trance Induction, Energy Modulation, etc. Here you will find an elementary description of what hypnotherapy and trance is and how you can use it.

Manipulation is fascinating, and motivational behavior. It's not manipulation, it's not just intimidation, and it's not really like deceit. It is a common phenomenon in nearly all areas of life. Politics, architecture, culture, and even intimate relationships. However, technical literature, which aims to resolve the difficulty of systematically characterizing and evaluating the very essence of the phenomena, remains inadequate. Very few academic studies have been undertaken to examine, analyze, and clarify the underlying importance of manipulation and its significance compared to other driving behavior. Most of the literature that aims to confront this problem takes the concept together and summarizes it in one final description. We want to start the discussion of manipulation by introducing three ideas that have much helped me to understand the essential aspects of manipulation, particularly in exploring the uniqueness of the phenomenon and the secrets behind its strong effect. Most people would discern bribery from intimidation, on the one hand, and oppression. Researchers highlight the complexities of the phenomena and suggest the following difficult definition: "An effort to control when A attempts the dynamic motive of S's actions through manipulation or by relying on the supposed vulnerability of S.

Many of these philosophers focus on various critical features and elements of deception, including complexity (Rudi now), trickery (Godin), and irrational patterns (Phillips). These variations tend to bring into motion the impossibility of gathering and summarizing the very nature of deception in one definitive and straightforward description. There will still be actual examples of manipulations (or, more specifically, what we intuitively categorize as manipulative behavior) that contradict any concept. At least do not fall within the meaning of that description.

Manipulation produces an idea of free choice
The manipulation aims to manipulate the object to act in a direction that, under normal conditions, it is likely to prevent. Besides, specific deceptive tactics are designed to drive the target to respond in a way that is not compatible with its purpose, motives, and best interests. This trait of deceptive conduct is somewhat paradoxical. On the one hand, forcing someone to behave against their desires and interests suggests that manipulation involves persuasive elements. On the other hand, the word deception itself, synonymous with an enigmatic definition such as "maneuvering," indicates some judgment and thought as it works? This conflict can be overcome by incorporating the "illusory free choice" aspect to our definition of coercive interaction.

In general, the skilled manipulator tries to intrude, intervene, and control the decision-making process of the subject by giving him the idea that he (the issue) takes his behavior freely and independently. To accomplish this result, the manipulator tries to maneuver the target to see the "intentional intervention" (i.e., the manipulator) as the best alternative possible in the current scenario. Following our simple assumptions, particularly those of optimizing expectations and mitigating risk, the target is obliged to take the best possible action in the light of its understanding of the circumstance. The realistic sense is that the target, subject to unseen manipulation, assumes that its decisions are taken openly and independently. Hiding the necessary facts to produce the desired decision exemplifies the concept of "illustrious free choice" in a deceptive relationship. The goal, which assumes that it chooses the right choice honestly and objectively, is, in fact, subject to unseen intervention in its judgment and rational thought.

Unfortunately, it is not impossible to envision opposite circumstances where a person is persuaded that he or she is on the right track, making the correct choices and not considering alternative alternatives. Ironically, and even paradoxically, encouraging him to explore the value of other possibilities involves applying unorthodox methods of control that some deceptive techniques can deliver. In the most challenging situations, the person is stuck in a skewed perception of the truth that he is not able to analyze objectively. There are several classic examples: an enthusiastic young gentleman who is determined to become a great musician even though he lacks any sense of rhythm; a brave soldier who refuses to believe that the enemy is going to attack; a conscientious businessman who wastes much of his money, time and effort to increase the quality of products that are no longer in demand.

Cases of tragic entanglement are expensive in that they restrict the world's view of the trapped man, disrupt his adaptation to the ever-changing conditions of life, and bring much hardship and suffering to him and his surroundings. The critical point is that, under certain situations, an innovative, manipulative technique will often be the only hope. An indirect form of control will convince the ingrained target to challenge the legitimacy of its bias. In this way, the manipulator could enable the entrenched objective to consider other possibilities that it had not yet accepted. Ironically, in its initial role, the target was persuaded that it was selecting the best possible option, while deceptive pressure allowed it to make the right decision. I mark this kind of "manipulation emancipation' technique,' and I'm discussing it thoroughly in the coming chapters. Here, I would like to note briefly that this approach includes methods of control in psychotherapy and education that are intended to give the impression that the aim is to make the best of the transition by it.

He should not note that someone else (i.e., the psychiatrist or the educator) is actually maneuvering the circumstance and invisibly helping him find the path towards transformation and progress. In the following pages, we would need to discuss various issues relevant to this strategy: how could the benevolent manipulator accomplish this effect? Is "democracy by manipulation" still a successful system? What are the dangers involved?

Manipulation is hidden with the target
Motivating by using a persuasive technique is meant to mitigate the likelihood of goal objecting to the movements of the manipulator. The manipulator tries to discourage the target from contemplating such organizational options. Instead, the manipulator attempts to manipulate the target to justify potential actions that it (the target) refuses to acknowledge. The manipulator tries to create a motivational result smoothly and elegantly. He wishes to make the impression that the target is choosing his actions

freely and independently (i.e., illusionary free choice). This effect could be achieved because, in the time of a manipulative interaction and the context of its subject, the manipulator's spectrum of vision is larger than the target's. It seems that the manipulator simply knows more. One of the functional consequences is that, at the moment of contact, the manipulator will change the point of view of the target, something that the target (who has a narrower range of vision) cannot do. The eventual inference is that, during a coercive relationship, the object cannot recognize that it works under a coercive control. A clear example of this is the act of seduction for indecent reasons. The sophisticated seducer forecasts potential reactions to her future movements.

And she thinks like a target when she's planning a con. However, the target, whose mind is overwhelmed by intense emotions of desire and affection, does not even consider the risk of being led astray. The willingness of the target to recognize the true motives of the manipulator allows it to explore alternatives other than the objective of the manipulator. This is just what the manipulator tries to prevent; otherwise, it will do. Don't choose to exploit it. The realistic sense is that the "scam" has been revealed, and the target may determine whether or not it wants to yield or fail to behave in compliance with the instructions of the manipulator. In other words, it's not a matter of "illusory free choice" but a genuinely free choice.

As a consequence, the coercive act fails or does not occur. According to our interpretation, comments like "you exploit me" are self-contradictions. It is not possible to be a survivor of manipulation and to speak about it at the same time. In comparison, this aggressive strategy may have been used to shift positions in interaction.

Effects of manipulation on the essential power
The critical capability is an essential function that allows us to choose our behaviors according to our goals and desires. It's expected to act as a devoted guard whose job is to hold our actions and conduct following our self-interest and world-view. A motivating activity designed to lead a person to work contrary to their preferences without noticing the distortion must interrupt, or at least bypass, the inspection process. As a consequence, manipulative actions inevitably seek to influence the strong potential of the goal. I have described two types of techniques that are intended to accomplish this impact. The first one is planned to cloud, blur, and reduce the vital power of the target while the second, unexpectedly, is oriented towards increasing the efficiency of the target. The first type is pretty straightforward. During the confrontation, the manipulator uses morally objectionable methods to mitigate potential objections to his target movements. However, as the following two examples illustrate, specific and even competing motives and intentions can be used to influence elemental power. It could be used for the advantage of the manipulator and to boost the position of the target.

Persuasion & Hypnotic Effect is almost like learning a foreign language
When you continue to take the ideas of this book and incorporate them, you're going to have to put off "travel time," which means that you're going to have to clock in hours with a clear goal and get the benefits of your preparation. In reality, many of the ways you learn how to form your language and sentences can run counter to how you communicate at the moment. This will force you to have to stretch

your imagination to comprehend the context of the ideas taught.

Mental Rehearsal: You should be an actor

When an actor appears on stage or in front of a screen, do you think they write their lines or use a script? The actor uses a script to practice their lines. When you continue to understand the boundaries of being able to convince or persuade, it's the same thing. You're going to have to practice the lines. Even when an actor puts on a person in the part they play, you're going to have to do the very same thing. You'll need to get out of your new comfort zone and start behaving outside the cage.

Get Out of the Comfort Zone

Everyone's in a safe spot. The purpose of this training is, above all else, the self-influence that you can gain to drag yourself out of your comfort zone. The comfort zone is the location, the mental state where you are residing in your mind. You need to have a mentality that you can sacrifice a bit to get the most value from this exercise. The rewards of this would well outstrip any discomfort you may face by studying it, but this internal training is the secret to concentrating on what you want, not what you don't want.

Start with the objective in mind

- What are you pretending to be?

- Where do you want to go?

- Who would you like to be involved with?

- What kind of job, company, or profession do you want?

This and several other questions are what you need to ask yourself because you know what you expect from this scenario of Hypnotic Manipulation and Hidden Intimidation. Set the target of where you want to be, the kind of skills you want to learn, and then post the date and focus. When the target is set, you should then reflect on how you're going to get there. Some have used this technique to become Stage Hypnotists. At the same time, some have used these techniques to find anyone of the opposite sex. And many more have used these essential ideas to build a lifestyle that exists within their minds and enables them to benefit from all aspects of life, from work or company to any relationship they have.

Become a Controller

The significant thing I'm explaining here is to show you how you can become a master. The manager is the guy who's going to call the shots in his life. If you get nothing but this idea from this book, it will be worth reading. Being a planner is a mind focused on the facts, although you assume, they are not really as they are now. To be a controller is a state of consciousness.

The Controller's Behavior

The Alpha is the controller. He or she is the key man or woman, the "Target Maker." This is the mindset that you are going to build when you continue the process. Don't ever make the opposite idea happen in your mind. You are "A Controller." This is something you need to affirm to yourself regularly. "I'm in the process of being a strong controller" "I'm the controller in all aspects of my life."

Pre-play & Rehearse Performance

Always set it on your mind to make a replay of success. Your conscious mind is potent, and you can draw from it so much energy than you can ever imagine. It's this confidence that's going to drive you to your idea of what success means to you. The subconscious does what it's supposed not to do what it's intended to do. That's why you're going to have to use replay to adjust it.

Regulation of Anxiety

The critical question I have from people is that they are sometimes scared to try these techniques to see if they will work. After all, we're doing a lot of this secretly, so it makes sense that you're still reluctant to use a new strategy or method. Bear in mind what was said about becoming an actor before. You've got to get into your job and make yourself happy at times. Consider this as you control the discomfort of the unknown. "It's not the absence of fear, but the overcoming of fear." It's taking action. The more effort you take, the more fear you lose. Everyone's scared. It's all going to be focused on the target ahead.

All knowledge is state-dependent

Whenever you discover something, it depends on what kind of situation you're in at the moment. When you understand that touching a hot stove makes you burn, you've learned a valuable lesson. Every time after that, as you get close to a hot stove, your subconscious can immediately warn you of the condition and keep your hands away from the fire. We're learning from our:

-Physiology

-Emotional Conditions

So that means, to comprehend those things, if you can place yourself in a mental condition like any time you've learned something or the same emotional state, then it's a possibility why you can understand it much better.

Body Language That Can Make You More Convincing and Pleasant

Will you want to reassure someone to be seen as more likeable? You do, of course! Here's an easy and effective way to make this possible. Do you want to learn about a body language method that can boost your likability and effect over others? There is such a mechanism, known as "Mirroring." This interpersonal communication strategy would help you to communicate with, connect with, and build confidence and respect in the mind of the person you're talking to. This isn't bad for the body language element that isn't on other people's radar screens. Body language is not just essential to get the message across. It also plays a part in how people view you and how you feel for yourself! From career interviews and in-person and interactive meetings, you learn more than you can.

The Strength of Body Language to Facilitate Person-to-Person Interactions

Mirroring involves copying the stance, the gestures, the verbal skills, and the vocabulary of the person you speak in interpersonal conversation. How is it working? A 2016 study using functional MRI showed that speakers and listeners "reacted and adapted to each other's signals." This result was published in The Wall Street Journal on the advantages of mirroring, especially in industry. This resonated deeply with me because it was the foundation of traditional acting practice. The exercise is called

Mirror and shows the same impact on the person-to-person interactions that the theoretical experiment has confirmed, even without costly equipment. In Mirror, one person (Person "A") stands in front of an imaginary mirror and moves instinctively ("Getting ready for the day" or "Arguing an argument" are appropriate examples here). Usually, this person is advised to step slowly. "A" is companion (Person "B") faces "A" and copies everything he does. The practice can be stepped up by telling "A" that he is unconsciously talking to himself. Again, "B" would imitate all that "A" is doing (and, in the second edition, the facial expression). The functions are often changed, often several times.

The fascinating thing about the Mirror exercise is that intention, sentiment, expressiveness, and energy level are all exposed by expression and movements. This is an invaluable lesson in itself for practicing artists. Equally significant, it is a fast-track illustration of the interconnectedness of human beings and how it can be fostered by exhibited and imitated actions. Both experiences are as invaluable to public speakers as to stage actors.

How to Develop Interpersonal Speech Report and Trust?

How do you use mirroring productively in your discussions and relationships with others? The secret to this is the sincerity with which you pursue and execute the technique. You should begin by not trying to mimic your conversational partner at all. Instead, work on knowing what the other person is thinking about and what their desires tend to be. If you stay open and fully involved in what the other has to suggest, you will improve your ability to practice mirroring. That is, if you are trustworthy of your purpose, what you present to your partner will come out of honesty rather than an attempt to exploit. As for the technique itself, begin by matching the voice tone and rhythm of the other person. Vocal signals are typically more precise than body movements and can serve to ease the first attempt at mirroring. Enable yourself to imitate non-verbal habits that you see. It may include posture and location, whether the person is sitting forward or lying back in the chair, the level of eye contact, head nodding or pacing, and the level of involvement or enthusiasm expressed emotionally and at the rate of the individual's voice.

Act to get the best outcomes spontaneously and genuinely

The theory is that you just want to be involved in what the other person does. Your speech, body, and emotional engagement represent that degree of dedication. You can be shocked how energized and concentrated you become in a conversational context. If that happens, you might forget that you practice mirroring at all. Mirroring can yield off in terms of knowing and listening to the person you're referring to. But it's also valuable teaching to simply become a more reflective person, one who reflects on others rather than on himself.

Persuade how to use body language in a convincing argument?

Whenever you're communicating, the material lies on the surface for everyone to see. But beneath that visible surface flows a healthy river of influence. The undercurrent that viewers can't as clearly identify: the influential underneath generated by non-verbal contact—these aspects of interpretation and power of the preceding language. In some instances, we can't name them or describe their exact influence at all.

Yet they still work throughout and under the familiar pieces of our speeches and presentations. Among the most important of these is body language. A good speaker must learn how to make the most of the body's language, for the body is an important communication medium. As speakers, we are bodies traveling through space, and audiences respond as strongly to what they see and understand from body language as they do to any other aspect in our speech. Here are four ways to use body language and talk with greater force and convince, empower, and encourage audiences. Three of these tips are about the sort of expression you're talking about in terms of your appearance. The fourth is a vital body language technique that you would use in any conversation, voice, or presentation you give in public.

For speaking when you stand
- **Ground yourself.** Stand with the legs apart at the armpit-width to establish a comfortable and calm appearance. In results, you get a portion of your energy out of the world. Don't be stripped of the power.

- **Move with Intent.** Too many speakers are walking, pacing, or going without Intent. Choose parts of the stage for some of the critical topics you address, and use visual aids and even crowds to give the message a tangible representation.

- **Make massive Signs Restricted**. The single expression that amplifies an essential argument is the one that gives value to it. Make it clean, and it's limited. Too regular or slow movements do not offer any physical expression to the above.

- **Do use facial gestures.** In part, the listeners determine whether to trust someone with facial gestures or look in the eyes of the speaker. An expressionless speaker has offered the crowd too little to move on.

For speaking while you're sitting down

- **Shift the back of the chair.** Getting too relaxed in a chair is a risk while you're talking. When you need to express motivation and enthusiasm, you need to go on, which is humiliating.

- **Get up and take Lean Forward.** Strong stance when sitting displays composure and brings authority. Leaning forward is an essential hint to your audience that you are committed and involved.

- **Open yourself for yourself.** A common mistake among speakers sitting at a board table is to hold their hands together or keep their arms in a "closed" pose. This establishes a physical distance between you and your audience.

- **Gesture.** Just because you're sitting down does not mean you can't make a move. Too many speakers become talking heads and do not have amplifying or encouraging motions. Always use your arms and your hands.

When you speak practically

- **Stand and move on.** Audiences who you talk to physically or over the phone can hear the emotional expressiveness that you use when you speak. If you intend to engage yourself when you talk in person entirely, why do you remove movement while you chat on the phone or in a webinar?

- **Use headphones**. Not only can the headphones set you up to switch and talk, but they make your voice sound louder and more substantial. When you fall in the rhythm, you're not going to want to be around them.

- **Try to ask questions.** Although listeners can't respond to the visual cues you send them (such as when they should respond), you need to send these cues outspokenly. You and your audience are going to feel like you're connected. And you're trying to get the audience out of multitasking!

- **Use speech power.** In the lack of essential contextual cues, the vocal capacity has to be consumed. And no movements for the audience to see. They need the voice to point and focus. Here are the 5 Main Techniques for Vocal Modulation to help you render more effective expression and presentations.

Observe the body language of the crowd
- **Focus the Energies Outward, not inward.** The body language coming from your audience is as essential as the non-verbal feedback you're sending. Don't care about how you're doing — watch how your listeners respond.

- **Take a look at how listeners react.** When you observe such motions, expressions, eye contact, and jiggling legs, pay attention as the patterns change. It's also a warning that you're losing the attention of listeners.

- **Change your rhythm and approach as appropriate**. When that happens, change what you do. Say a story if you've been talking in general; give an example; or turn off the system you're using or start using if you've been talking for too long.

- **Develop Interaction.** Keep the audience engaged above all. It may mean merely using body language, putting them on their feet, or engaging in an exercise. Audiences are often more convinced, empowered, and encouraged as they perform, not only listen.

Ever listen to someone talking and remember that something doesn't ring true about that person? Everything was in disagreement with his words and the way he handled himself. That may have been his reluctance to look you in the eye. Perhaps his hands have overwhelmed you. Or maybe it was facial movements that didn't reflect what he was saying? No, now you know it was his position; focused, honest people just don't conduct themselves that way. As you will see, the body tells a tale of its own. You will also do that.

- Listen and read others.

- Make sure whether the person is trustworthy or someone you're right to run away from right now.

The eyes do not deceptive
Have you ever spoken to someone who isn't looking straight at you? The person stared over your back, over your head, on the street, or at someone else anywhere except you. What did you make about that? The person made you upset with that. Very possibly, you doubted the person's purpose, integrity, and trust. Or you might have been neglected. Eye communication plays a vital role in how people view each other, and, as a speaker, you should pay particular attention to it. If you make eye contact with your audience, they will believe you're genuine, trustworthy, polite, and truthful. These emotions have a significant influence on how listeners interpret the message.

There are other advantages of eye contact:

- It helps you to create a relationship with listeners.

- It's catching their interest.

- It reveals that you speak frankly.

- Demonstrates self-confidence.

- Indicates that you're responsive.

- Recognizes individuals.

While communicating with a group of people:

- Look at the crowd before you start the speech.

- Check from one hand to the other before you speak.

- Communicate and respond to one user at a time.

- Keep your eye contact for 3 to 4 seconds for each individual.

- Use four connections, connect, chat, and begin.

Stop eye contact includes:

- Staring at one person for so long.

- Looking over the heads of the participants.

- Staring up at the roof or out of the window.

Show Commitment and Passion by Hand Gestures

Hand gestures are the most articulate component of the body's language. Make your hand movements above your elbow and away from your body to be most successful. They should be robust and healthy to demonstrate confidence and excitement. A sweeping wave of your arm to show space would bring more to the message than a half-hearted gesture of the hand. Hand movements can also be absolute and varied rather than minimal and repetitive; having the same action over and over is annoying. Make the hand motions smaller for large crowds so that even people at the back of the room can see them.

Display some simple hand gestures:

- Height, weight, form, direction, and location.

- Value or urgency.

- Comparing and Contrasting.

Hand movements to stop include the following:

- The parent pointing number.

- Fist, rage and stress.

- The karate chop is brutal.

Example hand placements shall include:

- Split palms, one is holding the other at the waist.

- Hand to foot, able to make a move.

Always sure that your facial expression matches your speech

Your face unconsciously conveys hints as to how the listeners are expected to respond or behave. When you're talking about a horrific traffic wreck, but you're laughing and nodding, the viewers would be curious, not upset. Your facial expression must be compatible with the emotions or details of your interaction.

Assume the rooted role of the Express Trust

- The position you hold while still standing is significant because it shows your level of trust and comfort. If you slouch your shoulders and fix your eyes on the pavement, the audience will think you're timid and frail. If you continuously change your weight from one foot to another, you look awkward and anxious, and your movement can distract your audience. But when you stand upright, your legs shoulder-length apart, with your weight equally balanced over each leg, with gaze squarely at your audience, you express trust and poise.

- It's called the rooted position. Imagine that the feet are firmly embedded in the earth. It's not going to be easy for you to sway or get off balance. This is the state of strength and wealth.

How to persuade people by using psychological theories?
Influence the crowd with these ideas without becoming sleazy about it. Here is a summary of each of the ten hypotheses, which may sound familiar to you. Because you've used them in the past or because you've had someone attempt them on you.

1) Hypothesis of Enhancement
When you show a particular behavior, your mentality hardens. The reverse is also true, communicating ambiguity softens the action.

2) Theory of conversion
The minority in a group will have a detrimental impact on the influence of those in the majority. Usually, those among the majority who are more vulnerable are those who could have entered because it was convenient to do so, or who thought like there were no alternatives. Consistent and positive minority voices are the most powerful.

3) Theory of Intelligence Processing

This idea entails a convincing person purposely violating one of the four conversational maxims. What are the four of them?

• Quantity: The details are complete and accurate.

• Quality: The material is real and reliable.

• Relationship: The information is essential to the discussion.

• Style: Detail is conveyed in an easy-to-understand style, and non-verbal acts reflect the sound of the sentence.

4) Priming up

You can be affected by factors that influence your understanding of short-term thoughts and behavior. Here's a very creative example of Transforming Minds. A stage magician says 'ask' and 'repeat' in separate sentences in the priming of a human to dream about the term 'tricycle' later.

5) Reciprocity norm

Widespread social practice, and reciprocity, requires our duty to share the advantages to others.

6) Principle of availability

I want to see what's in the short stock. This motivation grows when you foresee the disappointment you may have if you skip it by not moving quickly enough.

7) Sleeper Consequences

Persuasive communications appear to reduce persuasiveness over time, except for low-credibility communications. Messages that begin with low persuasion gain conviction as our minds steadily disassociate the source from the content (i.e., potentially a sleazy car dealer and his guidance on what the best car is).

8) External effects

We are heavily motivated by others based on how we interpret our interaction with the influencer. Social evidence on a web file, for example, is convincing if the testimonials and advice come from reputable outlets, major companies, or peers.

9) Change in Yale Mentality Approach

This approach, based on many years of study by Yale University, has identified a variety of convincing speech variables, including being a confident, competent speaker, whether it is essential to first or last, and ideal communities to approach.

10) Absolute terms and conditions

Some words hold more significant influence than many others. This definition splits the applicable term into three categories:

God's names: those words that bring blessings or require obedience/sacrifice. For example, development, importance.

Devil's words: certain words that are hated and provoke contempt, such as racist and pedophile.

Charismatic words consist of those terms that are vague, less measurable than either the names of Heaven or the Demon.

7 Forms Compelling Body Gestures Reinforce Company Presentations

If you're presenting a new plan to clients or heading a regular sales meeting within your own company, presentations are moments of your professional career. The basis of a fantastic presentation is your content, and the more you plan, the greater the end outcome will be. Still, there is another aspect of the overall performance as a presenter and implementing your presentation. Talk honestly with poise and elegance, and a decent performance will be a win. On the other hand, poor execution will undermine the efficacy of otherwise excellent materials. To make the most of your content and put yourself on top of it, consider these seven creative body language hacks.

Arrange your pose like a Superman

Before your speech starts, take some time in your bathroom or another private place to practice the best Superman pose. Step up straight on your chest. Either put your hands on your shoulders with your elbows extended or lift your arms above your head in a triumphant pose. The trick is to make you look and sound as big as you can. Doing this for a few minutes before a big event would inevitably make you feel more comfortable, which, in turn, would motivate your presentation?

Stand up straight

Squatting can be a difficult habit to break, but it's essential to do so if you want to look at your best during the presentation. Give the statement standing erect on the back of the head. Be careful not to widen your shoulders or exaggerate your height, but to straighten your frame. This has two clear advantages. Next, you will become more assured to your audience, which will increase the appeal of your content. Second, the airway will be balanced, and you can automatically sound louder and smoother.

Open up your muscles
It is necessary to keep your posture open. You can feel both more optimistic and more trustworthy to your audience, even though it is just on a subconscious basis. Don't stretch your arms over your body or place your hands in your back. Do not cross your legs and lean against the wall, either. Keep the arms free and comprehensive to show that you are a free individual. Your message is going to be best received.

Take a look in the eyes of the audience
Eye contact is a vital aspect of body language and behavioral guidance for one-on-one sessions, such as work interviews and business talks. Still, it is also helpful in a comprehensive presentation setting. When you communicate with a big group of people, you can't look at everyone's eyes at once. Instead, reflect on the principal members of the group and look in their eyes. Don't keep it for longer than a few seconds; switch around the room to reach as many participants as possible. Doing so adds an extra special touch to your pitch and reveals that you're genuinely involved in your audience.

Move around comfortably
The stage is your domain, so make use of it. Don't make this mistake of staying in one position, even though it's on the podium. Instead, walk around the stage to take as much room as possible. You would look more relaxed, more assured, more familiar in

your surroundings. It also helps the speaker to be reflected in various ways.

Use your hands

Get the hands involved in the talk to improve your arguments and keep the viewer's more involved. Place your finger in your palm so that you can bring a reference around. Open your hands to show ambiguity or indicate involvement. Possible gestures and implementations are unrestricted, so use them sparingly. Using hand motions very much can make you seem anxious or agitated. Using the same movements over and over again might make you seem gimmicky or repetitive. Instead, use various forms of expressions, and only at times of presentation that you need an additional "oomph."

Relax the facial muscles

People are searching for visual clues to the feelings, motives, and trustworthiness of another person. It doesn't affect performing in front of a vast crowd. To optimize the meaning and efficacy of what you say, keep your facial expressions loose as you pass through various areas of the presentation. It can make you sound more genuine and individual, which goes a long way towards persuading the viewer. Of course, it's not enough to understand these body language patterns. If you want to be genuinely successful in their implementation without acting like an insane guy, you will have to do it in the real world. Adjust it until it looks and seems familiar to you. They'll be a regular part of your speaking patterns before you know it, and you'll never have to think about them again.

What you're doing reflects just about half of what people hear. According to research, 55% of the message you convey comes from your body language. That's why understanding body language has such a long tradition. Over the last century, psychology has made a great deal of progress in understanding the various social implications of body language. Below are some of the most important observations.

The shake of the shoulder is a familiar gesture not to know what's going on

According to a study, everybody is shrugging the shoulder. The shrug is a "simple example of a common expression used to indicate that a person doesn't know or understand what you're doing." It's a different move that has three essential parts, and they're all going on. The palms open to reveal what is enclosed in the hands, the shoulders hunched to shield the throat from attack, and the brow lifted, a traditional, and submissive greeting.

Open palms are a typical example of authenticity

Ever note how, when anyone swears to tell the truth in a court of law, they place one hand on a sacred document and hold their other hand in the air, palm in front of everyone they're referring to? An open palm has been connected to "truth, integrity, patriotism and obedience" in Western history. "Just like a dog shows its throat to demonstrate obedience or yield to a victor," people use their hands to indicate that they are vulnerable and not a threat.

A pointing finger with a closed hand is an attempt to assert superiority

When someone closes their hand and points with their index finger, they attempt to show superiority, but it doesn't always succeed. The Palm-Closed-Finger-Pointing is a fist where the pointing finger is used as a suggestive weapon in which the speaker metaphorically beats his listeners into submission. Subconsciously, it evokes destructive emotions in others because it precedes a right overarm strike, a violent motion used by most primates in a physical attack.

Check for lack of wrinkles around the eyes to spot a false expression

A sincere smile, also known as a Duchene smile, is almost impossible to do on orders. That's why family pictures appear to look so uncomfortable. The grin, it turns out, is all about the crow's feet around your eyes. They crinkle as you smile joyfully. They're not because you're faking it. When someone pretends to look perfect, but they're not, you're not going to see the wrinkles.

Raised eyebrows are also indicators of distress
Much like real smiles form the lines around your eyes, research suggests worry, disappointment, or anxiety will cause people to lift their eyebrows in discomfort. So, if anyone acknowledges your new hairstyle or dress with their raised eyebrows, it might not be sincere.

They're probably concerned if their voice goes up or down

Either you know it or not, your vocal range indicates your curiosity. As soon as a discussion starts, besotted women turn into singing voices, Psychology Today states, "when men lower their octave."

If they mimic the language of your body, the conversation is generally going well
When two people get together, their postures and gestures mimic each other. When the closest friend of yours crosses their ankles, you will do the same. When you're on a date that's going great, you're both going to make the same ridiculous hand motions. This is how we mimic each other as we sense a bond.

Eye contact indicates curiosity, both positive and negative
When you look at someone in the eyes, it determines the body's state of enthusiasm. However, the perception of this stimulation depends on the individuals concerned and the circumstances.

But if they've been staring into your eyes for so long, they may be cheating
To stop becoming shifty-eyed, some liars would deliberately keep their eyes too long to make it mildly awkward. They can even stand still and not twitch.

Extensive posture signals strength and a feeling of accomplishment
How people hang on to themselves is a significant hint as to how they feel. Research has shown that broad poses improve testosterone and optimism. If they lay back and relax, they feel strong and in charge. Similarly, evidence reveals that even blind-born people raise their V-shaped arms and lift their head somewhat as they win a physical competition. On the other hand, a low-power posture seen as someone covers and wraps their arms around them raises cortisol, a stress hormone.

Crossed legs are typically a symbol of reluctance and low receptivity, which are a negative sign of bargaining.
There wasn't a single deal when one of the negotiators crossed his legs. Psychologically, crossed legs signify a person's mental, emotional, and physical closure — which could mean that they are less inclined to budge in negotiations.

A 'cluster' of movements reveals a strong sense of interaction
The attraction is not transmitted by a single signal, but by a chain.

Whether they laugh at you, they're definitely into you

If anyone is responsive to your jokes, they're typically interested in you. Evolutionary psychologists claim that laughter plays a central role in human growth. It acts as a means of signaling a desire for friendship, whether platonic or romantic.

A clenched jaw, a clenched neck, or a furrowed forehead indicates tension

Many of these are "limbic reactions" associated with the limbic system of the brain. Emotion, detecting and adapting to threats, and maintaining our safety are all the substantial duties of the limbic system. The bus leaves without us, and we're clenching our teeth, scratching our heads. We're called to work another day, and the circles of our eyes widen as our chin falls. Humans have been expressing pain this way for millions of years.

Expansive, influential positions demonstrate leadership

If they are natural or trained, there are various signs and actions people use when they believe they are a boss, or at least attempt to persuade you that they are. These include maintaining straight posture, walking confidently, steeping and palm-down hand movements, and typically accessible and flexible body postures.

A trembling leg signifies an unstable inner state

Your legs are the most significant part of your body, so when you walk, it's pretty hard for anyone not to notice. A trembling portion is a symptom of fear, frustration, or both.

Crossed weapons can indicate defensiveness, depending on the context

It's quick to grab body-language signals, but it's essential to be conscious of the context. Although crossed arms generally mean that someone is near, people are much more likely to cross their arms when it's cold, and their chair doesn't have an armrest. Be mindful of the surroundings before deciding or modifying a plan based on these types of behaviors.

Persuasive body language positions

Your body language cannot determine the effectiveness of your performance. A compelling body language makes the argument more convincing and engaging. At least, it's holding the interest of the public. Below is a situational persuasive body language proposed by the Center for Body Language.

The box position (trustworthy)

Early in Bill Clinton's political career, he would punctuate his remarks with bold, large expressions that made him seem untrustworthy. To help him keep his body language under control, his counsellor taught him to visualize a box in front of his chest and abdomen, and to keep his hand going inside it. Since then, "Clinton Box" has become a common phrase in the industry.

To hold a ball (Dominant, commanding)

Showing as if you were holding a basketball in your hands is an indication of competence and power. As if you almost entirely have the truth at your hands. Some people use this role often in their speeches.

Pyramid-hands (relaxes, self-confidence)

When people are anxious, their hands flit about and fidget. They're still there when they're confident. One way to do so is to put your hands together in a comfortable pyramid. Often business executives use this gesture but beware of overuse or combining it with superior or dismissive facial expressions. The intention is to demonstrate that you're comfortable, not arrogant.

Wide stance (in control, confident)

How people stand is a good predictor of their mentality. When you stand in this calm and confident posture, with your legs about the width of your shoulder apart, it shows that you feel more in control.

Palms up (accepting, honest)

This gesture shows transparency and honesty. A lot of people make excellent use of this in their interviews. They are robust and prominent figures, but they still seem able to have a genuine relationship with the people they are talking to, be it a single person or a crowd of thousands.

Palms down (emphatic, strong)

The opposite trend can also be interpreted positively — as a symbol of dominance, power, and aggressiveness.

Proven Convincing Strategies

Presentations are a danger. You are spending precious time and effort, so you can't predict the nature of the production you'll be struggling with. The precise disposition of the crowd cannot be determined, or all the factors of the situation cannot be managed. You have to be brave to excel and come armed with an ace up your sleeve. You've got to be a master of convincing. And if your goal is merely to inspire or educate, you will need to convince your audience to pay attention. If you need to push your audience to take action, convincing is necessary.

Use your hands during a speech

Let your hands make a natural gesture during your speech. Research has shown that the commentators are judged to be more effective and knowledgeable when they make hand gestures compared to when they keep their hands still. When you're gesturing, be particularly mindful of how you use your hands. There are more interactions between the brain and the palm of the hands than any other part of your body. Palms have developed as an integral component of human minds. The research reveals how a speaker's palm direction can send a signal that appeals to your primitive brain. Based on the signal being broadcast, the speaker will either win the support and interest of the audience or be dismissed by the audience. Palm orientation was evaluated in one of the case studies mentioned; the analysis concluded that the palm-up speaker had up to 40% more retention than the palm-down speaker. Speaking with your hands is going to make you more likeable and convincing. If you address your palms down, you are going to be viewed as intimidating and commanding. The motion of the palms down appears threatening. The crowd laughs because the updated greeting is humorous.

Be a Wordsmith

Be careful with the words you chose to use during your presentations. For example, focus mainly on terms that can hit an emotional chord with members of the audience. Compared to terms with neutral connotations, inspirational words have a more profound impact on members of the audience. More specifically, the analysis was concluded. In the present investigation, we investigated whether there was a qualitative advantage of emotional memory relative to neutral words. The findings of six tests indicated that there was such a benefit: overall tasks, the specifics of the interpretation of terms (assessed by subjective and quantitative measures), were more likely to be recalled for emotional than neutral objects. Take the word healing to the next stage by adding some of the most popular terms into the presentations.

YOU

Use the verb "you" during the presentations want your audience excited. Rewrite sentences, substitute the "I" word with your word, to concentrate on the listener and not on yourself. Besides, if you give a presentation to quite a few individuals, start using their first names during the presentation. Don't push it through; be normal when approaching the members of the audience directly.

FREE

The word 'free' is continuously thrown into our faces by advertisers and service providers. And the term holds specific forces of persuasion. However, be cautious with your free usage to preserve the importance of your message, while still tapping into the significant energy of the word.

SUDDENLY

Suddenly, the term makes activities or interactions look thrilling and straightforward. If you can use the word frankly and tactfully as part of your call-to-action at the end of your presentation, go for it. The chances are that the performance will improve.

Tap the sensory experiences
Use the strength of the five senses to manipulate the system for the next presentation. For instance, if technological problems interrupt the performance, keep the crowd entertained by playing some fun music. Pleasant music played while you're on hold wants to keep guests on the line length to escape the challenge of trying to convince an irritated crowd, use music to keep people happy for you. Use colours strategically, and optimize the compelling value of the presentation design.

Storytelling presentation
Studies prove that tales are more convincing than rational claims. The most popular presentations are around 65 percent stories and 25 percent statistics, with the rest an illustration of the reputation.

Use the Sensitivity to Failure
Ask the crowd to think that you're doing the role that you want them to accomplish. As weird as it may seem, the brain simply cannot tell the difference between dreaming reality and witnessing reality. When the viewer imagines an experience, they have it both physically and psychologically. As a

consequence, the group is less likely to condemn the response you are calling for. This is because our emotional reaction to loss is twice as strong as our pleasure of reward.

Be polite
Likeable presenters are more convincing than presenters who are unable to relate to the audience. People tend to prefer speakers who are identical, generous with compliments, and cooperative. Before giving a presentation, study the audience deeply. When you take the stage, be prepared to express commonality between yourself and members of the crowd, and praise the group. When you work in the room following the lecture, comply with demands from members of the public who require a final drive for convincing. Comfort is another trait of welcoming leaders. Researchers report that leaders need to be viewed as warm, possibly more than professional, convincing. While projecting credibility is necessary, neglecting to show trustworthiness/warmth, a psychological force makes it quite difficult for leaders to acquire allegiance and be convincing sustainably. Among other methods, experts recommend flashing a genuine smile at critical times of your performance to create a warm atmosphere.

Gestures certainly matter how messages are processed and received. New research on the interactive tasks of movements offers some handy hints for persuading to live. And considering that the study is about talking to the hands, it's unsurprisingly enough, a group of Italian researchers introduced what is likely to be the first fully-controlled experiment to look into the convincing efficacy of hand movements in isolation. That alone was enough to get me to hand over the $34 to see what they find.

- First, you should make an expression. Irrespective of the form of gesture, gesturing is more convincing than not making gestures.

- Second, you should stop making gestures towards yourself. Pointing to one, keeping your hands on oneself, or even self-referencing, produced lower perceptions of the skill of the speaker.

- Third, the best gestures are "related to expression." In other words, instead of meaningless motions that do not have the requisite significance, the best gestures are those that are "ideal" to express or validate the concept. When speakers related their movements to expression, the participants in the study saw them as more successful and more composed.

Not only do the movements help the listener, but they also help the speakers. Another research showed that using gestures when illustrating the idea contributed to a greater comprehension and learning of the speaker. Currently, nothing in this or any other study that I am aware of indicates that it is a good idea to plan or practice for movements properly. If you are a well-trained performer, such actions are hurried and awkward, which is the opposite of the natural confidence that you want to express.

"Beats" (or "Rhythmic Gesture")
They are punctuated up and down or side to side movements that complement speech like a conductor's baton. Since they are not equivalent to voice, they are not the most powerful emotions. Often, to the degree that they can accompany some form of material, they can be a favorite speaker and a diversion for audiences. They may play an essential role: think of them as a simple way to run a highlighter over sections of your post. If you use

them sparingly, and if you want to bust out one or two "beats" just before you hit a crucial stage, the audience will pay more attention and be more likely to recall the material.

"Points" (or "textual expressions")

The speaker doing these will suggest (with a finger, a fist, an arm, or even ahead) something present in the room.   Since they are indeed connected to speaking, they are more powerful, more capable gestures. They're explicitly letting the listener see what you're talking about. The target is important: an occasional finger poke to the rival can be successful as long as it is pleasant and offensive, but pointing directly at the crowd can be perceived as impolite or superior. The most vital "points" may be towards an idea or a position, helping to bring into motion something that may otherwise be hypothetical.

"The Designs" (or the Iconic Gestures)

Here, speakers use their hands like a sculptor to signify some shape ("All names were put in a large, circular bowl") or some method ("Then he quickly climbed up the tree"). You can easily picture a speaker creating a bowl in the first case, or wiggling a few fingers to signify a climbing motion in the second. These are the most influential movements in the Italian analysis above since they are most specifically linked to the meaning of the voice. It's not that the viewer wants a gesture to grasp the idea (the bowls and the tree-climbing are common enough). The motion makes the audience imagine and therefore engage in the message rather than only receive it.

"Metaphors" (or Analog Gestures)

An expression acts as a metaphor as it relies on a philosophical association with the meaning of your voice. Rather than drawing a particular entity or mechanism (like the "type" above), it has a symbolic relationship to what you mean. For instance, a gesture suggesting support (e.g., the picture on the left) may be accompanied by a general message conveying some help. But the trick to this approach is subtlety: instead of "and that's why you should endorse [gesture] my friend," you'd want to retain a gesture like this when presenting a longer subject that is geared towards assistance. But you should make a motion in favor of the term, not an actual phrase.

"Placeholders" (or Unified Gesture)

These gestures promote the contact process by allowing the audience to hang messages together. In the way that a storyteller can follow the same facial action when speaking to a particular individual, movements can be used to delineate your text. For example, if you debate with opposing counsel during a bench meeting, your opponent cuts you off mid-sentence. You may hold your hands in the same up-and-coming role you were in before you were interrupted, as opposing counsel continues to signal that you did not give up the floor. Or, if you're faced with a judge's question that causes you to step away from the mainline of your case, you may drop the gesture you've been using, and then revive the same motion once you're through with the side-issue and back on the main track of your case.

Look at movements with this amount of clarity, it's convenient to say, "No thanks, I'm going to concentrate on content ..." but it's crucial to note that the audience is observing and listening. Material is the ruler, as should be the case in the legal phase, and natural distribution will always be the highest. But to think about the pieces of communication held by the hands and body, particularly as it relates to gestures, is an essential part of the whole image.

No one should underestimate the importance of body language in public speaking and presentations. Pass out the wrong sensations, and you're going to end up driving the viewer away. Yet with the right body language, you will win them over just as quickly. Some people just try to get their speeches 'over and done with' without caring about movements and body language. It's essential for you to be cautious and want to hear more about how you can use body language to your benefit. When it comes to presentations, body language can make one successful or fail. We will excel if we learn and make fair use of our body language, and lose if we let our body language get the best. When you practice your voice, it's essential to focus on your body language as well. On the day of your presentation, you're going to be happy, relaxed, and assured that you've got what it takes to make your presentation excellent. Now, the thing is, there are two sides when it comes to body language presentations. There's the body language of the host (that's you), and there's the body language of the audience. Knowing how to read your audience is a unique ability that can come in handy later. You don't want to be one of those presenters who think they're doing an excellent job on stage when, in fact, their audience is boring to death.

The Empathy Theory
Part of the effect your physical activity has on the viewer can be demonstrated by the idea of empathy, the desire to express the thoughts or feelings of another person. When you talk, people in your audience appear to be representative of your attitudes. They instinctively sense what you're feeling and react accordingly. It is essential, therefore, that the body diligently reflects real emotions. If you look calm and secure, the audience will probably feel comfortable and optimistic. If you smile at your audience, they'll see you as a nice guy, and they'll smile back at you. Most notably, once they are persuaded that you are genuine and trustworthy, they will pay attention to what you say and judge it on their terms. Of course, this method will work the other way around. If you are uncomfortable, the viewers would probably be uncomfortable. If you frown – even unintentionally – your listeners will generally frown at you. If you don't smile at them, they're going to feel rejected. And if you avoid eye contact, they will sense a loss of self-control and lose trust in you and what you speak.

Why Physical Action Support?
When you show purposeful, constructive physical activity when speaking to the crowd, you have a real barometer of your emotions and attitudes. But there are also other benefits:

1. **Messages are more unforgettable than that**

People become bored with static presentations. That's why TV newscasts nearly often have a clip depicting some type of action. If there is a crash, protest rally, or any other visually entertaining incident, the newscast would usually lead – even though it's not the most important news item. A newscast that focused on "talking heads" will quickly lose listeners who could get as much information from the TV. On the other side, it's impossible not to stare at a moving target. You've already heard how people pay attention to visual disturbances at Toastmasters gatherings. Late-comer arrivals or flickering timing lights typically siphon energy away from expression. People understand signals that hit several senses, too. We recall more of what we can see than what we can hear. However, we remember better when both our visual and our auditory senses are concerned. As a speaker, you can capitalize on these patterns by presenting visual stimulation that catches the interest of your audience and increases the reception of your verbal messages. Gestures, body gestures, facial expressions – both of these can be useful resources when done with skill.

2.   Punctuation gives value to it

Written language has a wide variety of message punctuation symbols: commas, intervals, exclamation marks, etc. But when you speak, you use an entirely new set of metaphors to remind the listener what the most critical aspects of your voice are and bring strength and energy to your expression. Any of them are presented with a speech. Gestures, body gestures, and facial expressions are just as efficient. However, to have the best potential effect, you need to organize your voice and body and function together. The more communication tools you use, the more efficiently you communicate.

3.   Nervous Stress transformed

To a certain degree, you are getting anxious before a speech is safe. It indicates that you care about doing well. All of the world's best entertainers readily agree that they're worried about success. Yet real fear — the kind that ruins a speech — will prevent you from being a successful speaker—anxiety and nervousness in public speaking practice at three levels: mental, emotional, and physical. The mental and emotional concerns are overcome by self-confidence – a by-product of training and practice. The easiest way to regulate the physical signs of anxiety and nervousness is by the deliberate use of gestures and body motions. The adrenal glands are stimulated in public speech. Your pulse is quickening. Your breathing gets shallower and quicker. Your muscles are stressed. Since the body can do anything to alleviate anxiety, you will unintentionally practice mannerisms that will distract the audience – so you can dissipate the tension. Gestures and body motions will help you take advantage of your nervous energy to make it work for you instead of against you.

Five ways of making Your Body Talk Powerful

How can you marshal your non-verbal tools – posture, gestures, body movements, facial expressions, and eye contact – and use them effectively when you speak? In this segment, you will learn five general methods to improve your body's spoken picture.

I.   Eliminate the Distractive Mannerisms

Dr. Ralph C. Smedley, the founder of Toastmasters International, said, "The speaker who sits and speaks at ease is the one who can be heard without uneasiness. If his stance and movements are so elegant and discrete that no one acknowledges them, he can be counted as genuinely useful. "If your acts are paired with your words, you will enhance the power of your expression – even though the listener does not explicitly hear them. But if your site activity includes mannerisms that are not linked to your spoken word, those behaviors will draw attention to themselves and away from your speech. In reality, rather than incorporating physical characteristics, an entrepreneur must also seek to eliminate impediments. What are the obstacles? You can usually detect at least a few visual disturbances in the delivery of each individual. Such mannerisms include the whole body, such as:

- Rocking out

- Swinging

- Moving

Such usually incompetent or unsuccessful speakers include:

- The grasping or leaning of the rostrum

- Tapping the thumbs

- Biting or kissing the mouth

- The shift in Jingling Pocket

- Scowling

- Hair or garment adjustment

- Switch the head and eyes from left to right like an oscillatory fan

Both of these acts share two things in common: first, they are physical expressions of essential nervousness; second, they are done unintentionally – the person is not sure that they are doing them. Many of us are mindful of our linguistic faults. But unless we have access to camera devices and monitor our gestures, many of our annoying mannerisms are unchallenged. The first step in removing unwanted mannerisms is to achieve a correct view of the spoken picture of your body. And you need guidance to do this. Your next move is to remove all physical activity that doesn't contribute to the voice. You will do this by being mindful of the problem areas and by conscious self-monitoring of future presentations. When you have a lot of problem areas, focus on one at a time. When each of them is eliminated, move on to the next.

II.   Be Normal, Informal, Conversational

The single most significant law to make the body talk efficiently is to be you. Today's popular speech style can better be represented as an amplified conversation. It's much more casual than the exquisite style that has dominated public speakers in years gone. Focus is focused on collaboration and exchange of thoughts – not on success or demonization. Don't want to mimic the next person. Instead, let yourself react instinctively and naturally to what you see, feel, and tell. Try to be as honest and familiar as when you speak to friends or family members.

III. Let your body look at your emotions

A person under the influence of his emotions projects an authentic self, behaving instinctively and spontaneously. If you're passionate about your subject, believe in what you're saying, and want to communicate your message with others, your physical gestures will come from inside and be relevant to what you're saying. By investing yourself in your letter, you can be intuitive and spontaneous without thinking about it.

IV. Gain self-confidence through preparedness

Nothing affects the emotional outlook rather than the awareness that he or she is well trained. This awareness inspires self-confidence, a critical aspect of good public speaking. When you're well-prepared, your actions should be directed outward to your audience instead of internally to your anxieties. You will be less likely to give visual images that contradict what you think, and you will find it easier to be standard and intuitive. You can almost effortlessly project the beautiful characteristics of honesty, earnestness, and excitement. Train and rehearse the content before it becomes part of you, yet don't want to memorize the speech. This can defeat your preparation because the conscious effort you need to remember each word will make you nervous and tense. Instead, know the subject so well that you just need to memorize the chain of thoughts. You're going to see the words pop out randomly.

V. Use your club as a laboratory for learning

Training is the secret to enhancing your results throughout every attempt. Your Toastmasters Club gives you a real classroom where you can gain useful experience. This is where errors cost you nothing, and the crowd is still polite, tolerant, and encouraging. Assist sessions diligently and talk as much as possible. Welcome input from your evaluators and listen closely to suggestions about the actions of the physical site. By integrating what you understand from this tutorial into your daily tasks, you will become adept at public speaking.

You're Speech Style

How you hold your body as you talk sends its collection of visual signals to the audience. Rather than anything else, it represents your mood, asking your listeners if you are calm, aware, and in charge of yourself and the speaking situation. A healthy speaking posture has other advantages for a speaker. It lets you breathe better and effectively project your voice. It also offers a reasonable starting point from which to make a gesture or move the body in some direction. And by making you feel both alert and relaxed, it helps relieve nervous anxiety and minimizes random, disruptive motions. What is the proper speaking posture? Tell someone else to read the next two paragraphs aloud while you follow the instructions:

Stand upright but not stiff, with the legs about six to 12 inches apart and slightly ahead. Balance your weight equally on your leg balls. Lean in for a little bit. Your legs are meant to be straight but not closed. Relax the shoulders, yet don't let them go. Keep your chest out and your back up. Your head should be erect and your chin up, but it's not that awkward. Let your arms hang naturally by your sides, your fingertips loosely bent. Now, take a couple of long, absolute breaths. If you feel relaxed? Your attitude should be sensitive, but not static, calm, but not messy. If this posture doesn't feel comfortable to you, consider repositioning your legs slightly, so your body feels relaxed. Do not hold the same role in the presentation. But if you move from one position to another, make a gesture, or shift your posture, be sure to align your body until your step is done.

Expressions

A gesture is an essential body expression that confirms a verbal statement or conveys a particular thought or emotion. Simultaneously, motions can be made with the head, shoulders, or legs, and thighs. Most of them are made with the hands and arms. Your hands can be great instruments of expression as you talk. But many novice speakers don't know what to do with their paws. Some people want to get them out of the way by putting them in their pockets or behind their backs. Others unintentionally alleviate emotional anxiety by making painful, disruptive gestures. A few performers over-gesture out of nervousness, shaking their arms and hands frantically. The movements of a speaker will provide a particular interpretation of the audience. The Indians of North America devised a sign language that would enable people with very separate spoken languages to converse. Sign language has made it easier for deaf people to communicate without speaking. The use of gestures in conversation differs from one society to another. In certain cultures, such as Southern Europe and the Middle East, people use their hands openly and expressively when they speak. In other countries, people use movements less often and are more subdued.

The essential gesture that we make and the significance that we bind to them are the results of our cultural experience. Just like cultures are distinct, so are the assumed meanings of gestures. For example, nodding one's head up and down means approval or permission in Western societies – but in certain parts of India, this gesture means the exact opposite. In certain parts of the world, a common symbol used in the United States that form a circle with a thumb and a forefinger to signify acceptance – is considered a provocation and an obscenity. To be successful, the movements of the speaker must be purposeful – even if they are done unintentionally. They ought to be clear to the public. They have to say the same thing to the listener as they do to the speaker. And they must represent what has been said, as well as the overall personality behind the post.

Why Gestures?

Many good speakers use actions. Why? Gestures are perhaps the most evocative type of non-verbal expression that a speaker may use. No other kind of physical movement will improve your voice in as many respects as your movements.

- Clarify your comments and help them. Gestures will enhance the audience's interpretation of your spoken word.

- Dramatize your thoughts, please. Along with what you mean, movements tend to build vibrant visions in the minds of your listeners.

- Give focus and energy to the spoken word. Gestures express your thoughts and attitudes more plainly than you speak.

- Give support to dissipate nervous energy. Purpose movements are a suitable medium for the nervous stress found in a speaking environment.

- Act as a visual aid. Gestures enhance the attention and retention of the audience.

- Stimulate the engagement of the group. Gestures will help you show the reaction you are expecting from your audience.

- Gestures offer visual help when you reach a broad group of people, and the whole crowd cannot notice your eyes.

Gesture Categories

Despite the significant number of movements that count as gestures, all gestures should be classified into one of the following main categories:

Descriptive expressions explain or reinforce spoken signals. They help the viewer understand similarities and parallels, and imagine the scale, form, motion, position, feature, and number of objects.

Emphatic expressions underscore what has been said. They point to earnestness and belief. For example, a clenched fist shows a positive emotion, such as rage or resolve.

Suggested movements are indicators of thoughts and feelings. They allow the speaker to establish the perfect mood or convey a specific opinion. An open palm typically means offering or accepting a view, while a shrug of the shoulders implies confusion, perplexity, or irony.

Prompting movements are used to help elicit the audience's desired reaction. If you want listeners to lift their hands, cheer, or take a particular action, you're going to improve the response by doing it yourself as an example.

Gestures made above the shoulder level indicate height, enthusiasm, or spiritual exultation. Gestures made below the story of the shoulder suggest denial, apathy, or condemnation. Those made at or above the status of the shoulder indicate calmness or serenity.

The most commonly used movements include an open palm kept forward to the viewer. The purpose of this kind of gesture depends on the location of the palm. Keeping the palm upward signifies offering or taking, even though this gesture is often seen as an unconscious action, with no clear intended purpose. A palm holding down can convey repression, confidentiality, completion, or stabilization. The palm holding out to the crowd indicates stopping, repulsion, rejection, or hatred. If the palm is placed perpendicular to the body of the speaker, it appears to show dimensions, space, or time constraints, parallels, or compares.

How to Treat Efficiently?

Gestures reflect the individual personality of each speaker. What's right for a speaker is not going to be for you. However, the following six principles apply to virtually anyone trying to become a creative, successful speaker.

1. React to, of course, what you hear, feel, and tell

When you make an expression, you instinctively express yourself by gestures. No matter what our attitude or cultural context may be, each of us has a strong tendency to punctuate and reinforce our words with gestures. The key is not to counteract the urge by hiding behind a mask of impassiveness; it will only produce a build-up of suspense. At the same time, don't make gestures from a book or another writer. Be yourself, really and instinctively. If you force unnatural movements on your natural style, your audience will notice it and call you a fake. Some are naturally animated, whereas others are naturally reserved. Use your hands openly when you talk informally, use them frankly when you chat. By default, you are a quiet, low-key guy, don't change your demeanor just to fit public speaking circumstances.

2. Establish the conditions of management

Your movements can be a mere outgrowth of your particular thoughts and emotions. They should emerge spontaneously and habitually from your approach to the message you are addressing. When you communicate, you're meant to be ultimately interested in talking – not worrying about your hands. The substance of the presentation must inspire your movements. By immersing yourself in your subject matter, you establish the conditions that will allow you to react spontaneously with appropriate actions.

3. Follow the term action and the occasion

Your visual and verbal signals must serve as collaborators in the expression of the same mind or thought. If a speaker struggles to fit words with gestures, the effect may be wooden, fake, and sometimes comical. Any gesture you make needs to be purposeful and representative of your comments. In this way, the audiences will recognize the result rather than the motion. Be sure that the vigor and strength of your movements are suitable for your phrases. Using powerful, emphatic gestures only when you sense the message is calling for them. You will need to change the activities to suit the scale and function of the audience on occasion. Generally speaking, the bigger the crowd, the broader and slower your actions should be. Bear in mind that young people are usually drawn to a speaker who uses aggressive motions. Still, older and more conservative groups may feel annoyed or intimidated by a speaker whose physical movements are too strong. The logistics of the speaking situation also influences your voice movements. When speaking from a physically constrained location, you can be prevented from using broad, sweeping motions. A typical example of a restricted speech role is the head table, where people sit next to the speaker.

4. Keep Your Actions Compelling

Your movements should be vibrant and distinct if they are to create the desired effect. A half-hearted motion suggests that the speaker lacks conviction and earnestness. A hand motion should be a whole-body movement starting from the shoulder – never from the elbow. Shift your whole arm out of your body comfortably and quickly. Hold the wrists and fingertips gentle, rather than rigid or tight. Efficient movements are energetic enough to be compelling and subtle sufficient to be broad enough. It's quickly apparent. Your actions should be distinct but not crazy, and they should never follow a fixed pattern.

5. Make the movements quick and time-consuming

Every single gesture has three parts: the approach, the stroke, and the return. Your body starts to turn in the expectation of the gesture during the procedure. The stroke is the action itself, and the return takes the body back to a relaxed speaking stance. The rhythm of a motion – focus, approach, stroke, recovery, balance – must be seamlessly performed in such a manner that only a stroke is noticeable to the viewer. Just as pacing is an integral aspect of comedy, the pace of a move is just as crucial as its consistency. The stroke must come with the right term – not before nor after it. However, the approach should be started long before the stroke; in fact, you should produce a particularly useful result by approaching the motion several seconds in advance and keeping the approach until the precise moment of the stroke. The return means keeping your hands on your sides smoothly – it doesn't have to be rushed. Don't want to memorize the expressions and blend them into the voice. Memorized gestures typically miss, since the speaker refers to the term that the gesture is intended to punctuate. This results in a motion that accompanies a phrase that seems fake and stupid.

6. Make natural, natural gesturing a habit

The first step in being adept at gesturing is to decide what you're doing right now. If you do, attempt to erase from the body's spoken portrait. Train to strengthen your movements – please don't delay for the day of your expression. Keep study to develop your gesturing capabilities in front of strangers, family members, and co-workers. Relax your inhibitions, make a move when you feel like it, and let yourself respond instinctively to what you think, feel, and say. It would help if you made acceptable movements a part of your everyday actions through knowledge and practice.

Body movements

Body movement – shifting your position or location during the speech is the most comprehensive, most noticeable type of physical activity that you, as a speaker, can do. Because of this, it can be either a massive advantage or an enormous disadvantage for the distribution system. If you turn your whole body in a calm, purposeful manner during the speech, you will gain three ways. For instance, body movement will help and strengthen what you say. And, of course, the motion would almost always draw the interest of the viewer. Finally, using body movement is the quickest, most effective way of burning up nervous energy and alleviating physical stress. However, both of these features can have the ability to work against you. One law that makes body movement your partner, not your opponent, is this: never move without a cause. Inevitably, the mind is drawn to a moving target, so every movement of the body you make while speech attracts notice. Moving along with your verbal message for a cause enhances the alertness and attentiveness of the viewers while at the same time strengthening what you tell. Seeing a fixed object is tiring, so you don't want to hold to a particular spot when you're chatting. On the other side, your body's activity should be controlled by moderation.

So much body activity, for the right kind, can be disturbing to the audience. Ideally, you should pursue a middle ground that consists of enough action to hold your listeners' attention, but not enough to divert them away from what you're doing. And as purposeful gestures call for attention, so make spontaneous gestures. The body would do about anything to get rid of the stress. Inexperienced speakers typically execute body motions such as rocking, swaying, and pacing without being conscious of what they're doing. If public speaking makes you anxious and stressed, aim to integrate sufficiently purposeful body activity into your expression so that your body does not unintentionally engage in distracting mannerisms. Another good explanation for body activity is to increase the comprehension of your message. The forms suggested that several ways of body movement are less reliable than those caused by individual actions. Still, body movement can also be an essential visual complement to the spoken word.

Stepping ahead during a speech indicates that you have passed an important point. A move or two backward suggests that you have come to an end and can let the crowd rest for a moment and absorb what you've just learned. A lateral change means a transition – where you quit one mind and take another. In some instances, body movement may be used to demonstrate or dramatize a particular concept. E.g., whether you're explaining a physical event, such as tossing a ball, or a runner straining to smash the tape to win a close-up race, you can help your listeners better imagine what you're doing by acting out your explanation. The final answer for body movement is probably the simplest: to get from one position to another. In virtually any speaking case, you have to walk to and from the stage, and you give your message. And if you're adding visual aids into a presentation, you're going to switch around while you use them. The trick to successful movement is to make these movements fast, standard, and smooth. When changing your speaking posture during a sentence, always lead with the foot nearest your target. If you're going to jump to the side, take your left foot.

Facial Movement
Impassive speech can be an advantage for a successful poker player, but for a speaker, it is an obstacle to efficient communication. People are watching the speaker's face during the presentation. Politeness, of course, is one of the reasons for this. Still, equally significant is the desire to collect the visual evidence that would be made available to the speaker a more meaningful message. Facial language is also the primary determinant of the context of a word. Here's an indication of this. When a friend grinned warmly at you and said, "You're mad," would you feel insulted? Possibly not; in truth, you may even take it as a token of love. But what if a sneer of contempt followed this comment? Verbal communication would be the same, but there's no question that your answer will be profoundly different.

When you speak, your face expresses your behaviors, feelings, and desires more plainly than any other aspect of the body. According to behavioral psychology, people need to identify – by merely studying the facial expressions of the speaker – such distinct emotions as discomfort, anxiety, pleasure, uncertainty, resentment, curiosity, disbelief, rage, and sorrow. Your face acts as a barometer to the public on what's inside of you. Your audience will watch your face for hints about your honesty, approach to your message, and your earnestness in sharing your ideas with them. Erase gestures that don't apply on your lips. They involve irritating mannerisms and implicit gestures that are oblivious to the thoughts, behaviors, and emotions. Both forms of unnecessary facial expression are typically signing of nervousness. Just as nervous speakers display disturbing motions and body expressions, they can also release excess energy and anxiety by subtly shifting their facial muscles. Examples of spontaneous facial gestures involve chewing or clicking the tongue, twisting the jaw, lifting the corners of the mouth, and twitching motions on some part of the face.

The audience finds these gestures to be indicators of nervousness and loss of trust, knowledge, and readiness. Such behavior may also leave the audience uncomfortable and less receptive to the verbal communication of the speaker. When you know that you're showing disruptive facial gestures, work on managing your apprehensions about speaking. Detailed planning and participation with your subject matter would allow you to develop trust and influence. The trick to conveying friendliness is to try to smile. It's still unwise to do that – you could be branded as inconsequential, and it would be unacceptable to do that during a critical presentation. But, by all means, smile when it's necessary to the situation. Show your audience that you are happy to have the chance to share your thoughts with them, that you enjoy yourself and that you are interested in them. There are no laws regarding the use of particular terms. By releasing your inhibitions and encouraging yourself to react spontaneously to your feelings, behaviors, and emotions, your facial expressions would be acceptable, generating authenticity, confidence, and integrity.

Eye contact

Each of the categories we've just addressed physical appearance, stance, motions, body motions, and facial expressions contains essential non-verbal elements for your vocabulary. But after your voice, your eyes are your most effective contact weapon.

Why is communication with the eye essential?

When you talk, you engage your audience with your eyes and make your presentation clear, specific, and conversational. One sure way to sever the contact bond is not to glance at the target. No matter how big an audience can be, every listener needs to feel important, to feel intimate. Link to the speaker, and to believe that the speaker interacts personally with him or her. There's an amplified conversation. Much as a small, casual community feels disconnected from a discussion if the speaker doesn't reach his or her eyes, people in the crowd will feel cut out if you don't make eye contact with them. In most cultures, the act of staring at others squarely in the eye is a sign of honesty. Failure to hold another's eyes while communicating indicates disinterest, loss of faith, insincerity, or deception. The same social correlations can be observed in public speaking. In one analysis, those who developed eye contact were judged to be more accurate, trustworthy, reliable, polite, and skillful than those who did not.

Only by looking at your audience as individuals can you persuade them that you are serious, that you are interested in them, and that you care whether they support your message or not. Your eyes also act as a control system when you talk. Only by looking at them, you affect the focus and concentration of your audience. On the other side, if you don't look at them, they're not going to look at you, and you're going to suffer response to your word. In turn, the interest created by your good eye contact will serve as a source of strength and inspiration to you. When you see that your message is essential to the public, you will build trust and feel more relaxed. Eye communication will even help you conquer your nervousness. Fear is the most common source of anxiety in voice, and stress is caused by the unexpected. Eye interaction makes an amount transparent to the viewer. If you look at your audience and know that most of them are engaged in your message, your anxiety will evaporate, and the nervous stress will be minimized. Not only can your eyes transmit crucial signals when you're talking, but they're also still getting them.

Sufficient eye contact is an input system that renders the speech situation a two-way communicating operation. Only by looking at your listeners can you decide how they respond. Are you doing well? Will the listener get what you're talking about? Are you having the interest of the audience? Is your message accepted? By watching the responses of the crowd, you will make instant changes to the presentation. Experienced speakers believe this tactile input to be the best advantage of eye contact. If you have mastered the confidence to gauge the response of your audience and adapt your language accordingly, you can become a much more successful speaker.

How to use your eyes efficiently
1. Well, know your stuff

Preparing yourself maintaining the power of your verbal messaging is a requirement for creating successful eye contact with your audience. You should know your voice so well that you don't have to dedicate your mental resources to recalling the chain of thoughts and phrases. Your perception must be external to the viewer – not inward to inner chaos. If you can talk easily without words, do so by all means. But if you need to use an outline or any other sort of written reminder, go ahead. Just don't let it be a replacement for planning and rehearsal. You can use your eyes successfully when making notes, but it takes skill and deliberate effort. Many skilled speakers are incredibly competent at this practice, taking advantage of such regular breaks as the laughter of the crowd or the after-effects of an exciting topic to take a quick look at their notes. It would help if you kept your letters short a few essential words or symbols keyed to the order of your message to make this strategy effective. If you know the content and are well-prepared, these cues can be enough to keep you on track and prevent breaking eye contact with the audience.

Build a relationship with you. When you talk, you interact with a group of individuals, not acting in front of a single team. Efficient eye contact means more than just transferring your eyes around the room; it means reflecting on the individual listeners and establishing a person-to-person interaction with them. How are you doing this? Start by choosing an individual and talking to him or her directly. Keep the person's eyes long enough to create a conceptual bond, maybe five to ten seconds, or the time needed to utter a sentence or express a thought. Then shift your eyes to another guy. You may have observed a speaker waging his head from side to side, or slowly turning his attention from right to left like an oscillating fan. Often note that while your eyes ought to shift from one person to the next, they should not follow some pattern. For an audience of the size of a traditional Toastmasters club, this is reasonably easy to achieve. However, if you select one or two people in each part of the room and create personal relations with them, each audience can get the feeling that you're talking to him or her directly.

Visual input control

When you give a speech, your listeners respond with their non-verbal messages. Use your eyes to find this useful help. Through watching these visual signals, you will gauge the responses of the audience to what you say, and then change your layout accordingly. When people in the crowd are not smiling at you, they will not be listening to you either. It's often so you can't be heard when you don't have a microphone, sound loud to see if there's a good response. They might just be bored. If that is the case, you'll need to recover their attention, maybe by using acceptable language, increasing your vocal variation, or making some purposeful movements, or the body's motions. If you think the listeners are puzzled? If that is the case, you will need to have more clarity about what you said. Monitor them as you do, and when their faces register recognition, switch to the next stage or thought. Are your listeners frowning at you? Note the viewer is unintentionally mirroring the speaker. You might be unintentionally glaring at them. Smile and see how their gestures alter. The same holds for members of the crowd who are nervously fidgeting: you might have been disturbing physical mannerisms. On the other hand, if their expressions reflect joy, curiosity, and near attention, don't change it. You're doing a fine job.

How to make the first impression?

First experiences are somewhat meaningful. People meeting for the first time make instant assumptions on each other that permanently color their relationships. When you give a speech, you will be judged by the people in your audience, and the initial effect you deliver on them will significantly influence the performance of your presentation. One of your goals as a speaker is to create a visual picture that complements and strengthens your verbal message. You want your audience to respect you, to believe you, and to hear what you say. You have already made your first impression on your fellow club members as a Toastmaster. Know though, that your club is a learning workshop that trains you for outside speech offered to other people, and in the future, you will be presenting to business associations and the neighborhood. You're going to be a mystery to all of these viewers, and having a strong first impression would be significant.

Appearance matters a lot

Like it or not, your body image has a significant effect on how people evaluate you. When you give a speech, your presentation conveys a compelling visual message to the viewer that is crucial to your performance as a communicator. You can't change your age, height, or facial features so that you can improve your appearance through proper clothes, grooming, and exercise. This manual cannot contain extensive information on these subjects. The types and interests differ considerably over time, place, and socio-economic conditions. There are few common remarks for both speakers. A strict thumb rule for the dress is to be at least as well-dressed as the best-dressed person in the crowd. When your listeners are wearing suits and ties, eat the best case or dress to get you the most compliments. Make sure that every piece of clothing is tidy, well-tailored, and well-fitting. Don't wear jewelry that glitters or jingles when you're driving or make a motion. It could divert attention away from your voice. For the same purpose, clean your pockets of bulky items or stuff like pocket changes or keys that create audible sounds as you walk. Audiences want speakers representing mental health and physical vitality. Research has found that the listener correlates the well-being of a speaker with the soundness of his or her verbal messages. So, watch your diet and workout daily.

When you speak to the audience
Part of your first impression is made before you begin your voice. As the crowd enters, the plans should be finished. It would be best if you did not have to research the message. Instead, mix with the group and express the same fun, optimistic personality that will make the speech a success. Be attentive and courteous as the conference or curriculum starts. If you're anxious, relax gently and deeply. One speaker is advised to do isometrics. These unobtrusive training gestures go unnoticed by some and are useful for helping to dissipate nervous energy.

The first-minute importance
When you talk, mainly if you are not well known to the crowd, the most critical part of your performance is the first minute. In those few seconds, the people in the group are going to make important decisions about you. They will determine if you are confident, genuine, polite, willing to answer them, and deserving of their consideration. And to a large extent, they're going to base this decision on what

they see. After your introduction, walk deliberately and steadily to your speaking role. Balance your body while you take your speaking part. Keep immediate interaction with the viewer, incorporating direct eye contact with a friendly smile. Keep your expressions and emotions to a minimum during the first few moments of your speech; let the crowd get used to you first.

Thumbs up on expressions
As speakers, we need to note that much of our message is not just in our voices, but also in our visual presentation. For some of us, this involves extending our expressions and facial gestures and cultivating a better understanding of eye touch. For some, it means modulating the very one's same characteristics as well. Whatever your physical strengths and communication skills, your ability to physically articulate your concepts through gestures and other modes of body language will improve not only your appearance but your overall success as a speaker.

The dominant trend of psychology over the last few decades has been that individuals do not necessarily work at their maximum mental potential. That is, often people think carefully about things, but they can't think carefully about every piece of knowledge or message they receive. Instead, people often rely on algorithms or shortcuts in decision-making. This differing degree of thinking or elaboration has repercussions about how evidence is obtained and its convincing effect. The ELM (Elaboration Likelihood Model) is an early example of what has been an eruption of dual-process and dual-system decision-making and assessment theories. However, rather than suggesting that people thought only in one manner or another, it presents a continuum of thought (elaboration). With different reasoning (or "route") taking place at either end of the continuum and a mixture of the respective techniques at either direction at a moderate level of thinking. Persuasion based on comparatively high degrees of thought is considered the critical path to influence. Whereas effectiveness, which happens with very little thought, is called the Peripheral way of convincing. These different routes mean that different people can respond to the same information very differently, or the same people can respond differently to the same information in other conditions. Importantly, whether persuasion emerges from comparatively high or low levels of thought can have somewhat different effects.

Primary Route

When inspired and willing to do so, people appear to closely examine the facts provided to them, analyzing the presumed core validity of the premises in the light of pre-existing expertise. Importantly, this improved thought does not immediately translate to an improvement in persuasion. An assertion (or piece of evidence) is only convincing if it gives rise to beneficial ideas in the receiver. A statement may be counterproductive to a persuasion effort if it is deemed to be wrong or, for the most part, causes unfavorable responses, such as counterarguments. Under the central path, the degree of change in mood depends on the importance of the thoughts generated in response to the message (favorable or unfavorable), the number of them, and how secure people are in their studies. The clearer thinking generated, the more confident it is, the more convincing it is. Since the central route depends on the assumed rather than the real nature of the main merits of the case, its persuasiveness will vary from person to person. It also means that high reasoning does not inherently amount to objectivity or fairness in judgment. Careful judgment may be impartial or may be skewed.

Peripheral route

Since people cannot give their full attention to every message, they are introduced. They frequently focus more on simplistic heuristics or peripherals, like the experience or popularity of the speaker or their current mood (e.g., "I liked that rally, so I must like that candidate"). In the political sense, a variety of reasonably necessary cues are available, which, in the absence of much thinking, may cause favorable judgments. The clearest example of this is the Democratic Party. Other powerful cues include likability, resemblance, and trust heuristics, including voting for someone because they seem likeable, close to themselves, or trustworthy while not learning anything about the candidate's policies. Indeed, the essential assumed trustworthiness of the candidate's face has been shown to forecast election results. While simple cues, such as likability and confidence, often bring about improvement when people do not think much about the peripheral path, as will soon be discussed, these same simple cues may often affect attitudes through the central route.

Determinants of progress

If a message is interpreted through the central or peripheral route is determined by the degree of improvement it receives. Factors such as political engagement and expertise may decide the path to persuasion by influencing how often people are inspired or willing to learn about political messaging. In addition to information, the capacity to interpret a message may be affected by variables such as time constraints, obstacles, and the "channel" of communication. (self-paced media such as written materials are more straightforward to interpret than audio or video, the speed of which is fixed in production). In addition to political interest, motivational considerations influencing the amount of thought include such aspects as to how the receiver finds the subject to be individually significant, whether there is any perceived standard of appraisal (i.e., accountability), as well as some personality distinctions. Three characteristics that are extremely important and have generated a great deal of attention are the need for cognition (how much someone likes to consider and solve problems). The need to analyze (how much someone wants to assess things and make firm decisions on concepts). And the need for clarity (how much someone likes to get a prompt answer).

Elaboration implications

As factors enhance the probability of reasoning by increasing one's motivation or skill, essential signals become less critical determinants in attitudes, while meaningful roles and claims become more acute. Since political material (and one's reaction to it) is more closely evaluated in the sense of improved planning, this information is more likely to be adequately incorporated into the pre-existing mental structure of the recipient for assessment. Behaviors formed or modified by the central route are more expected to be stronger and more significant than the same attitudes developed or altered peripherally. This implies that actions in a prominent way would be more accessible (come to mind quickly), more optimistic (seen to be more legitimate), more consistent over time. Thus, while the two paths of influence can lead to what seems like the same mindset, they can have very different and significant implications? Next, we can see how the same variable can lead to convincing by either the central or the peripheral path.

Several functions

To date, we have noted two ELM (elaboration likelihood model) claims. Two simple convincing routes function at the end of the elaboration spectrum and vary in related issues. They consider necessary to result in a change of attitude; and while both routes may result in straightforwardly similar outcomes, the primary way of persuasion, with its more elaborate processing, results in a strong one.

How better you react to body language?
Depending on Your Personality Style Body Language is a big part of your conversation, but certain people don't pay enough attention to it. Here's how you react to body language, depending on your form of personality.

INFJ:

INFJs are sensitive people who pay attention to their environment. They pay attention to the descriptions and attitudes of people, which is why they can interpret them so well. INFJs will identify those actions in body language and can use them to help understand others and what they experience. INFJs are in contact with other people's feelings, and while verbal responses are a bit part of how others perceive each other, their body language is much more critical. INFJs are also not the most articulate individuals, which is why others must be able to pick up body language.

ENFJ:

The ENFJs are undoubtedly fantastic at interpreting body language, which is why they are so good at reading the feelings of others. Although ENFJs pay attention to what people think, they spend much more attention to their body language. They know that the way people act emotionally will sometimes reflect how they feel a lot more than what they think. Body language is essential to ENFJs, and they naturally can identify people's physical indices.

INFP:

INFPs are socially isolated people, but they sometimes tend to take a look back instead of getting to the middle of the thing. This will help them pick up the signals that other people are communicating with themselves. They positively respond to body language, but they don't like to pull, either. They want to provide people space, which is why they are not continually paying close attention to the inner feelings of others. INFPs would like to let people show themselves as they can do so.

ENFP:

ENFPs consider the body language of others, even though they do not make this explicit on their own. They don't want people to know how much they pick up and love giving people rights. They will pay attention to people's actions and lock it up if they need the detail later. ENFPs like to reflect on their freedom and do not want to linger or smother people with their thoughts.

INTJ:

INTJs always tend to pay attention to as much information as they can acquire, but only when it appears to be relevant. INTJs should not often pay careful attention to the body language of other people, since they may not understand. They don't like trying to read into the tiniest aspects of someone else's actions, so they want people to be upfront and honest. If for some other reason, the INTJ feels it is relevant, they will take the time to find out what's going on with that person. INTJs are perhaps not the most articulate people themselves, so body language can be the only way to interpret their actions or emotions.

ENTJ:

ENTJs are more focused on paying attention to their ambitions and working on getting something done. They like to reflect on their interests and obligations, and they don't like having to pay close attention to the feelings of others. The ENTJ must retain a sense of space from those around them and enjoy freedom. ENTJs are not effective at understanding people, and they tend not to pay constant attention to their actions because they are someone they care deeply for.

INTP:

INTPs will undoubtedly continue to pay careful attention to details and sometimes want to interpret body language rather than verbal answers. INTPs know that not all people say is what they think. They are well aware that body language is an essential way of communicating oneself, and they will undoubtedly attempt to read it in others. They're certainly trying to pay careful attention to the body language of the people around them to get a better reading of their actions. INTPs are just not excellent at interpreting feelings because what they pick up will be difficult for them to handle.

ENTP:

ENTPs certainly know that body language is an integral aspect of the comprehension of others. They're likely to pay careful attention to someone's actual behavior as they learn to read them correctly. Although ENTPs may pick up on body language and attempt to better interpret someone's actions in this manner, they can lack understanding of their emotions. It may be difficult for them to process what they see in that person because feelings are not always their strong suit.

ISTJ:

ISTJs aren't efficient in reading body language, so they want people to be upfront on what they want. They're not fans of trying to dig further, so reading thoughts can be challenging for them. The ISTJs want the people around them to be transparent and frank with them about what they want and what they believe. This way, the ISTJ will find a realistic solution to any dilemma that the individual is having. For the ISTJs, getting to pick up on hidden clues is not exactly their most vital point.

ESTJ:

ESTJs are certainly not fond of trying to pick up on body language and more apparent habits. They'd rather be with independent people and upfront with their desires. If someone is frustrated or in need of help, the ESTJ needs the person to make things understandable to them without holding back. People who continually need others to translate their body language may be incredibly irritated and puzzled by the ESTJ.

ISFJ:

ISFJs are compassionate people who like to pay careful attention to the needs of those around them. The ISFJs understand the value of body language and will undoubtedly pay careful attention to it. They know that collecting the physical actions of the people around them can allow them to consider what they experience. People don't show themselves honestly, and their body language will give away what they feel.

ESFJ:

The ESFJs adapts well to body language and take time to understand the physical reactions of others. The ESFJs also do this instinctively, which allows them to understand the feelings of those around them. The ESFJs are in touch with the emotions of others and are profoundly concerned about the wishes of their loved ones. Because of this relationship with the feelings of people, the ESFJs pay particular attention to their body language to understand what they experience and not merely what they verbalize to others.

ISTP:

The ISTPs just don't pay much attention to the feelings of others, so they tend to preserve a sense of individuality. They don't like trying to pick up on the overt actions of someone, and they like people that are upfront on what they want. ISTPs are physical beings, but they understand when people have different physical reactions. They're just not great at deciphering feelings, which makes it impossible to bring things together.

ESTP:

ESTPs certainly understand that someone shows a different body language than usual. They know when someone doesn't respond to them the way they usually do, and they will react to it. They may become very depressed if their loved ones begin to be emotionally distant, as ESTPs are closely linked to the physical world around them. They will naturally be conscious of the material changes in others, and they will want to react accordingly.

ISFP:

The ISFPs note the body language and subtle variations in people's physical actions. They like, however, when people can articulate themselves freely because interpreting these signals can feel intrusive. The ISFPs want their loved ones to be upfront and frank with them, and to share their emotions more freely.

ESFP:

The ESFPs also understand body language better than anything else, since they are in touch with the real world around them. They will also note that someone behaves weirdly or not feeling right, purely based on their body language and outward appearances. For ESFPs, it is often better to understand people based on how they express themselves visually than verbally.

A persuasion is an act of persuading others to change their views or to do what you say. Influence has always been represented as a delicate type of art, but what makes it so healthy? Understanding the art of persuasion cannot only help you know how to manipulate people; it can also make you more aware of the strategies that you may use to try to alter your values and attitudes.

Is persuasion an art, and why?
To understand the art of persuasion, you must first understand the broader meaning of philosophy. Art is a method and a commodity that:

- Expresses intense feelings

- Intellectually demanding

- Complex and consistent

- Conveys confusing signals

- Shows a single point of view

- Produces an entity or output that involves a high level of ability

It is still clear how many of the above characteristics refer to types of art such as painting and playing music; they do not all refer to the art of convincing. Persuasion is not an art form in the same way as painting or music but instead includes highly tuned artistic skills-or the art-of language and conversation. However, persuasion does contain some of the characteristics of more conventional types of painting. It's mentally demanding, challenging, articulate, and loyal to your character.

What is the point of persuasiveness?
You may consider why you should want to learn how to impress others. You may also think that such a "craft" is diabolical or deceptive. The reality, though, is that any successful person has been able to convince others of something at one time or another. For example, most people have to ask the boss to hire them before they can even start working and making money. Persuasion is moving to several humanitarian efforts. Salespeople convince customers to purchase goods or services. Politics are persuading voters to help and vote for them. Con artists are persuading people to fall for scams and waste money they don't have. You may convince your teacher to take a makeup exam, encourage your girlfriend or partner to marry you or persuade others to assist with your service program. It's pretty hard to find people getting something done without any sort of persuasion. So, it's just not a matter of whether you can practice better methods of convincing. The concern is that you haven't already done it.

Factors to be considered in the art of convincing

All should learn the art of convincing. It needs determination to know how to do it successfully. Some people seem to have the ability to persuade people to see it that way. If you find it hard to remember, it's not the end of life. You can and will learn how to master this kind of craft. Here are several things to remember when you decide to convince someone:

Evaluate how simple the convincing can be

You should begin by feeling how difficult it is to win over the audience. Researchers have described many influences that affect how easy it can be to persuade others of something. All you need to do is follow the correct instructions and strategies.

Group member

When you are a member of a group, you are objectively less likely to be convinced of topics or ideas that run contrary to the opinions to your fellow group members.

Low self-esteem

People with low self-esteem are significantly much more comfortable to persuade than people with higher self-esteem. This is more likely because they appear to trust the views of others more than they do their own. The biggest obstacle you're going to face here is to assess the level of self-esteem of the person you're trying to convince. You will also do this by examining variables such as body posture, voice confidence, and dedication to the audience's point of view.

Inhibiting aggression

If you don't want to display confrontation, you're more likely to be surpassed by a smooth talker fluent in persuasion. And if they make you feel dissatisfied with something, they're trying to persuade you of, lack of provocation will make it easy for them to manipulate your decisions. People who are not inclined to violence don't argue what the other person suggests.

Depression and anxiety behaviors

Research suggests that unhappy people are more readily persuaded to accept someone else's opinions on their own. This is primarily attributed to factors such as lack of violence and self-esteem, as described above. However, you can find that certain people who suffer from depression will not be convinced by you, but rather cooperate with you to prevent confrontation.

Social inferiority

Many of those who think themselves socially insufficient appear to be more readily convinced. Even if they are no more socially incompetent than most, the fact that they perceive themselves in this manner causes them to put the responsibility of interaction on the person they communicate with. This makes it easy for the person to reassure them without being challenged.

How to Practice Persuasiveness?
Get the Appropriate Introduction
It's incredibly difficult to persuade an outsider of something. For example, salespeople dislike cold calling because they never know the kind of person they're dealing with on the other hand. They don't know their beliefs, interests, or whether they belong to a party that rejects what / how they're offering. Just as essential, the person calling does not know, and the salesperson does not trust. If you can get an introduction from a mutual friend or colleague, you have a lot better chance of persuading others to consider your perspective. If you can't find an opening, it allows you ready for something before you try to convince yourself. This is where outstanding listening and leadership skills come into the frame.

Worth of the hearing
When you first listen, you collect the details you need to build a customized presentation that makes sense to the person you're trying to convince. Skilled election candidates don't just turn up at the door and start to read. Instead, they usually ask a few questions about your beliefs to reach a starting point for their persuasion. In addition to the knowledge you get from listening, you build the feeling that you trust the other person and agree with their views. On the other hand, they are more inclined to shape a complementary view of you and listen to what you have to say.

When you don't believe, be respectful

It's important to discuss your consensus with the person you're trying to reassure as much as possible. This shows that you value them and that you are broad-minded. Everyone needs to be thought of as wise because if you're going to contradict anything anyone does, they're just going to ignore you. Of course, on anything, you can't compromise with anybody, nor should you have to. Although you did, you wouldn't have been able to persuade your group to change their stance. You should maintain a kind approach that respects the rationale behind what they believe and the decisions they make.

Subtlety is essential

If you can say precisely what you want someone to believe, and they think it right away, there's not much need for convincing. More often than not, you ought to convince them in positive ways that your point of view is right. There are several different ways of convincing to be used, but the most powerful are those that are not obvious or apparent. Instead, they are based on making associations, sharing stories, and understanding the other person and where they stand.

Persuasion and Values

The art of convincing involves persistence and dedication to the method. If it were a matter of just saying, "Believe me!" there wouldn't be a lot of justification involved. You ought to take the time to formulate your points and justify your logic, implicitly, and consistently, to change someone's mind. If it's a short letter, it does not take a long time to send. But if you want to express anything more complicated, you need to be careful and engage with your audience.

Whose opinion matters?

If you bring your argument to a close, you can represent your conclusion as entirely right. However, people are more quickly convinced if they feel that they are coming to their judgment. They like to think that they decide to change their views, values, or behavior. The good news is, if you put out your point in a manner that makes sense to your viewers, they're likely to believe that their change of mind was their own choice. They would also be more likely to continue to hang on to that belief and, most critically, to act on it.

Legal issues

There are a few legal dilemmas to examine if you intend to learn the art of convincing. Many individuals have mischievously used manipulation methods to harm or take advantage of others. Before you decide to persuade others to work with you, think about the effect they will have if you succeed.

Undue interference

Undue interference is a legal concept that implies that you persuade others to behave according to their own free choice, without regard to the consequences. This becomes a matter of interest because someone is affected in a way and unable to make their own choices. For example, a caregiver may persuade an elderly adult to change their will and leave it. If you suggest studying the practice of persuasion, it is a spiritual necessity to resist excessive control. It'll keep you out of legal trouble too.

Misrepresenting statements

If you're in court or making a social media post, it's unethical to make misleading claims, papers, or pictures to support your case. If you wish to be responsible and considerate in your practice of convincing, you need to make sure that the facts or keeping information you give are reliable and valid to the best of your ability.

Perpetual Scams

People who use their convincing fluency to scam others don't care if what they do is harming someone. Sometimes, the people they end up persuading try to convince others of the same stuff without realizing that they were conned. It is essential to keep the facts straight and alert to the potential of deceit.

Is convincing positive or negative?

Just like every other type of practice, persuasion is neither positive nor negative in itself. It is how you use the art of influence, and for what reason, that decides whether you are adding something valuable to the world. The failure to impress others can be a considerable handicap in life. You may have problems finding a job, buying a house, or taking the next step in your relationship. On the other hand, you might find that you are so easily swayed and fall for any trick you have been faced with. If so, there are various ways to reduce the vulnerability to falling because of any slick come-on. A therapist will help you develop your self-esteem, strengthen your life skills, and learn how to handle your depression. These variables are going to make you less vulnerable to deceit.

Secrets of persuasive people
If you encourage your boss to finance your initiative or your preschooler to wipe away his tush after using the toilet, convincing is an ability that is integral to your progress in life. Persuasive people have an uncanny tendency to make you lean toward their way of thought. Their hidden weapon is the possibility. They're trying to get you to like more than their ideas; they're going to get you to like them.

Here are the 15 trading tricks that incredibly convincing people use to their benefit.

1. They know about their audience
Persuasive people know their listeners inside and outside, and they use this information to express the language of their listeners. If it's toning down your aggressiveness when talking to someone who's reserved or churning it up with an angry, high-energy sort, everyone is different, and keeping up on these subtleties is a long way to getting them to hear your perspective.

2. They connect with the audience
People are much more likely to consider what you have to say because they feel what kind of person you are. In a negotiating report, Stanford students were asked to agree in class. Without some sort of training, 55 percent of students have successfully reached an agreement. However, when students were told to identify themselves and discuss their history before seeking to reach an agreement, 90 %

did so effectively. The objective here is to stop getting too entangled in the back and forth of the conversation. The person you're talking to is a person, not a competitor or a target. No matter how exact the point is, if you don't communicate on a personal basis, he or she will doubt anything you say.

3. They don't push others

Persuasive people develop their ideas confidently and enthusiastically, without being hostile or violent. Pushy people are a drastic shift. The in-your-face technique begins with the receiver backpedaling, and they're heading for the hills before long. Persuasive people don't demand anything, and they don't require vigorously for their role because they realize that the subtlety is what wins people over in the long run. If you want to be more hostile, concentrate on being optimistic yet relaxed. Don't be anxious and stubborn. Know that if you genuinely have a good idea, people can catch on if you give them time. If you don't, they're not going to catch on at all.

4. They're not the mousy

From the other side, delivering the concepts as questions or as if they required validation makes them seem to be incomplete and unconvincing. If you seem to be quiet, concentrate on expressing your thoughts as claims and fascinating information to the other person. Also, exclude the qualifiers from your speech. When you're striving to be compelling, there's no room for "I guess" or "It's likely."

5. Using constructive body language

Becoming familiar with your movements, expressions, and tone of voice (and making sure they are positive) will attract people and open them to your points. Using an enthusiast accent, uncrossing your arms, keeping eye contact, and moving into the person who speaks is supportive body language that convincing people use to impress others. Strong body language will motivate the audience and persuade them that what you say is true. When it comes to compelling how you say things may be more important than what you say.

6. They are both straightforward and precise

Persuasive people can express their thoughts quickly and simply. When you have a good understanding of what you're talking about, it's fun and straightforward to explain to those who don't understand. The right approach here is to know the subject so that you can describe it to a child. If you can easily justify yourself to someone who has no experience on the subject, you can make a convincing argument for someone who does.

7. They are real and honest

Being real and genuine is essential for us to be persuasive. No one ever likes a fake. People gravitate to others who are sincere, and they feel they can trust them. It's hard to accept someone when you don't know who they indeed are and how they think. Persuasive people are mindful of who they are. They are happy enough to be relaxed in their skin. By reflecting on what inspires you and makes you comfortable as an entity, you become a far more engaging and convincing person than if you try to win people over by pretending to be the person, they want you to be.

8. They consider your point of view

The argument is an incredibly useful technique of persuasion. Please accept that your claim is not good. This indicates that you are open-minded and able to make changes instead of arrogantly sticking to your cause. You want your viewers to know that their best interests are at your heart. Consider using comments like, "I see where you're coming from," and, "It makes a lot of sense." This shows that you're listening to what they're saying. And you're not merely trying to push your thoughts on them. Persuasive people encourage others to be entitled to their views, and they accept personal views as genuine. They do this because it displays appreciation, making the other person more inclined to consider their perspective.

9. They ask good questions

The most significant mistake people have when it comes to listening is not hearing what they're saying, so they're focused on what they're going to say next, or how the other person is going to influence them. Words come out loud and straightforward, but the sense is lost. An easy way to prevent it is to ask a lot of questions. People want to hear that you're listening because anything as fundamental as a clarification question demonstrates not just that you're listening, but also that you care about what they're saying. You'll be shocked by how much appreciation and respect you receive from raising questions.

10.Visual presentations

Research indicates that audiences are far more likely to be influenced by something that has graphics that carry it to life. Persuasive people use strong graphic representations to focus on this. Real photographs are not accessible or necessary; they tell vibrant storylines that breathe life into their ideas. Good tales create memories in the minds of recipients that are easy to connect to and hard to forget.

11. They leave a positive first impression

Research suggests that most people decide whether they want you in the first seven seconds of the meeting. Then they spend the remainder of the discussion mentally explaining their initial response. This can sound scary, but by understanding this, you will take advantage of it to make substantial progress in your resilience and willingness to convince. Initial experiences are intimately related to constructive body language. Strong expression, a firm handshake, a smile, and opening your arms to the person you're talking to would help guarantee that your first impression is a positive one.

12. They know how to stand in front of audiences

Insistence is a direct challenge of persuasion, so move softly when you want to convince people to decide immediately, finding demonstrated that they are often more likely to endorse their original view. Your impatience leads them to fight your points for their own sake. If your place is right, you're not meant to be scared to back off and give it time to sink in. Good ideas are always challenging to process immediately, and a little effort will go a long way.

13. They recognize people by name

Your name is a vital part of your personality, and it sounds terrific when people use it. Persuasive people make sure they use the names of others any time they meet them. You're not supposed to use someone's name when you meet him or her. Research indicates that people feel valued when the person they're referring to speaks to them by name. If you're brilliant with faces but have difficulty with words, have fun with them and making people remember their names a brain exercise. When you meet people, don't be scared to ask for their name a second time if you forget it right after you hear it. You're going to have to keep the word handy, so you remember next time you see the person.

14. They are pleasers

Persuasive people never fight a battle only to lose a war. They know how and when to hold their ground, but they are continually making sacrifices to support their cause. They still give in, give land, and do things to those that make them happy. Persuasive people do this, and they know that this won people over in the long term. They know that it's easier to be good than to be "right."

15. They always keep smiling

People usually (and unconsciously) reflect the body language of the person they are referring to. If you want people to respect you and trust in you, smile at them during a conversation, and, as a result, they will automatically return the favor and feel happy. Persuasive people laugh a lot, and they have a real passion for their ideas. This has a cumulative effect on all the people they meet.

How to read and persuade people with six robust courtroom techniques?

Recognize the 'three personality positions'
Image of three chairs lined up in a row. The first chair is your public face, the way you want to look to everyone. The second is your secret face, the feelings of inadequacy that you keep hidden or only share with your friends. The third is your hidden identity, the thing that motivates you to make fake fronts, for example, something that happened to you as a teenager. Start by reflecting on someone's first chair in an initial conversation. Encourage them to chat about what they think is fascinating. Let them show their greatness, and they'll be flattered that you're involved in building confidence.

Understand and sympathize
To link to a deeper level, speak to your second chair next. Place yourself in the hands of the other person: consider how they feel and talk about those feelings. You don't even have to ask questions; just make observations. For instance, you might say, "It must be a struggle to run your own company with so many people dependent on you." So shut up, listen, and let them express themselves. You know, when you respect their role, it shows them that you see them. Be kind and speak to the person's heart. If you're not sure how they think, share the analogies of your life and see how they align with them.

Be honest
You have to talk from your own to someone's third chair. Conversely, to what we're sometimes instructed, it's all right to express your feelings about communicating with others. Being vulnerable to your insecurities or worries is the perfect way to create confidence and allow others to open up. When we start a courtroom, we first tell the jurors what we fear the opposing side will do. For example, if our

client were prosecuting a dishonest business associate, we could suggest to the jury, "You should sure the prosecution can tell you that our client wasn't affected by this crime because he's wealthy and prosperous." When they hear that, the jury would think, "We're not going to fall for that."

Focus on body language and voice tone

"Mirroring" is a common practice where you unconsciously imitate the pose of the other person, such as leaning back or avoiding eye contact. You may sense how someone feels by watching their body language and listening to their speech. Does it sound familiar and fit with what they say? For example, if their words represent confidence, but they cannot meet your eyes, they may lack confidence. Focus on their facial gestures and glance at their eyes. We shake hands with every member of the jury by eye contact, focusing on someone until we see their head turn subtly, signaling that we are related to them. Be mindful in your voice, including your accent and intonation. For example, you might lower your voice to establish a sense of intimacy and deliberately pause to lead a discussion.

Address your objections

Through power and justification, you may counter the preconceived objections, statements, and prejudices of the other individual. That's why we ask the jury early in the trial to uncover all their biases to fix them. E.g., "Some people believe like wealthy business owners don't deserve the significant awards we are aiming for. Can you feel like that? "Listen to them and thank them for expressing their viewpoint. To resolve objections, do not undermine their beliefs; only encourage them to be open to your point of view, reframe the issue, and answer their concerns. Describe what you should do with them instead of selling them. Paint an idea of what their life would be like if they knew of what you were offering. Ask them to explain their experiences in detail despite their current problems, using the five senses and the present tense.

Principles of persuasion

Why is it that some people are so highly persuasive? Should we all take advantage of those abilities? After researching the most influential political, educational, business, and religious figures and testing countless strategies out of me, these are the 21 crucial lessons that I've found for persuading people.

1. Persuasion is not manipulation

Manipulation is intimidation by pressure to get others to do something that is not in their interests. Persuasion is the art of convincing people to do things that are in their best part and help you.

2. Convince the Persuadable

Everybody can be convinced, with the correct time and meaning, but not always in the short term. Democratic candidates spend their time and money on a limited collection of swinging electors who plan to vote. The first step in persuasion is often to recognize specific individuals who are convincing to your point of view at a given moment and to concentrate your energies and attention on them.

3. Timing and Context

Context and pace are the fundamental building blocks of persuasion. Context provides a clear norm of what is appropriate. For example, the Experiment has demonstrated that overachieving students could be shaped into dictatorial correctional officers. Timing determines what we expect from people and our lives. We choose to marry a different sort of person than we do when we're younger because what we want is a transition.

4. You've to be involved in being convinced
You will never convince someone who isn't interested in what you're saying. We are always most interested in ourselves, and we spend most of our time worrying about the future, love, or health. The first art of convincing is learning how to speak to people about them all the time; if you do that, you'll have their captive interest.

5. Cooperation obligates
When someone do something for you, you feel obligated to do something for him or her. It's part of our evolutionary DNA to help each other survive as a community. More specifically, you can unduly exploit reciprocity in your favor. By making small gestures of kindness to others, you will ask for more back in exchange, which they would gladly give.

6. The Consistency in a work
The person who can continue to question what they want, and who continues to show importance, is essentially the most convincing. The way too many historical personalities have eventually convinced millions of people to remain vigilant in their actions and message. Remember Abraham Lincoln, who lost his mother, three sons, his sister, his spouse, fell in

business and lost eight consecutive elections before he was appointed president of the United States.

7. Perfectly complement

We are also profoundly influenced by compliments, and we are more likely to trust people with whom we have positive feelings. Try to congratulate others honestly and sometimes on something they're not generally complimented with. It's the best thing you can do to convince someone that costs nothing but a moment of contemplation.

8. Place your objectives

A lot of persuasions are balancing the desires of others to trust your decision. The CEO who guarantees a 20 percent rise in revenue and a 30 percent increase is rewarded, while the same CEO who offers a 40 percent increase and produces 35 percent is fined. Persuasion is essentially about knowing and over-expecting the perceptions of others.

9. Don't presume

Don't ever think about what someone wants; only show your worth. We often avoid selling our products/services because we feel that others don't have the money or interest. Don't guess what someone will or may not want, give what you can, and leave the decision.

10.Build your scarcity

Apart from the need to live, nearly everything has a perceived meaning. We like things because these things are what other people like. If you want somebody to want what you've got, you've found ways to make the item scarce, even though it's yourself.

11. Build Emergency

You ought to be able to induce a sense of urgency in people who want to move right away. If we're not inspired enough to do anything right now, we're unlikely to have any incentive in the future. We have to reassure people, and desperation is our most important card to play.

12. Graphics matters a lot

What we see is more effective than what we hear. That could be why pharma firms are now so close to the potentially terrible side effects of their medications as they set the backdrop for people watching the sunset in Hawaii. Your first thoughts are perfect. And master the ability to build a picture for others, the vision of their eyes, of a potential event that you will have for them.

13. Tell the truth

Often the most powerful way to reassure someone is to teach them things about themselves that nobody else can admit. Faced with harsh facts are the most prevalent, essential incidents that have taken place in our lives. Truth-tell without bias or agenda, and you will also find the responses of others fascinating.

14. Develop a relationship

This applies to our unconscious actions outside our deliberate decisions. By mirroring and balancing other regular habits (body language, intonation, voice rhythms, etc.), you will create a sense of relationship where people are more relaxed with you and are more open to your ideas.

15.Flexibility of actions

It's the most versatile, not necessarily the strongest, who's in charge. Children are also compelling that they tend to go through a litany of actions to get what they want (pouting, screaming, negotiating, begging, and charming), while adults are left with a simple "no" answer. The greater the collection of actions, the more compelling you would be.

16.Learn how to pass energy

Some people strip our energy away from us, and others infuse us with it. The most successful people know how to shift their motivation to others, inspire, and invigorate them. It's often as simple as eye contact, body interaction, humor, interest in verbal response, or even active listening.

17.Communicate clearly and effectively

If you can't describe the idea or point of view to an 8th grader in such a manner that they can tell it to another adult with ample clarification, it's too hard. The art of convincing is to simplify everything down to its heart and explain to people what they truly care about.

18.Being organized give you the edge

Your starting point ought to be to know something about the people and circumstances around you. Planning and preparation facilitate a successful argument. For example, in a work interview, you significantly boost the chances of being well versed in the company's goods, programs, and history.

19. Keep calm and isolate in confrontation

Nobody is more successful when they are "On Tilt." In conditions with remarkable ability, you will still have the most influence through remaining relaxed, detached, and compassionate.

20. Use frustration for intent

Many of the people are unhappy with the confrontation. Whether you're able to intensify the situation to a heightened level of uncertainty and conflict, in certain conditions, some will come back down. Using this sparingly, and should not do so from an irrational point of view or lack of self-control. But note, you can use rage purposefully to your benefit.

21. Conviction and self-assurance

Performance is not as persuasive, intoxicating, and desirable as certainty. It is the one who has an unbridled sense of confidence that will always convince others. When you genuinely believe in what you're doing, you're still going to inspire people to do what's best for them while getting what you want in exchange.

Psychological convincing strategies

Every day, we are faced with persuasion in a wide range of ways. The average citizen is subject to thousands of advertisements a day. Meat producers want us to purchase their newest items, while film companies want us to watch the next blockbusters. Since manipulation is such a ubiquitous aspect of our lives, it is also all-too-easy to forget how we are affected by outside sources. Persuasion is not simply helpful to advertisers and salespeople. Learning how to use these methods in your day-to-day life will help you become a successful negotiator and make it more realistic that you'll get what you want, whether you're trying to persuade your baby to eat her vegetables or to force your employer to grant you the bonus. Since persuasion is so effective in so many areas of everyday life, the strategies of persuasion have been practiced and experienced since ancient times. It wasn't until the beginning of the 20th century, though, that social scientists started to research these effective strategies systematically.

Main Persuasion Strategies

The end aim of convincing is to persuade the target to internalize the convincing claim and to accept this new mindset as part of their core value system. The below are only a handful of the most powerful means of convincing. Other approaches include the use of incentives, penalties, constructive or negative expertise, and many others.

Trying to create a need

One form of convincing requires the development of a desire or an appeal to an established desire. This kind of persuasion relates to a person's simple needs for shelter, affection, self-esteem, and self-actualization. Marketers often use this tactic for marketing their goods. Remember, for example, how many commercials indicate that people choose to buy a certain product to be satisfied, healthy, loved, or appreciated.

Adjust to societal needs

Another very successful persuasion tactic is appealing to the desire to be famous, respectable, or equivalent to others. Television advertisements include many examples of this form of manipulation, in which audiences are persuaded to buy products so that they can be like someone else or be like a well-known or admired individual. Television ads are a huge source of convincing publicity.

Use words and pictures

Persuasion sometimes uses filled words and images. Advertisers are well conscious of the influence of encouraging terms, which is why so many advertisers use expressions such as "Fresh and improved" or "All Natural."

Put your foot on the doorstep

Another method that is also useful at getting people to comply with the order is known as the "foot-in-door" strategy. This persuasive technique entails getting a person to commit to a specific request, such as asking them to buy a small object, followed by a much larger request. By getting the person to consider the tiny initial favor, the claimant already has his "foot in the door," making the recipient more likely to cooperate with the larger offer. For instance, a neighbor wants you to take care of her two children for an hour or two. After you commit to a lesser offer, she wonders if you would only take care of the children for the remainder of the day. Since you have already committed to a specific request, you might feel obligated to consider a larger request. This is a clear example of what psychologists refer to as the law of loyalty, and advertisers also employ this tactic to persuade customers to purchase goods and services.

Go large, then little

This strategy is the reverse of a foot-to-door strategy. A seller may begin by making a big, frequently impractical request. The person responds by refusing to sell, figuratively closing the door. The salesperson answers by making a much smaller offer, which sometimes tends to be conciliatory. People always feel they pressured to respond to these deals. Since they rejected the original offer, people always feel obligated to support the vendor by approving a smaller appeal.

Use the force of mutual support

If people do you a favor, you typically have an almost irresistible responsibility to return the favor in kind. This is regarded as the practice of reciprocity, a social duty to do something for someone else because they did something for you first. Marketers may take advantage of this propensity by making it seem that they are giving you good, such as providing "extras" or discounts, and would force customers to consider a deal and make a purchase.

Establish an anchor point for your corporation

The anchoring bias is a subtle cognitive bias that can have a strong effect on agreements and decisions. To make a compromise, the first bid appears to become a focal point on all future discussions. So, if you're trying to negotiate a pay rise, being the first one to propose an amount, particularly if that amount is a little high, will help you impact subsequent talks. The first number is going to be the starting point. Although you do not get the number, starting high, do lead to a higher offer from your employer.

Limit the availability

A psychologist has established one of the main concepts known as scarcity or restricting the supply of something. Research shows that when things are scarce or reduced, objects become more desirable. People are more likely to purchase anything if they hear that it's the only one or that the deal will soon be over. An artist, for example, might only produce a small run of a single print. Because there are only a few prints left for sale, customers will be more likely to make a buy until they're gone.

Spend time notifying convincing communications

The examples above are only a handful of the numerous methods of convincing mentioned by social psychologists. Search for indications of persuasion in the day-to-day experience. A fascinating procedure is to watch a half-hour of random television shows and to remember any instance of convincing ads. You could be surprised by the sheer number of effective strategies used in such a short period.

How to detect emotions, deceit, and distress?

In your professional and personal life, you need to know who's a friend or an adversary and show you the truth or a bunch of lies. Various records may suggest whether people are excessively upset or nervous, which may be the product of their deception. However, only because you see a sign of deceit, the person might not be lying. There may be other situations at function, which is why it is important to resist generalization and try to search for signs of deceit in the proper sense. The more signals of deceit you see, the better the chances are that the individual is not real to you. Let's assume, for example, that you ask your buddy if he was at the bar last night and, in answer, he's rubbing his nose. The action might not be important on its own, but if it also blushes, stammers, swallows loudly, blinks a lot, and shuffles its legs, then you have ample proof that it hides something from you. If you learn all the signs of deceit and stress, you will become an extremely astute and effective human lie detector. If a person has cheated, the body responds, and there's a disagreement between what's wrong a guy doing and telling the facts.

What Breathing and skin alteration means?
Our ways of breathing change depending on the conditions, such as whether we're under severe stress or lying. You could observe people filling their lungs with the appropriate volume of oxygen and instantly releasing their breath. The explanation for this is that they are oxygenating their bodies when stress and fear have propelled their autonomic nervous system to work overtime. It takes a great deal of energy to fabricate and mislead. Every organ in the body — respiratory, skin, digestive, and neuromata — goes into high gear in reaction to elevated stress. You will even unexpectedly see people's faces blow out as they expel oxygen. This move, too, is the effort of their bodies to relieve the anxiety they accumulated during the discomfort of their deceit. When individuals get highly nervous, they undergo other changes, including altering the color and brightness of their skin. For example, in fair-skinned individuals, the color will shift from a soft shade of pink to a bright red to white and even a greyish brown. When their blood supply increases, their skin represents this transition. You may see a shift in color in those with light skin, but it is much harder to observe in darker-skinned individuals

whose skin color can darken further or appear ashen (greyish).

In addition to seeing changes in the color of the skin, you can see sweat. When you see someone being dishonest, you can see tiny dots of sweat come out of the person's upper lip and then on his forehead, making it look shiny. As the sweat falls, you'll see her clean the sweat from her forehead and forehead, just another sign of deceit. The sweat also migrates to the palms of the hands, leaving them clammy if you shake their hands or brush their palms. Then you'll see them wash their dirty hands together or pull on their dress.

Shaking body
Shaking is also the reaction of the body to terror. In the case of a liar, it stems from the anxiety of being caught. When the body temperature of people who are under tension or lying is increasing, they can do what they can to relieve themselves of the pain of feeling hot, such as loosening their belt or placing their finger under their collar to loosen it. It is also not rare to see the skin broken out in red patches or bumps due to temperature variations. Stress and fear will make them swallow hard, so they feel like their throat muscles are contracting. There are unconscious behaviors that look like life-saving gestures to them, but which translate into warning signals of deceit for you.

As the flow of blood varies, the veins and capillaries expand. People experience pain in tiny capillaries in their bodies, like the sensitive mucous membranes around the nose. That's why to reduce their pain, and people would immediately start pulling on or scratching their nose, eyebrows, ears, or cheeks and around their mouths. Because of this itchy or awkward feeling, you can see their lips swing to the side, pinch together, or spread, which is a common sign of deceit when it comes to questioning.

Shaking of muscles
As muscle tension is considerable, it is not rare for muscles to contract and become weaker. As a consequence, the individual feels uneasiness or shakiness. You will also see that in their hands as they lift something like a cup of water. You can see it in their legs as their posture becomes relentless. Shaking is also the reaction of the body to terror. In the case of a liar, it results from the anxiety of being caught. The body undergoes a temperature shift as it learns that something scary or unpleasant is going to happen. So, a trembling or vibratory motion may be produced to better control the temperature rise due to anxiety. Most generally, someone who experiences nervous anxiety is deceived by shakiness in his or her voice. Vocal muscles, which are the size of a thumbnail, get strained, sparking vocal tremor, and the pitch breaks as the person talks.

What the eyes can reveal?
When people blink a lot, it's a protective reflex. For instance, if someone unexpectedly raised a fist and came to you, you'd instantly come back and start blinking. The response is nature's way to clear your eyes for clearer vision, so you're ready for what the other person may do to you. The same thing happens when you're nervous. You twitch a lot to protect yourself from someone who is challenging you about your misdeeds. This behavior can also indicate feelings of ambiguity or vulnerability. If people feel humiliated, embarrassed, or anxious, they will automatically look away from you. Some people find it impossible to keep eye contact, which is why, when

you ask someone a question and lie in response, they're going to change their line of vision.

How people show self-soothing habits?

Feeling discomfort makes people anxious, and they want instant relief from these emotions, and they will naturally do actions that cause fun experiences. For example, they can rub one or both of their eyes, much as babies do when exhausted or angry. They can frequently stroke certain parts of their body, such as their forearm or thigh. They could scratch their heads, not because they're scratching, but because they feel fine. Initially, the body temperature increases during tension and gradually goes into what is known as homeostatic equilibrium and starts to cool down. A depressed or lying person may begin to feel a rush of coolness in his body and start constantly rubbing his fingers or palms of his hands together to generate heat.

Similarly, as people indulge in self-sustaining actions, they can often threaten to harm or even mutilate themselves to escape them—the pains of their fear that will make them feel better. Some are self-mutilated and feel bad as a way of humiliating themselves. You may have seen people pick their palms and fingers until they bleed. More often, you see them pinching or twisting their skin, dragging their ears, chewing their lips, scraping their fingers or toes, scratching themselves violently, or even bashing their heads.

Eye contact is a prove to truth

It doesn't matter whether people turn their attention to the left or the right or up or down. The important point is they've changed their eyes. There is a line of thought and misconception perpetuated in several body language books that were looking up implies that people are visually-oriented and need to be referred to in visual words, such as "I see" or "Look at this," while looking to the right or the left implies that they are auditory people who can connect to words such as "I hear you" or "Listen to this." When somebody unexpectedly squints his eyes, and a furrowed line emerges in the center of his forehead when asking, it's typically a giant tale of deceit. Their eye expression shows that they're frustrated, irritated, or angry that you're asking questions. You can even see their forehead lines as they wide open their eyes, all of which reflect confusion at your probing awareness of their lie. Some people will avoid eye contact with you constantly to make you believe they're telling the truth. This is a big thing to say, and no one who is saying the truth is continually looking at you, whether he or she is blind.

The response of mouth and lips
The best thing to say about whether people lie or are under severe stress is that they have trouble lubricating the interior of their mouths. Their mucous membranes dry up, and they have trouble swallowing and forming phrases. Their tongue becomes stiff and starts to cling to the inside of their upper lip along with their teeth. That's why you see liars or people who are stressing out lick their lips and swallow them, pinch their lips, and even swing their lips in an unconscious effort to generate more saliva to ease their embarrassment. With little saliva in their mouth, the liars become thirsty, and it is not rare for them to put down a bottle of water in one sitting room. This is commonly done while a convicted suspect is being interviewed during a criminal inquiry.

Involuntary muscles action
The most common muscle twitches occur on the temples and jaw lines, particularly when the jaws clench together. This, too, is the autonomic nervous system that functions while someone is under threat. When you see someone's temples pulsating, they are mostly the product of elevated blood pressure and muscle strain. When the jaws clench tightly, this is also the product of muscle strain. Muscle tension is also prevalent in the spine, particularly in the back. It is not surprising, however, to see people frozen the back of their necks or put their hands there while they indulge in deceit. Another significant to say when a person lies is the shrug of the shoulder. That is how the body loses muscle stress that happens when a person formulates a lie or when they are confronted about non-truth. Liars can suddenly move or shuffle their feet if they ask a critical question or make a lie. It's their body's way of suggesting they want to run or leave the scene to get away from the interrogation.

Deliberately misleading talk
There are many sayings in a person's speech where that person is not real. Here are some of the things they're trying to do:

- Answer a question with your question.

- Send a roundabout answer or get off the tangent instead of sticking to the point while answering a question.

- Repeat the terms and phrases.

- Make psychodynamic slips in which they will confess wrongdoing and then quickly right themselves.

- Talk loudly to pretend confidence, particularly when challenged or confronted.

- Vocally perish after important words or sentences.

- Speak too much and offer too much knowledge that is not important.

- Pause and stammer about main topics, using a tone of "yeah" and "um."

- Stop for a long period during which they create their lie.

- Go on the protective and turn the tables.

- Talk in a trembling voice.

- They also clear their throats.

You can notice these people in your personal life, your business affairs, and even your family. They can be male or female, young or aged. To give you the Body Language Advantage over these toxic styles to quickly identify them and interact with them accordingly — by setting limits or not allowing them to join your life.

Almost 93 percent of the conversation is non-verbal, indicating that it has nothing to do with language. When it comes to conversation, what you say doesn't even mean so much. It's more about how you say it. Yet non-verbal contact is not a conventional language. It is abstract, complicated, and often confounding. There are six keys to sharpen your non-verbal communication skills.

Get some encouragement

Learning the non-verbal language is not a challenge for the faint-hearted. You need to be inspired, and you just want to improve the ability to communicate non-verbally. There's nothing simple about it, of course. You're going to have to invest a lot of effort and energy into it. You will need to set goals, get guidance about your mistakes and achievements, and work.

Strengthen your body language for your reading skills

If you wish to practice non-verbal communication, the most important thing you can do is try to 'read' the non-verbal signals of other people. You need to be observant and attentive, and you need to be focused on getting through with this. You're going to want to get feedback and focus on consistency. That's why it's a smart idea to look for a coaching mentor who can help you climb the ladders and sharpen your skills.

Convey body language to others

This is the encoding, or more, the capacity to convey non-verbal information to other people through posture, facial expressions, movements, and tone of voice. Research suggests that non-verbal encoding and decoding abilities are related. If you're very good at decoding the body language of others, you'll note that you're still very good at conveying body language yourself. To make the best out of body language, you need to improve the capacity to communicate the emotions authentically and learn to be a strong emotional performance.

Remove micro-expressions

There are tiny gestures that can be very confusing. Micro gestures misrepresent your motives and can even ruin the picture you're trying to portray. You should learn to keep your face calm, rock-solid while you talk. Start by practicing with a mirror. Take a look at your reflection in the mirror, and start talking. Concentrate on some odd micro-expressions on your face when you're going through specific emotional states. Try to say the same thing again while keeping your face stable and strong. You should do this work out for about 15 minutes a day.

Understand ethical values
To send correct non-verbal communications, you
need to grasp social norms. Of course, different
signals can mean different things depending on the
context of their use. To be a more effective
communicator, you can consider the communication
context. There is no way you can learn body
language without knowing social conditions.

Non-verbal regulatory skills
You must be able to control your non-verbal actions
based on social efficacy. You may have to hide your
feelings sometimes. If your emotions are very
strong, you won't be involved enough to consider the
non-verbal interactions of others. Learning body
language is not easy, but it can be achieved all the
same. You're just going to have to do the training
and be dedicated to learning.

**Different ways constructive body language will
make your life a better one**
You possibly now know that constructive body
language will have a significant influence on your life.
Research explains that constructive body language
will have a strong influence on everyone. Good body
language refers to aspects like constructive listening,
appropriate eye contact, and some targeted
movements that can make someone more
professional, likeable, and convincing.

1. Change the behavior
Studies suggest that the implementation of
constructive body language has a significant effect on
the hormones. Research also explains that changing
the body's vocabulary to make it meaningful

strengthens the attitudes. This is a significant advantage, provided that a good outlook will make you more effective in addressing the problems of your career and your personal life.

2. Enhance the presence

By changing your body language to make it more optimistic, you will significantly enhance your image. You will give out stronger messages and alter the way people see you. Whenever you get a little down, you should still use power body language to get your life back. Trying to get up, stretch your chest, and keep your head straight for just two minutes. More often than not, you will note how much stronger and more secure you are. You will also have a strong effect on the people around you by practicing a constructive body language.

3. Tends to increase testosterone

Testosterone is an essential hormone in the body, whether you are a male or a woman. It's not just about sports, rivalry, and athletics. It boosts your confidence and makes you feel more secure and trustworthy around the board. Scientific tests have shown that positive body language will increase testosterone levels by up to 20%.

4. Prevent confrontation

Whenever we are irritated or frustrated, we use a particular body language. By mastering defensive body language, we can say it when the people we communicate with get offended. Just assume how many unpleasant experiences you would prevent in this manner. Improving your body language and having a clear perspective of the body language of others is a good way to stop the confrontation.

5. Talk better to people

Up to 93% of all human contact is non-verbal. By following a constructive body language, you will become a more effective communicator. This, in particular, will help you to interact with the people around you and broaden the scope in a professional context.

6. Decreases the stress hormone

Studies have found that positive body language reduces cortisol levels (a stress hormone that adversely influences output and induces detrimental health effects over time) by up to 25%. While using this hormone in your body, supportive body language will reduce discomfort and improve your performance in daily activities.

7. Improves emotional, intellectual ability

One of the core aspects of emotional intelligence is the ability to express thoughts and feelings accurately. People with negative body language have a damaging and spreading impact around them. By learning to strengthen your body language, you will increase your Emotional Intelligence and be a happier person around others. By taking a few minutes per day to develop your body's vocabulary, you will transform your life better.

Unusual facts about body language reading
Non-verbal communication is a social language that is stronger than our vocabulary will ever be. Non-verbal communication mastery will give you specific advantages in both your personal and corporate life.

Perhaps this is why so many life skills coaches discuss the value of knowing body language. As you continue on your quest to learn body language, so that you can make your life a lot easier, it's crucial to keep the following body language details in mind.

It's not all black and white
What many body language specialists don't advise you is that everything is not black and white. Specific gestures have no specific significance. Rather, they're undefined. For, e.g., if anyone crosses their arms, this may be taken to indicate that they indicate defensiveness. But they might be freezing, too, or they might just want to get relaxed. If you strive to improve body language, keep in mind that movements can only be understood based on particular situations. There is no single law that applies to all of us.

Facial body language can be tricky to read
Most adults have perfected the art of masking their real emotions, rendering the face a poor place to start interpreting body language. People just like to get along at home, at work, and in diverse social environments. For that cause, they still appear to smile and believe that their faces are soft when they're genuinely pissed. Much of the time, the face is a friendly mask that veils our real emotions from the outside. Understanding this will come in handy when you continue to develop your body language reading skills. Even the face can carry away some of our deepest emotions, even if they are related to micro-expressions. These are all the unintended releases in our true feelings that break through the shield of the mind. Such micro-expressions can occur for a fraction of a second, and it will take you a lot of

training (and practice) before you can understand how to pick them up.

Body language indicates the purpose
A general idea out there is that body language is a symbol of intent. Instead, body language conveys emotional meaning, with some pretty decent precision. Scientific experiments indicate that our emotions first reveal up in the body, before appearing in the conscious mind seconds later. If you are impatient, frustrated, satisfied, or starving, your body will reveal these emotions to a considerable extent. So, trying to master body language has more to do with learning to decode other people's behaviors, not their conscious thoughts.

Read the body language of the people you know
People can more easily tell when their partner is pissed or when their child is bored. You can also see when your employer wants you to do something. Because you've spent a lot of time around people in your close circles, you've gained a wealth of information about their body language cues. Also, the people we know well, though, can betray us.

Body movements hack to control frustration and other aggressive emotion
Emotions, both positive and negative, are helpful. These should be articulated acceptably. It exists, however, that a lot of people prefer to control frustration and other feelings to match what they believe is 'socially-approved' behavior. The theory is that by suppressing anger (or other negative emotions), you won't be seen as a 'cry baby.' The resulting embodiment of feelings is dangerous and

sometimes leads to conflict between partners, difficulty sleeping, and a lack of confidence in the things you enjoyed doing.

Lookup

There is a persistent feedback loop of body language and emotions. Each of them appears to influence the other. The next time you feel like anger is getting the better of you, and you should use this to your benefit. There are few things worse than doing negative things because you're upset and apologize later when you didn't mean it. Looking up at the ceiling or the sky is a perfect way to use body language to unleash frustration. People appear to look down when they're in a negative condition. Think of a kid who's been reported misbehaving. What's the body language? They're more likely to look down and avoid eye contact. This is one way the body communicates negative feelings. Looking down continues to give way to negative feelings. So, the next time you find yourself squarely trapped in the grips of rage, translate the negative body language and do the reverse (which is looking up). Essentially, you're going to disrupt the depressive feeling and cause pleasant hormones to be released.

Keep smiling

Did you know that having a smile or laughter can heal from aggression and other negative emotions? Laughter is a perfect way to improve your mental state. The next time you find yourself getting upset or having a really bad mood, think of something that made you laugh. You can display something funny on your computer, too. It's going to be tough to remain angry while you experience something that makes you smile or laugh.

Take a deep breath

Take a long breath away; anger and frustration continue to make our breathing shallow and quick as the body slips into its battle or flight reaction mode. You should deny this effect by deliberately altering the breathing patterns so that it's longer and stronger. This helps you get back to a state of mental balance while you calm down. When you breathe slowly, concentrate on lengthening the time of your exhalation. For, e.g., you should count to 4 as you breathe, and then ten as you empty your lungs when you're exhaling, pretending that you're blowing out your frustration into the breeze.

Write it down

Scientific evidence indicates that creative writing has therapeutic advantages. Any time you find yourself getting upset or feeling bad about something, write it in your diary. This tends to flush away negative feelings and can also shift your outlook. If you've finished writing your feelings, feel free to get a fire, and burn the page. Visualize all the rage (or some other emotion dragging you down) flying up in the smoke. All of these basic exercises will help to disrupt the depressive state so that you will feel awesome again. Bottling negative thoughts does more harm than good. Instead, work on releasing emotions that drag you down positively and productively.

How to use nonverbal communication to improve the mood?

Your body communicates to both the inner and outer environments. Your body language has a significant influence not only on how people view you but also on how you are. Poor posture affects your physical fitness, affects your emotional disposition, and tells others a nasty tale about yourself. Many of life's greatest players have used body language to convey thoughts, win debates, and get what they want. Body language to combat anxiety. Do you know that your facial expression could affect your mood? Scientists found that patients with depression could improve their situation by presenting fewer frown lines on their forehead. Your body language has a strong impact on your feelings. If you follow a body language of trust (good stance, power pose, etc.), you begin to feel more secure.

On the other hand, if you curl up (poor balance, slouching, etc.), you appear less confident and uncertain. You owe it to yourself to use constructive body language to improve your mood. Start by enhancing the stance and other supportive body language features.

Move and free up your mind
When people are extremely upset, we frequently suggest, "Take a stroll." Why? Because a simple walk will change the state of their minds. Data shows that when people walk comfortably (right back with easy, light steps), they appear to be happier. People who walk unhappily (heavy knees, dangling shoulders) become more aggressive. Your posture influences your emotional state and also determines whether you are likely to pay attention to positive or negative facts.

Force a smile to raise the mood
Try to force a smile or a joke (for long enough) the next time you find yourself down. You're going to be shocked to know that this is lifting your spirits (even if for a moment). You will make this work much easier by attempting to take a picture of something

you find amusing (or make you laugh). It's a perfect way to disintegrate a negative feeling and improve your attitude.

Trying to dance to stay positive

Have you ever been with someone who's been trying to cheer you up? And you never knew how pervasive their passion was? It was the body language of communicating. Everything beautiful about a little dance (either you or someone dear to you) prevents a negative mood. But what if you're in an atmosphere where dancing is not appropriate? You could be working in the workplace where there are clients and wanting to change the attitude. Consider walking a few paces or jogging softly. It's going to have the same impact as a dance. Body language has a huge influence on how you think and how others perceive you. Invest a little time every day to check your body language to identify things that need change to concentrate on it.

So, friends, we hope you've had a fun and insightful reading about body language fundamentals and how to use them in business. Note, the trick is to learn body language in series, not in isolation. Only looking at the angled movement of the head, but missing the cynical tone might offer a false impression of honest conversation. Perhaps most critically, you have to realize that when you research the body language of others, some will be actively scrutinizing yours, too. Try to take some time from your routine to focus on your body language to avoid providing intimidating or offensive messages by your movements to expressions. However, you don't mean any damage. In short, body language is non-verbal communication consisting of kinesics (movement of the body), haptic (touching), and proxemics (distance). It's very present in our daily lives, as many signs of body language can already be seen in half an hour. The role of body language can be to communicate meaning, to manage the flow of information through the use of eye behavior, and to have the potential to influence others. Most notably, body language communicates the emotions/identity and can control our interactions through signals of attachment, the immediacy of action, and recognition of our feelings. Body language is an integral aspect of the communication process. It not only does facilitate verbal expression to be conveyed more easily, but it also provides a voice to express feeling and message. However, the sense of body language varies based on community, gender, or age, which makes it more complicated and confused. To use it effectively, people should understand and develop their understanding to prevent this dilemma. Applying body language to regular contact is a wise and insightful way to get in touch with someone; let's do it and make sense of it. Language consists of spoken and non-verbal languages. Non-verbal-language, or body-language, plays an essential role in transmitting signals as people communicate with others. Data reveals that 7 percent of the overall effect of a message is verbal, 38% is oral, and the remainder is non-verbal (55%). Moreover, the main field of face-to-face communication, more than 65 percent, is non-verbal, while verbal is less than 35 percent. The influence of body language is important in everyday life. This book addresses what body language is, what particular impact it has on communication, and how to use body language effectively.

©Copyright 2020 by "Craig Cialdini."

All rights reserved

This book:

"Manipulation and Persuasion bible: Art of Persuasion and the Body Language Mastery on Human Behavior."

Written By

Craig Cialdini

This document aims to provide precise and reliable details on this subject and the problem under discussion.

The product is marketed on the assumption that no officially approved bookkeeping or publishing house provides other available funds.

A legal or qualified guide is required. A person must have the right to participate in the field.

A statement of principle is a subcommittee of the American Bar Association, a committee of publishers, and is approved. A copy, reproduction, or distribution of parts of this text, in electronic or written form, is not permitted.

The recording of this document is strictly prohibited. Any retention of this text is only with the written permission of the publisher and all liberties authorized.

The information provided here is correct and reliable, as any lack of attention or other means resulting from the misuse or use of the procedures or instructions contained therein is the total, and absolute obligation of the user addressed.

The author is not obliged, directly or indirectly, to assume civil liability for any restoration, damage, or loss resulting from the data collected here. The respective authors retain all copyrights not kept by the publisher.

The information contained herein is solely and universally available for information purposes. The data is presented without a warranty or promise of any kind.

The trademarks used are without approval, and the patent is issued without the trademark owner's permission or protection.

The logos and labels in this book are the property of the owners themselves and are not associated with this text.

TABLE OF CONTENTS

The mind is one of the highly complicated aspects of human characteristics. The functioning of the mind has perplexed and intrigued humanity for as long as we will remember. Philosophers, psychologists, and scientists have tried to unravel the mysteries of the mind. It is widely believed that the human mind influences our behavior and actions. Hence, tons of research work have been devoted to understanding the process an individual goes through before acting permanently or maliciously.

Some attempts to review the human mind have focused efforts on the brain. These studies look at the brain's physical aspects, which specializes in how information is acquired, processed, interpreted, and stored. Essentially, they hope to know better how the brain can affect an individual's way of thinking. Analyzes like these have paved the way for advances in managing debilitating conditions such as Alzheimer's, perception difficulties, and even amnesia.

The most familiar aspect of the study of the human mind is psychology. At some point in our life, we consulted a psychologist or met someone who needed to consult one to face our most challenging emotional battles. Repeatedly, the experiences of life destroy us in ways we cannot fix on our own. Sometimes, the failure is the result of some biological markers we inherited from our parents. Emotions such as depression, anxiety, and fear cloud our daily experiences making growth difficult. With a mix of medication and therapy, we will protect ourselves from the inner darkness.

But what about the darkness in others? Everyone can do good. We also have the power to attempt to commit great evil. Underneath emotions such as sadness, depression, joy, and happiness, there can be a deep seething desire that will lead us to hurt others if these impulses are not held back deliberately. These darker desires are rooted in other primitive instincts, such as our response to flight or combat, promoting our survival. Sometimes, there is only one word that qualifies the human response to those dark and evil emotions.

Dark psychology can be a search for the individual state of human beings' psychological nature to feed on others. In secular terms, dark psychology explores that aspect of the attribute that allows us to deliberately and voluntarily take actions that harm our fellow men. Mind you, the use of prey in this context does not necessarily translate into physical harm to an individual. However, there is a branch of dark psychology devoted entirely to the present. Next, we will briefly touch on these areas to raise an understanding of the topic.

Those cases are just triggered responses to external situations. The pot was stirred, and the dark emotions of the people hiding beneath it boiled to the surface. They typically withdraw once control is exercised. Each has a latent tendency to be medium touch or just plain evil if the appropriate "buttons" are pressed. Other individuals, on the other hand, are in full control of those dark emotions. They feed them, feed them, and release them voluntarily at another person's expense when it serves their purposes.

Sometimes, these emotions are cured at an early age. A child learns that if he cries in a particular way, the adults in their life rush to follow their orders. If the old folks don't impress the kid early enough for the mistake of this, the child grows up thinking that the people in their life are often manipulated to try to fulfil their orders. Crying will stop being a weapon as they get older, but they may continue in their manipulative ways. Where they don't use tears, they use emotions to blackmail their victims. Thus, what began as innocent childish behavior becomes a dark need for control.

The lengths this individual would imagine exercising their control would define the intensity of their actions. Dark psychology is based on studying the thought process of an individual like this. Get to know the rationale behind these actions. The patterns shown before these acts are performed after and shed more light on how individuals can intentionally see those actions to conclude by knowing the pain and pain they might cause to a different individual. Dark psychology illuminates the dark side of the attribute.

CHAPTER 1: MIND AND CONTROLLING IT

When we try to rise above being human animals, we are animals under human skin. We are subject to the wishes and desires of any being with a genetic makeup and vertebrae. To rise above this is an admirable aspiration and one that we encourage anyone to undertake as a worthy spiritual endeavor.

But to deny that we are genuinely animals is to lie to ourselves. We need to interact in a social environment and deal with people who may not be enlightened and spiritually advanced. They may want what we have and secretly be filled with envy and contempt. The worst event is having these suspicions satisfied and then being drawn into the politics of man.

In this case, what are the options? Do we deny this is happening and hope others will be touched by our honesty and goodwill enough to change? Or do we abandon our higher spiritual ideals and play their game? We could like to advocate for a fundamentally different approach. Take the manipulation game and mind control and make it part of your spirituality.

In this way, we do not deny manipulation and mind control or give up. As an alternative, we comprise it and see it as a tool for our growth. We describe the spiritual life of the warrior who embraces life and considers each battle an expression of life, not death. For this warrior, every moment is an opportunity to live fully and aspire while walking in the world but guided by something higher. If you are courageous and daring enough to embrace mind control in this way, each interaction is lifted above the mundane and mundane and becomes a vehicle for your spirituality. You will be relieved and remain intact even in the most vulgar of human politics. Your war will be your temple.

You should be warned. While reading, there is nothing that will be held back. Like the combatant, there are many unpleasant things you need to learn about this life you choose. Although you are obligated to learn these secrets, you are not obliged to use them.

Know Controlling Mind

Mind control, when you hear these words, a myriad of images come to mind. You could imagine a sneaky man using the power of his mind and the will to control the acts of some unsuspecting and innocent women. You might think of some clandestine cabal of world leaders secretly planning the next steps towards a unified world economy. Or maybe you are the cult leader with a gathering of loyal followers ready to hear every word. You are not likely to have in mind a loving parent who reads to their children or an alcoholics anonymous meeting that helps its members live a decent and sober life.

Likewise, improbable that you will recognize the hold that mind control has on you while in your favorite church of worship. Or, as you sit down with your psychiatrist, you are unlikely to be aware of the subtle acts of mind control being used on you. But there is. Any attempt can cause a change in your thoughts and feelings, and therefore in your actions, is an act of mind control.

It may sound shocking because most people see mind control as a bad thing done by bad people. So, let it be clear; the controller's intention and motives do not apply to this symposium. The regulator may be encouraged by the most altruistic ideals, or he may want your money.

We will try to find out how these thoughts and feelings are instilled to achieve the controller result. Mind control is different from vulgar actions and coercion tactics. Coercion is when all a controller wants to take a specific action and don't care about their motivation. Threats, guilt, and humiliation usually do their job. But pressure lacks any form of grace or elegance.

Pressure does not care about the thoughts and feelings of the people who are forced. It is the main difference between coercion and mind control. As many so-called cults use intimidation to gain compliance from their followers, the topic will be discussed, but the goal is to aspire to something higher, namely mind control.

It requires knowing how people think and react and knowledge of individuals' impulses and weaknesses. More importantly, you need to know yourself and be able to control your urges to react. Your goals, your highest ambitions, must be kept secret, and every action measured by how close you are to your destination. One way to distinguish the way people reason is in sequential, linear, and non-linear reasoning. Sequential thinking is the act of thinking and replying automatically. A serial review is the result of our evolution and is very useful. Simply reacting to the current situation prevents us from having to overthink. It is also the way sheep are led to slaughter.

Linear thinking is a step forward and requires foresight and the ability somehow to predict the consequences of the activities and numerous ways to advance our objectives and wishes. For the regular chess player, the game is an excellent example of extending linear thinking to its limits.

Non-linear thinking doesn't stop at the chessboard. In its pentacle, it incorporates all the dimensions of space and time. Simultaneously, a linear-thinking chess player may aim to win every game and become a world champion. The non-linear player will see how losing a game will position him to play an opponent who will be easier to beat and give himself and the game more significant publicity. A player who thinks non-linear can also see so far, knowing their limits and the limits of the game, that at some point they will stage a considerable outburst promising never to play again and the player's exposure to one of their ambitious others.

The ability of mind control is more than just responding to the situation (serial thinking) or having a structured plan to get your result (linear thinking). It is the capability to be smooth when responding to a fluid environment. You have to know your goal, you have to know yourself, you have to know your environment, and you have to know the people you influence in every possible way. And you have to do everything while appearing to be like everyone else around you.

It is not an everyday task, but it is worthy of your efforts. To aspire to these ideal promises that you will learn something about yourself and your world at every turn. Of course, if you are concerned in mind control, it is perhaps rational to discuss mind control ethics. I am not one to preach morality, and you will not read how you should use mind control.

If you're not bothered by Mind Control being used on you and generally a happy person, then it's possibly okay to do similar things with others. As a common rule, if you decide to use mind control and are motivated by anger or grief, you will likely hurt people in the process. Maybe that's not a problem for you. So be it. It would help if you were cautioned never to underestimate people's desire to equalize and change your actions accordingly.

What you will find is that sleep (metaphorical sleep) is the natural state of mind. People will parallel your attempts to arouse them with an effort to change them. While people don't mind changing, they resist being changed. Consequently, it is finest to stick to your advice. Do people need to wake up? Sure, but let them do it when they want. Until then, it will be you and I who benefit from these insights.

Assuming you are an insignificant energy source subordinate to an enormous machine dominating the world, would you have swallowed the red pill like Neo's main character, to be "woken up" and realize it?

Controlling Mind And its Introduction

To understand the Mind Control process, it is necessary to understand the human mind. People make decisions at every level in a way that is unique to each of them. These determinations are centered on mind dribbles that are spent to identify the self and its situation. These filters are best comprehended in the form of questions people ask themselves. Preserve in mind that these questions are asked unconsciously because people are not aware of them, but they can be inferred from their behaviors and how they respond to events.

These inquiries are not the same in every perspective. A person can make essential relationship decisions based on the query "Would this person arrange me with security?" but from the perspective of buying a car, the question might be, "Will it get me consideration?" or vice versa.

These questions can be numerous and have a hierarchy of priorities. For example, defining whether to consider someone as a sexual partner may involve answering the following questions.
* "Am I attracted to their looks?"
* "Do I feel unharmed with this individual?"
* "Can I see myself having aroused with this individual?"
* "Can I view myself being intimate with this individual more than once?"
* "Will I feel good about me if I have sex with this individual?" etc.

People will reply contrarily to the same situations depending on the questions (filters) they ask. A person facing job loss may ask, "What did I do wrong?" in which case they noticed, found, or created what they have done wrong. In the same situation, another person may subconsciously ask, "How is this a chance for me?" and view the same position as an opportunity.

To the astonishment and enjoyment of many rational thinkers, there is no end to people who routinely focus on problems rather than solutions to the thing's life throws at them. None of these queries are asked on an awake level. Many of these queries /filters are so deeply entrenched that it could upset people if they are asked to view the situation in any other way possible.

The grade you can express a person's filters and the unconscious questions that arise is how you can direct their thoughts and actions. In other words, Mind Control. By understanding this, you can begin your mind control learning journey by examining your filters/ queries that lead you to make conclusions and, at the same time, also perceive the people around you.

A pair of filters/questions you could add to your personal repertoire to learn mind control are: "What can I assume is true for this person that is not overtly obvious?" and "How can I be through their attentiveness to get my result?" Mind control has many names, persuasion, seduction, manipulation, sales skills, politics, advertising, etc. The desire to change the minds and behaviors of people was the only thing.

It is one of the main tasks of communication. Yes, even when you talk to yourself, your motive is to direct your thoughts, actions, and behaviors. The sour truth is that we use mind control every time we open our mouths to speak. While these two words, "Mind Control," may have a grinding ring to very our ears, it doesn't avert it from being a reality of everyday life. Many people will violently deny using it.

It's time to lift the phrase "Mind Control" from its misplaced sewer and subject it to scrutiny as a mere fact of human nature. It means being truly honest with ourselves by keeping our intentions close to the vest. While this is ideal and few people will enthusiastically tell you otherwise, the opposite is usually true.

To show that all you have to do is be completely honest about your intentions every time you go on a first date. Maybe you have visions of marriage in mind with your date. Or perhaps your only goal is to bring your date into an unbridled expression of sexual debauchery. Truth, it turns out, is a caustic and volatile chemical when added to most human interactions.

When administered without limitation, the only specific result is that the work will be uncertain. Thankfully, the truth is also very malleable and relatively safe when administered with caution in deluded forms. Therefore, it is best to be judicious with your expressions of honorable intentions and feelings until a reliable answer can be concluded. In the interim, we can look for proof of how pervasive Mind Control is in our daily life.

Universally Using Controlling Mind

Here is how mind control is worked in ordinary life:
- Motivate a child to improve in school enthusiastically
- Create obedience to a religious or political figure
- Create a feeling of superiority towards a group
- Motivate a potential customer to purchase a specific product or service
- Create panic to sell a particular stock
- Instil confidence in the authority who is speaking to you on television
- Create contempt for competition by establishing greater customer loyalty
- Bring more revenue
- Bringing an attractive person to a romantic or sexual encounter
- Selling an undervalued product at a higher price
- Discuss a cop about a fine
- Make a viewer believe in psychic abilities
- Get someone to reevaluate their previous beliefs

The list can go on and on. In all these cases, the controller knows his results and objectives. It is safe to say that whenever you want something that involves motivating someone to do something or when people do something without asking why they are doing it, some form of Mind Control is engaged, whether deliberate or not. So, we are applying Mind Control all the moments. Even the function of having your partner take out the trash couldn't happen without some form of preparation, conditioning, and mind control.

If in doubt, ask a stranger to take out your trash and see what kind of agreement you get. As you will study, mind control requires thinking at a higher level than the subject and veiling the strings of control with everyday life's daily distractions. When one tries to control the higher levels of a power hierarchy, something interesting happens. The visibility of control becomes less evident to individuals as they become more involved in their daily concerns.

Mind Control is around us. Once you understand the intensity of Mind Control in your life, your only option, outside of paranoia, is a calm, almost Buddha-like omniscience that recognizes the ubiquitous presence of Mind Control and sets out to use it to your advantage. Although this mentality can be encouraged, no one can teach it. Only through patience, effort, and a little bit of suffering can you get this priceless prospect.

Mind Control Models

If mind control controls others' thoughts, emotions, and actions, several functional models will help you do this. To determine how mind control creates the degree of compliance you want, let's consider some standard mind control models.

Behavior Variation Model

As in any case of Mind Control, the controller identifies what he needs people to do and needs them to do it willingly, and for what they think, it is their reasons. The behavior modification/conditioning model works with stimuli in rewards and punishments based on their behaviors. In much the similar way you would train a dog to do tricks, you can voluntarily prepare a person to participate in some action. Behavior alteration/taming needs a sequence of steps that repay good conduct and penalize lousy performance. But let's speak. You want your follower to steal candy from a store (or worse). Using the behavior modification model, you would first reward them for "thinking creatively" outside the norm of social, ethical behavior.

After they have gotten used to thinking outside the norm, and you reward them with every step for it, it's time to move on to the next level. In this next phase, rewards are given for taking actions outside the norm but sanctioned within a social structure or group. University hazing is a good example. It wouldn't take much more than many of these exercises to get them to do something even more harmful. When an action is not taken, a punishment could be as mild as having group members scoffing in contempt. They will also be allowed to deal with the consequences of not acting as required. It creates the illusion of free will.

The controller must make the remunerations huge and the punishments mild but memorable to use the behavior modification/conditioning model skilfully and stealthily. It will prevent the follower from believing that he has been coerced in any way. Scientology has an extensive behavioral conditioning process called "The Training Routines" or "TRs." TRs are presented as communication training at the beginning of someone's interest in Scientology.

Connected Pattern

A doctor can tap your knee, and this is often reflected with a snap of the leg. So we, as humans, also are programmed to answer. The hard-wired human answer to the present is one among conformity and a sense of gratification. The scapegoat is that the fundamental human got to know that our problems aren't our fault, albeit they are. There are tons of conversations among the Human Potential Movement to "take responsibility for one's life," On an understanding level, it makes perfect sense.

If we glance at our life as something that we've complete control over, we feel more empowered, and that we tend to act more decisively and be happier people just because we elect it. However, the planet has other plans and can often throw us a curveball that we didn't expect; people we trust will rob us, we'll affect bills and financial worries, and love relationships will end. It's still a relief to understand that "it's not our fault" altogether these cases. We'll gladly take the side of strangers who will support us by throwing stones at our enemies.

Model of Neuro-Linguistic Programming

NLP stands for Neuro-Linguistic Programming. It's a field of study developed within the late 1970s by two scientists, Richard Bandler and John Grinder. They wanted to work out why some therapists could affect their clients and obtain speedy results were other therapists seem to require months and years. During this way, they found that we all undergo specific mental processes to form decisions and make changes. If someone (someone) knows about another process to develop changes, they need to conform to that process, and therefore the change will happen. It's essentially having the road map for someone's mind.

You can guide the person to try too many things without even knowing what you're doing. As a result, many of us have applied NLP to sales and persuasion, while others have used it for seductions. What makes NLP unique as a mind-control model is that it treats people as distinct individuals, not as a mass of wired robots. It means everyone has their change processes and these processes are unique to them. The central key to using NLP as a mind-control tool is finding ways to stimulate people's processes. These processes are often within ideas, personal assumptions, trends, values, and strategies for creating decisions. Once the unique techniques of a private are discovered, the doors are wide open for mind control.

Controlling the Atmospherically Model

The environmental control model is often tons of fun and challenging. It requires the controller to think about everything the topic will experience so that he can, of course, conclude what the controller wants and, consequently, achieve the controller's goal without considering other possibilities or options. It's essential to ascertain a way bigger picture of what's happening. Believe how wizards control the environment to form you think the effect. an honest magician won't tell you, "This may be a normal deck of playing cards." Instead, he'll fan them out for you and even cause you to manage so you'll find out what he wants you to believe on your own. The bridge might be marked, rigged, or support of 1 kind. To use the conservational mind control model, consider this sentence: "Nobody can resist what they cannot detect." The environmental control model is additionally a favorite of scammers. Suppose you substitute a hospital parking zone and see a person during a white coat with a stethoscope dangling from his pocket. This label says, "Samuel Wallis, MD, Urology," posing for jumper cables to start his car, of course. In that case, I assume that's a doctor. More importantly, don't suppose he is not a specialist.

The pentagram of the control model is that the film "The Matrix." For people that lived linked to the Matrix, everything was even as they thought it had been with everyday life's worries and desires. All the while, they were shielded from discovering that they were nothing but AA batteries won't power a worldwide machine. To effectively use the Environmental Mind Control model, you initially got to ask what you would like your follower to try and what to believe and then create the environment that will naturally make him finish what you would like.

Doing this on an outsized scale can prove difficult thanks to the various variables required to be controlled. On a smaller scale, however, it is often relatively straightforward. Let's take the instance of getting to a spiritual retreat. Participants are isolated from the remainder of the planet. No TV or newspaper. No cell phones or computers. They are then asked to require off their shoes and shut one's mouth when in certain places as a symbol of reverence.

After doing this for any length of your time, it doesn't take long to believe what they're told to think. A scammer will also use isolation by ensuring his brand is continuously occupied by his scammer co-workers, whose job is to provide the brand's attention is continually directed where they need it. These are Mind Control models only, not techniques and tactics. As models, they supply suggestions on possible strategies that make mind control possible.

Controlling Mind and Memes

It signifies a replicator of cultural information that one's mind transmits (verbally or by demonstration) to another reason. Examples of Dawkin's memes are melodies, slogans, dress fashions, ways of making vases, or building bows. Other examples include divinities, concepts, ideas, theories, opinions, beliefs, practices, habits, dances, and moods propagating within a culture. A meme propagates as a cultural evolution unit analogous in many ways to the gene (the division of genetic information).

Memes often propagate as more or less integrated cooperative ensembles or groups, referred to as memeplexes or meme complexes. The theory itself proved to be a successful meme, gaining a rare penetration into a scientific theory's popular culture. Some meme theorists argue that memes most beneficial to their hosts won't necessarily survive; instead, those memes that replicate the most effectively spread the best, which allows for the possibility that successful memes could prove harmful to their guests.

An instance of this is the meme of a faith that states, "something wonderful is about to happen." This belief can benefit all rational analyzes regardless of its truthfulness, but healthier thoughts such as the "Everyone wants to get me" idea can win. Suppose this is true when designing a meme (or belief system) for Mind Control purposes. In that case, one must consider increasing the meme's ability to replicate itself and increase the belief system's lifespan.

Some memes' supporters propose that they develop through natural selection, very similar to Charles Darwin's biological evolution ideas on the premise that variation, mutation, competition, and "heredity" affect their replicative success. For example, while an image may become extinct, other ideas will survive, spread, and change for better or worse through modification. It has some practical applications when applying your mind control skills. If the beliefs you instill in people are beneficial to you, you need to find a way for them to persist and replicate.

Give sense, not just to the faith, but to the maintenance of the idea. For example, a religious group can call itself a "believer" to empathize their beliefs' value, especially of particular thoughts in the leaders' words' correctness. So, because they appreciate calling themselves "believers," they understand the leaders' comments as truth without stating it. Perhaps a more straightforward process for making a meme replica is the initiation process. During a typical initiation, the initiate is subjected to emotional stress. This procedure inspires in the new initiate a deep sense of personal worth for the group and initiation. It makes him eager and willing to participate in the subsequent initiation ritual of initiates.

Controlling the Minds: Only Cowards Suffer

When human behaviors extremes are considered, the foremost brutal actions to know are seemingly ordinary people acting in ways contrary to even what they might think they're capable of. Cults are the simplest example. No average person would tell you that he plans to become celibate and kill himself in hopes of reincarnation on a spaceship journey by angelic space aliens.
But this is often what Charles Manson forced many of his followers to try. Once we attempt to add up to those acts, we are usually amazed and quickly classify them into one among two categories; they're "crazy" or "monsters." therein act, we inadvertently prevent ourselves from learning the foremost valuable lessons of Mind Control. So, we enquire you to think about what if they weren't crazy?
Can they be Fanatic?

It is where we run into the most crucial obstacle to understanding how Mind Control works, which is morality. Whenever we use our righteousness to gauge an action, event, or situation, we unconsciously block our ability to know it and involuntarily limit our ability to speak effectively. The very fact is that anyone is often influenced, moved, and manipulated by Mind Control. Like Archimedes, who realized that he could move the world if he could stay within the right place within the universe. No man can't be moved with the proper pressure within the right place at the appropriate time.

Controlling Mind: Would You Use

On many levels, the study of mind control can benefit anyone. At the main basic level of our needs and desires, it seems straightforward that the more quickly we will influence the people around us, the more comfortable we'll meet our needs for money, love, sex, and security. But this is often only the foremost obvious. It's also the smallest amount necessary. While I've managed to urge everyone studying the topic in my life, the maximum significant benefit I've gotten is that the hardest to quantify.

It is the peace of mind that will only come from long years of using and using power. Most humans are hungry and crave the facility that Mind Control can give. That hunger, though irresistible, is additionally the result of lack. Not enough money. Not enough sex. Not enough certainty. Not enough security. Just like the child who continually tries to convince their parents that they're okay while they enter the third, fourth, and fifth decades of life.

After maintaining power and influence over others for a short time, you quickly find out how simple it's. It seems that most people go around with their duct in their hands, trying to find someone to attach it to it. Power and influence are not any longer goals to be achieved but become tools to be used. A bit like a drill in the hands of an honest carpenter learning to hammer a nail with the smallest number of blows, so too power becomes something you employ less and fewer to indicate your skill. It's just a tool. And just like the carpenter and his hammer, you'll earn a living using it effectively. Once you first start using mind control, your goals are usually predictable and straightforward; usually more sex and money. But eventually, all of this becomes old and familiar.

The goal then becomes to work out the minimum amount of power (and mind control) is required to urge what you would like. Another advantage may be a quiet detachment from the foremost significant suffering of humanity. It's noted in particular because of the smug feeling of superiority from knowing something forbidden from others. Distinction later gives thanks to a way of fun within the way people do "little things" about life and death. They panic about renting, relationships, and seeking approval.

Eventually, people will come to you wondering how does one stay so calm and poised during the turmoil that seems so evident to them. In truth, all they need is to be within the presence of that calm because there's nothing you'll tell them, which will give them what they need.

Controlling Mind: Would you learn?

It is an honest question, and that we can say that if you never learn the art of Mind Control, life is going to be more or less an equivalent. You'll run with an equivalent sort of people doing comparable belongings you have always done. You will have similar frustrations you've ever had and, therefore, the same rewards. It's very likely that outwardly you do not seem to miss everything. Your life will be like prominent people, thinking that what you see is real, and you'll not be curious or disturbed by the subtle and sometimes devious things that happen beneath the surface.

You will see people as people, and that they will inevitably live up to your expectations. If you do not learn mind control, you'll still be distracted and bothered by politics or advertising, but you'll never realize or consider why. If you never learn mind control, you'll evaluate yourself and confidently conclude that you simply are very almost like most people, you know, and you'll be right.

Controlling Mind: Why Should I learn?

We distinguish between learning mind control and being good at it. Mind control learning falls into two categories. Reading it and studying it. As far as we do know, you're only willing to examine Mind Control. It means you'll be ready to tell folks that you recognize somewhat about mind control. Learning mind control is an order of significance beyond reading. Studying means dedicating oneself to understanding the concepts of Mind Control, a minimum of on an intellectual level.

Studying will cause you to an honest commentator on the topic. Being good at mind control is another quantum jump. You do not realize it at this level, and you'll mention it. You are doing it on every occasion. You see each social interaction as a chance to witness some aspect of Mind Control in action or, better yet, to check something about Mind Control that you simply have learned. So, if you would like to be good at Mind Control, it'll take time and study, reading (of course), and teaching concepts, but even more, it requires an adventurous attitude and a desire to attach deeply with people.

It is a decent idea to revise everything you'll consider about hypnosis, NLP, social influence, brainwashing, cults, unclassified government interrogation documents, and more. You'll also strive to ascertain mind control in action. You'll visit and join cults. You would possibly even attempt to climb the cult's hierarchy to determine how far you'll go and the way much you'll learn from experience. You'll make every plan to enrich your life with differing individuals' types to understand the principles and exceptions that apply to human behavior and thinking.

To be truly good at Mind Control, you've got to swear to measure your life, trying to know and control people in ways in which make them enjoy your presence and are grateful for your attention. When you're wrong, you objectively review the results and make changes. There's a mindset that anyone who wants to find out mind control is probably going to evolve.

Inquisitiveness

Mind control information does not have any boundaries, which will be studied and tested. It's why curiosity is so important. Interest is that the quality that will allow you to check everything you research mind control.

Companionability

If you're getting to learn mind control, you better enjoy being with people. It doesn't suggest you will not have a personal life. A life crammed with personal self-discovery will surely benefit you. The chance to be within people's presence is usually taken as a chance to check your ability to steer and influence. Your goals do not have to be great during these interactions. Sometimes it's just a matter of observing which individuals answer your influence.

Intellectual

Mind Control is limitless. You'll study. It's inevitable that as you delve into the depths of research and experimentation, you'll discover new and unedited information.

Purposefully Not Just Strategically

The tactic is about the items you are doing to urge a result. The strategy is to regulate the entities that influence the achievement of the development. A simple plan will make it appear to be the planet that offers you everything you would like as if it were a present, but you've seen the critical picture of what affects things. A small push using the strategy will produce even as much like an active push using the tactic and make your power feel almost magical.

Silent

It may seem contrary to the mentality of sociability, but it turns out that creating a balance between these two extremes offers excellent strength. It is perhaps the most challenging part to learn: keeping quiet about things you know. Several who have just acquired their first magic trick are often inclined to reveal the secret in exchange for short-term attention. However, in the long run, we forgive because the sense of awe you can create is replaced by the awareness of being a cheater from that moment on. Thus, you learn that keeping a secret has power, and giving it way limits that power.

Given the little we now understand about dark psychology, we know that some of the most shocking crimes are rooted in some personality traits related to dark psychology. But this is a broader side effect. We need to fetch it nearer to home, to you and me. How does this dark psychology affect us, if it even affects us? We can assure you that there are no "ifs" to this question, and in a few moments, we would understand how. The effects of dark psychology are experienced by both the author and the victim. To know the impacts, we need to explore some elements of dark psychology. Folks who display specific behavior characteristics that are considered obscure such as narcissism, psychopathy, and Machiavellianism, are prone to experience difficulties in all aspects of their relationships. If all three traits are present in a person, they have a greater propensity to commit a crime. The three personality traits mentioned have specific characteristics grouped under them.

Narcissism, for example, is characterized by a sense of entitlement, feelings of superiority, deep seething envy for the success of others, and exploitative behaviors. Psychopathy has an absence of guilt, a lack of empathy, destructive impulsive behavior, self-centeredness. And an inability to accept responsibility as some of the characteristics. Selfishness, cruelty, and manipulative behaviors are indicators of Machiavellian traits. Separately, these traits are problematic but put together; they can cause trouble. Especially in a person's relationship with others. In the office, for example, that individual would do it;

- Insufficient performance in the office, even with the most mundane tasks

- They disrupt the flow of work due to their inability to get along with others

- Others would intensely detest him

- Their impulsiveness would lead them to make questionable and unethical decisions

- If placed in an administrative capacity, they are more likely to commit white-collar crimes

- But it's not just their working relationships that suffer. In their relationships, they are bound to encounter the following problems

- Their constant need for attention and validation can be exhausting for their partner, resulting in faster relationship expiration dates

- They resort to physical and emotional blackmail to manipulate their partners

- They tend to be verbally, emotionally, or physically violent with their partner or children

People who come into relationships with them pay a high emotional cost. If you've met someone whose relationships are characterized by these experiences, for the sake of your sanity and general well-being, avoid them. But if you are the one experiencing this, seek the psychological help you need to get better. No matter how ingrained these problems are, you can improve your behavior and experiences with the right form of therapy. The initial phase is to recognize the situation for what it is, recognize that you have a problem, and seek help promptly. For our respite, exchanging with people who have the traits I mentioned above leaves us emotionally and mentally drained. Sometimes, the effect can be physical and, in extreme cases, fatal. His home, his business, his finances, but his loss was much more profound and more significant than these. We did not have a relationship with the author of the act, but we also became victims. Our losses weren't as monumental as yours, but we also suffered losses. For starters, we've lost our sweet neighbor. She is not dead, but she never recovered from the experience. We have lost our ability to trust strangers. Our mutual relationships also seemed to require an additional layer of trust to thrive.

The most significant impact of dark psychology on anyone is that it produces a strong sense of loss. We lose our valuables, we lose relationships, we lose ourselves, and for those who are extremely unfortunate, they lose their lives. It is secure to say that the impact of this darkness is profound.

If a person exhibits one of the dark personality traits, there is a very high tendency to show others. In society at large, if the larger community members display these traits, it is safe to say that the crime perpetration rates in that society would be significantly high. It is not to say that people living in cities or towns with higher crime rates are more prone to crime. There are other contributing factors to consider. But not even the prospect can be excluded entirely.

However, one thing that cannot be ruled out is the ripple effect of actions directly related to or due to dark personality traits. Some destructive behaviors even turn victims into predators, and this cycle continues well into the future until someone takes courage and takes the courageous step to break free. Children from abusive families, for example, more often than not grow up to be abusers. In some cases, in an attempt to break away from their parental mold, they find themselves trapped in equally abusive relationships, even if they are not the abusers themselves. It is virtual to have an influential gravitational pull towards the violent elements that characterize their childhood homes.

For others, becoming victims can have such a tremendous impact on their psyche that it triggers something inside them. I have read that the "click" can be temporary. In a short moment, they lose all control over their primitive instincts and act exclusively on the strongest emotion that emerges, which is usually anger. This condition is what causes some people to declare temporary insanity. But some people embrace the dark emotions that arise when they "snap." The absolute sense of morality comes out of the window. The consequences of this are usually devastating.

Dark Psychology and Its Manipulation

Put, manipulating someone means controlling or influencing that person intelligently or evilly. Like it or not, we've all manipulated a person or situation to achieve a desirable result. It sounds grim but let me lighten the mood with a story from my mischievous childhood.

The art of manipulation is part of our nature. However, when it comes to psychological manipulation, things get darker and more sinister. In this situation, a person's actions or thoughts are influenced by the use of underhanded tactics that are offensive, deceptive, or even both. In this context, the manipulated person does not choose to accept or reject the manipulator's will. They are forced to comply.

Manipulators have their reasons for doing what they do. Sometimes, it's something as fundamental as making financial gains like the fictional soldier who cheated my neighbor out of all her life savings. In the workplace, people are committed to promoting their agenda, even if that would mean banging a few heads against each other. Their principle is straightforward; if you want it, you have to reach out and take it. In relationships, it's usually about gaining power and staying in control. The need to be responsible fuels everything they do, and sometimes they can go out of their way to achieve this. And then you have those who love to manipulate people for recreational purposes. They are just bored and use their manipulative games to pass the time. It's crude and vicious, but that's just the way they think.

One of the usual utmost tactics used by manipulators is lying. A master manipulator is well versed in the art of deception. They are adept at making up fantastic stories that have no bearing on the truth. Or they subterfuge and lie by omission. Some people are so good with their lies that you rarely notice until it's too late. Another tactic employed by manipulators is guilt and shame. When confronted for something they did wrong, they would immediately deny it and then promptly change the situation, making you feel bad for questioning them in the first place. To further strengthen their grip on the victim, they denigrate her, turning the victim into a rapist. You will find this type of manipulative technique in domestic cases where the abuser would claim that the victim's character, words, or actions are what prompted his behavior in the first place.

Other subtle techniques used in manipulation include the use of evasive and undemanding responses to the questions posed. Rationalize actions if they are captured and rotate reality to fit their narrative. Some manipulators use sex and seduction to accomplish their ambiguous goals when trapped, anger, and guilt projection are quickly used to manipulate the situation in their favor.

However, manipulators are not always casual in their selection of prey. There are specific traits in their victims that attract them, and some vulnerabilities also make it easier for the manipulator to perpetrate their crimes. Lonely people with low self-esteem and a desire to please are more comfortable to control than the bold social type. However, some people show similar characteristics to later ones who end up being manipulated. For these people, manipulators study their personality flaws and weaknesses before using them against them. Impressionable people are likely to be fooled by appearances. Cheeky people who tend to make compulsive decisions are more likely to be manipulated to make quick decisions with a long-term impact. Greedy and materialistic people have a greater tendency to be scammed.

Importance of Hypnosis

The idea of hypnosis has been relegated to the world of belief. That the swing of an object can control a person's mind, and a finger's snap was considered an incredulous idea.

No amount of denial can change the fact that hypnosis is real and used far more frequently than we care to admit. In today's modern psychology, hypnotherapy has effectively treated certain skin conditions and manage pain associated with childbirth, dental procedures, and even rheumatoid arthritis.

Hypnosis and psychology are described as a cooperative interaction in which participants respond to suggestions from the hypnotist. That is to say, when a person is hypnotized, the hypnotist firmly guides his actions. In films, we are led to believe that a person under hypnosis becomes sleepy and disoriented. In reality, people react differently under hypnosis, but they are not as clueless as they seem. Indeed, psychologists refer to this as a state of hyper-awareness. In this state, they experience focused attention, heightened suggestibility, and vivid fantasies. People are brought into this state through the use of visualization and verbal repetition.

Here are some of the most common misconceptions we have:

- Hypnotism Puts You Under Complete Control of Your Hypnotist In the movies, and we are made to believe that a depressed person would have their actions controlled by the hypnotist. It is not valid. Although hypnosis relies heavily on suggestions, if your mind disagrees with these suggestions, you would openly reject it. Then no. You won't crawl on all fours and moo like a cow, not unless you want to.

- The brain is more complicated than we think it is. The same self-protection mechanisms that make it nearly impossible for your hypnotists to control your actions keep you alert, and if there is immediate danger, you can get rid of it in an instant.

- Hypnosis is a kind of pure science. It is based on the research work of renowned psychologists such as Sigmund Freud. There are a method and a process, and none of these require wooden dolls and red candles. All it takes is your consent.

- Hypnosis can improve your skills. It dangles on what you are viewing. Hypnosis can improve your memory, but it can also give you false memories or even distort that memory itself. Hence, the results are not as great as you would have hoped. It has also been linked to improved performance but doesn't expect to run the 5km marathon overnight.

Hypnosis does not always imply that you enter a trance state for it to be effective. The critical elements of hypnosis are the power of suggestion and the repetitive use of words that resonate deeply with the victim. Politicians, for example, exploit this aspect in their campaigns. They use words like change, make a difference, and so on. These words trigger a more in-depth search within oneself, and unconsciously we find ourselves longing for that change.

Challenging Behavior

The subject of criminal behavior is not our focus, but it cannot be overlooked because it constitutes an aspect of dark psychology. Profilers, criminologists, and law enforcement agencies benefit immensely from studying criminal behavior. In psychology, criminal behavior is not often thrown around because it is believed that crime is behavior. However, engaging in a crime doesn't necessarily make you a criminal. Sure, there's a lot of debate about this kind of thinking, but we should leave it to the experts. Our focus here is on those elements that cause a person to commit a crime.

Some people do things merely because they can. Not because they were driven by some childhood wound, by the need to take revenge for an offense you may or may not have committed. They do it simply because they can. As individual persons, it is in our nature to try to understand why. We want to make sense of our situation rather than believing that we are just victims of random acts. However, we should be prepared to accept that the problem is sometimes only as it appears—a person guided by his desire to hurt others. If you are trying to find answers to such questions, you should also open yourself to the possibility that this person was just plain evil.

For a person to commit a specific type of crime, there are usually some characteristics that indicate that this person may be capable of this. It goes beyond judging a book by its cover because prolific criminals are often mastering of disguises. They fascinate you before they disarm you. In our daily life, these people disguise themselves as one of us by pretending that they have your best interests at heart. Given what we now know about manipulation, deception, and hypnosis, we know that predators are not always strangers. So, how can you identify those things that help you make better choices in relating to people? We will explore the traits in detail.

Relatives and Companions

In addition to yourself, examine the circles in which this person runs. Do they come from a close-knit family? How is their relationship with the family? Have you met their friends? If this person has no friends, it could be a red flag.

Memoire

We like the idea of a person being wholly reformed and, in all honesty, this happens. However, it would help if you didn't ignore that a person with a horrible history has a greater tendency to become a repeat offender. If the person was abusive in their previous relationship, there is a possibility that they would be the same as you. No, unless they have undergone or are actively undergoing treatment.

Control and Its Problems

People who cannot control themselves in situations that cause them to have a propensity to inflict harm on others. Likewise, people who have trouble giving up control have the nerve to snap and lash out at the closest victim when they lose it, and that person could be you.

Unsociable Morals

In social settings, monitor their interactions with others. People who don't generally like everyone are red flags. If the person is typically obnoxious, rude, and low at getting along with people, you may have a problem on your hands.

Substance and Its Abuse

Addiction to any form of drug or alcohol is a clear indicator that this person struggles with specific problems. Substance abuse negates their ability to reason correctly and make correct decisions. An individual who misuses drugs or alcohol may not be able to make your relationship a priority in their life. And unless they have a way to support that lifestyle, you may end up paying for it directly or indirectly. It can lead to years of abuse and neglect.

These are just indicators of criminal elements in the people we relate to. As with all human things, there are exceptions, and there are variables. However, the major fault you can make is seeing precise pointers and then rationalizing them. We tend to make excuses for others. The first thing we rush to tell ourselves is that no one is perfect. But that ideology can quickly take us to warm waters. Get informed, be aware, and then make informed decisions. These do not guarantee that you would stop these types from hurting you and taking advantage of you. But you can protect yourself from them 100% better than if you were acting from a place of ignorance.

Some of us are inherently hard-wired to want to fix the people in our life. We see someone who is broken, and we think that if we love him strong enough, we can bring him back from the edge of whatever precipice he is in and begin our journey to a happy ending.

Zones Susceptible to Dark Psychology

The chances of things getting this creepy are pretty slim. But never make the mistake of assuming that you are immune to the powers of dark psychology. Its influence is much closer to you than you think. The most common place where elements of dark psychology manifest themselves.

Affection and Relationships

Love is a universal language. It is a primal emotion that we all instinctively desire. As human beings, we are designed for love. We want to love and feel loved. Nobody is as content as a man or woman in love and knows that he is loved in return. Some people mate for procreation purposes. Some people mate to deny social pressure. Some even mate to promote the alliance of powerful families. But the main reason for relationships, namely how to get a mate, is love. That said, it is easy for things to degrade to the point where love is used as a bargaining chip to have more power over another individual. And this is where the elements of dark psychology come into play.

Communal Taming

Social conditioning refers to the impact society has on your life as a whole. While social movement looks more at your social status in terms of income, living conditions, and so on, its reach can go deeper. Your society can and does affect your beliefs and your religion. You may not be a direct practitioner of those beliefs, but you are indirectly affected by them. In certain cultures, certain days are considered sacred. It means that doing business in those days could be regarded as a crime.

There is a general misconception that being part of a more advanced society makes you impervious to cultural influences. How can a company that gave birth to characters like Albert Einstein and Neil Armstrong be influenced by something as ridiculous as culture, right? Well, you're wrong about that. If nothing else, you are even more vulnerable.

The most significant advance our society has made today is in the field of technology. We exist in a world where things get done in a flash. Money transactions are completed at the push of a button. If you are working out a business plan in this era, your products and services need to match the same speed we are all used to. Otherwise, you are preparing for failure. Unfortunately, this speed that characterizes our daily life makes us vulnerable to get rich quickly with schemes. We hear all these fantastic stories of people who became millionaires overnight, and, on a subconscious level, we want the same thing.

The only coherent explanation we can give for a situation like this where a company with almost no recorded documentation of its existence comes in and scams the hard-working people who are usually smart in their relationships is social conditioning.

Aspiration and Individual Ambitions

We altogether have a to-do list. Occasionally, this list is just a group of activities designed to help us get through the day. And sometimes, it's a roadmap towards where we would like to be soon. Draw up a business plan for your startup? It is an entirely different game. You are trying to prepare yourself for the future financially and, most likely, by providing a product or service that influences people's lives. In today's terminology, we call it "head moves." Ambition is what drives you towards the goals you have set for yourself. Do you want something? You strive to achieve it, and for the more ambitious people, when they reach their goals, they push a little more. Ambition is an attractive trait in every human being. The aspiration to be better than who, what, and where you are now often putting you behind the wheel that directs your life. Nobody needs to be with individuals who are content to sit on the couch all day and do nothing but eat chips and browse the channels. People want to be with someone genuinely excited about the beautiful future they envision for themselves and who are working meticulously to achieve it. However attractive as ambition is, it can attract the wrong kind of people into your life when put into overdrive because it leaves you open and vulnerable. It may seem like a contradictory statement because ambitious people are described as anything but powerless. Where ambition drives your goals, your aspirations can instead be seen as indicators of success. There are many similarities between aspirations and dreams, but the main difference is the successive ones' magnitude and intensity. Your ambition may be to move up the managerial ladder before the end of the year, and your aspiration may be to open up more job opportunities when you reach that position. Ambition is more concrete in its desires, while aspirations are those noble notions, we nurture to make us feel better about ourselves. By themselves, neither ambition nor aspirations should harm you, but when other elements come into play, they can be expended to operate and deceive you. Most organizations believe that ambition is one of the most desirable qualities in a potential employee. And this is usually because ambitious people are more willing to do what needs to be done to move the company forward than their seemingly more docile counterparts. People like these are very focused and have a one-sided mind regarding fulfilling their responsibilities, sometimes not considering what it would take to do it even if it would mean stepping on some colleague's foot. In some contexts, this can be good. After all, the workplace and the world at large aren't a playground where the rules of what's right for everyone is applied. But this attitude can quickly create a hostile work environment that makes it difficult for employees to grow. The organization's goals can be achieved consistently but at the expense of its employees. That's not the immediate danger, even if that doesn't mean a situation like that isn't a cause for concern. A person who does not reign in their ambition can be persuaded and manipulated to do morally and ethically wrong things to achieve their goals. The people with high dreams and aspirations are most likely to fall into the manipulative techniques that involve blackmail. For example, a young career man with an excellent reputation and a good position within a company is more likely to do anything to maintain that status quo if he is ambitious. However, those things he is required to do would further taint his reputation if knowledge of those actions came to light. It is not to say that the rest of us are less likely to become victims of blackmail and other forms of manipulation.

Manipulation is not about physically wielding a large and dangerous ax on a person to force them to do somewhat they typically would not do. It is a game of fraud and deception. The manipulator acts as a mirror that captures the victim's desires, ambitions, and aspirations and then threatens to realize that vision by showing its weakness. The victim is forced to falsely believe that his only hope of saving his dreams is to fulfil the manipulator's wishes. The stronger the ambition, the more likely the victim is to obey, especially if they believe they can get away with it. The acts that could be manipulated into performing could be anything from undermining the authority figure in their life, committing an action that could be offensive, or any of the other things the manipulator may have in mind. Let me resize it to relatable proportions. In all our relationships with people, there is a measure of trust. No matter how unreasonable you may be, the working relationship you have with your tailor is also an indication of a certain level of confidence as you trust them to help you cover up your nudity without being harmed in the process. But as there is trust, there is also distrust. Nevertheless, we strive to process these feelings to maintain the bond/bridge between the people involved.

Emotive Traumata

One of the most significant residual effects of any experience we have is emotions. They say experience is the best teacher in life. We are having used above than a period trying to understand human nature. There are some experiences in life that would promptly cause you never to react again. Those experiences are so deeply etched in our minds that we immediately interpret sure signs as a precursor to the event that scared us in the first place. And the second we observe these signs, our fight or flight instincts are unleashed, especially if those experiences threaten us. This predictable pattern of behavior is meant to protect us in times of perceived danger. Think of it as a biological defense against what could harm us or that emergency exercise your body goes through when your brain feels you are in trouble.

A woman in love memorizes her lover's scent. And every time he smells that perfume, his mood changes. Sometimes it induces joy, and on certain occasions, it can trigger lust. If that relationship builds up, the scents could cause sadness or anger, depending on how severe the breakup was. All I'm saying is that emotions are part of the human experience. When we feel a certain way, we act a certain way. Some events can trigger emotions that cause us to react abnormally. People can disguise themselves and turn into something they are not. They wear clothes and perfumes that look rich, and because you have a strong emotional connection to wealth, you look past the other warning signs and make a sorry decision. Whether they are good or bad, your emotional scars can make you vulnerable to deception and manipulation.

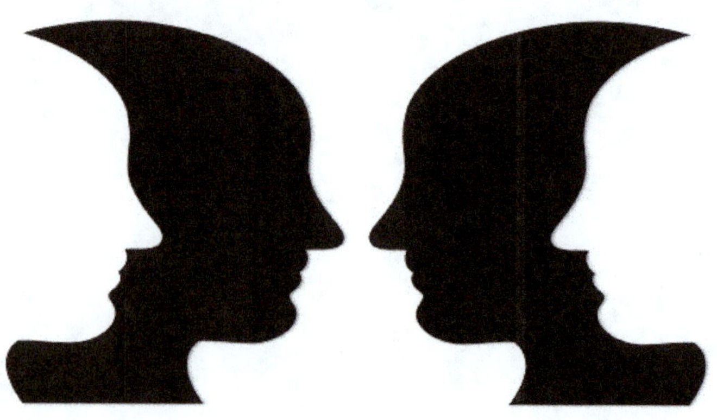

It is of primary importance to establish a clear definition of manipulation. Without understanding what constitutes manipulation, there will be many difficulties separating manipulation cases and other forms of influence.

In a broad sense, manipulation is the effort to influence the behavior or perception of others. Most definitions extend it to include "through the use of abusive, deceptive or otherwise exploitative means" or something similar, as a means of differentiating between manipulation and other influencing behaviors, such as persuasion. It raises even more questions, such as what constitutes "exploitation." Deception is relatively easy to define as intentional concealment or distortion of the truth. But does deception preclude persuasion?

It could be argued that anyone taking on a job is already operating, knowing that people are likely to highlight their positive traits and divert attention from the negative. In this sense, it is not necessarily dishonest to omit certain information in that situation. So, expectations can also play a role in determining the ethics of manipulation and where the line is drawn between manipulation and other forms of influence.

There is another word in that broad definition worthy of attention. Defining manipulation as an "effort" suggests that manipulation is still manipulation regardless of success or failure. The act of manipulation is defined as attempting. Ironically, those who are less successful at manipulating others, who are discovered more frequently are more likely to gain a reputation as manipulators than those who are successful.

You can probably point to someone in your orbit, perhaps a relative or colleague, who you consider manipulative. However, consider how others view them. Are they known as manipulators? Does this affect their success? The answer to this can also be complicated. If colleagues see someone at work as a manipulator and yet dominate the boss, they could still be judged successfully. When thinking about manipulating others, it is vital to set clear goals. It will allow you to make rational and objective decisions, which is the key to success.

Influence vs. Manipulation

The modern world has adopted the term influencer for people with a large following on social media, able to influence others with their content. It doesn't take a particularly critical mind to recognize the source of this term as advertising. As consumer behavior evolves, advertisers have noticed and seek increasingly to harness influencers' power to draw attention to products. It is done in various ways through paid or unpaid sponsorships, promotional deals, and agreements.

In some cases, influencers disclose these deals while, in others, they don't. Ethical issues are raised again, mainly if an influencer is just a happy consumer but secretly on the company's payroll selling the product.

The goals of many influencers, especially those who work with advertisers, are fundamentally manipulative. It's not even a gray zone problem. Influencers aim to pass products to their followers to make money. It is impossible to know whether everyone they influence would benefit from the work, nor is it possible to understand their financial situation or specific circumstances. In this case, the influencer puts their interests first.

Manipulation does not necessarily include an attempt to harm others. However, to some extent, efforts must put to goals and interests first. It is part of the puzzle.

Furthermore, it is safer and more logical to refer to the flu as a parent term of manipulation, including manipulation and other influence methods, such as inspiration and emulation.

Persuasion vs. Manipulation

These terms might seem opposed, with persuasion serving as a form of "honest" manipulation, in which the actor is at the forefront of his own goals and opinions. However, it will be more useful to consider persuasion at a lower level than manipulation. Persuasion, therefore, becomes a method of manipulation, which is a form of influence.

Persuasion is also one of the least effective ways of manipulation. How many times have you been in a debate with someone else to raise your hand and say, "I admit, you're right"?

It is probably possible to count these instances on one side. It can be easy to convince someone that smoking is unhealthy, but is it easy to get them to quit? If so, governments would see no need or benefit to imposing heavy taxes on tobacco products to discourage their use.

And what about other forms of flu? And other methods of manipulation? Well, manipulation must have intent, and it should have some way of goal, even if the goal is to create anarchy. A great director can influence the work of many others, but it is different from manipulation. The director does not set out to influence others (although they can). Instead, he gains influence through others' reactions to their work, resulting in inspiration and even emulation. Persuasion, likewise, is not the only method of manipulation that could be employed.

An easy alternative is to lie, a form of deception. Lying and being believed will inevitably change the perception of those who believe the lie. As has already been established, it is still a manipulation, whether successful or not. Persuasion, like influence, does not suffer from the same image problem as manipulation. It is seen as a good thing to be able to make a "persuasive argument." Even if it has a sinister tinge; the phrase "I can be very persuasive" implies an effort for power over another party - perhaps even abuse. Furthermore, when employers refer to the soft skill of "persuasion," it is correct to interpret it as a euphemism for manipulation.

Manipulation and Its Definition

A manipulation is a form of intentional influence. It is characterized as an attempt by a person or party (the manipulator) to change another person or party (the target), typically to achieve an objective in the manipulator's interest.

This definition is useful because it is objective and transparent. Also, it's helpful because you'll learn manipulation techniques that will help you achieve your goals.

However, two problems remain. The first refers to the "desired influence." The intent is problematic because it implies responsibility. Everyone manipulates everyone around them all the time, even from a young age. It would be wrong to exclude a child's whims from the manipulation umbrella, just because they are not old enough to rationalize their behavior. The same goes for adult outbursts, after all. The intent, therefore, does not imply conscious action, but it can also be instinctive. It also allows for the authentic presence of "naturally manipulative" people.

The second problem is the disappointingly vague ending: "typically to achieve a goal in the interest of the manipulator." Not only is it problematic to define "the interests of the manipulator," but there is also a general ambiguity in the inclusion of "typically." This part only creates a normalized idea of manipulation and would not fit into a more general definition. After all, how can anyone know their interests perfectly? Of course, it is possible to manipulate someone successfully, and the result is still one's death.

By successfully manipulating others, you can change their behavior, opinions, and achievable goals to promote your interests. It's that simple. Effective manipulation, however, is about improving the success rate. It could be that everyone is manipulating the boss, to some degree, to get that promotion, but only one candidate will get the job. Working hard is the right place to start, and working effectively is even better. However, letting it be merit alone may not make it. How can you make your boss want to promote you, rather than anyone else? Understanding this will give you the edge.

Be careful about Other's Manipulation

The more you understand manipulation, the better equipped you will be to avoid being manipulated by others. Recognizing manipulative behaviors in other people will not only protect you from their influence, but you will learn more about their goals by feeding your mind with the information you can use to manipulate them. It is not hard to be conscious of the situations you can expect to encounter manipulative behavior. The hardest thing is always identifying how you are being manipulated.

A vital part of this is understanding other parties' goals and how they attempt to achieve those goals at any given time. With this information, you can not only recognize and capitalize on the behavior of others, but you can develop the ability to predict the future actions of your opponents. It requires emotional intelligence, as it is necessary to put yourself in your target's shoes. In developing this ability, a good starting point is to evaluate one's behavior through one's actions and learn to understand one's choices from an objective point of view.

Your Targets

Since you are probably already manipulating the people around you to some degree and being manipulated yourself, the first significant step in achieving effective manipulation is understanding and defining your goals. Without setting goals, it's impossible to measure the effectiveness of your current manipulation efforts. It is not to say that you are not already manipulating with some level of significance. Some people are naturally more manipulative, and some people are natural manipulators; however, the two don't always overlap. Start by thinking about your actions and behavior towards others.

Consider who you see positively at work or in your social circle, and who you see negatively. Also, consider how you deal with different people and whether it aligns perfectly with your opinion of them. There is a good chance it isn't. You are probably already doing working to gain others' reasonable statements who you believe hold power and influence. It is a very general approach that everyone in society takes. To use an obvious example, your boss's behavior is likely different from that of your peers, regardless of your personal opinion about them.

You May Also Set Targets

Otherwise, you might just be trying to impress. You might also try to carve out a comfortable work-life by shedding responsibility and doing what you can to obscure your low productivity. Maybe you are taking action to get closer to a colleague you are romantically interested in. These are just ideas. Every day before going to be, think about your behavior. What have you been thinking about and trying to get the day too? These are the goals you are already naturally working towards. When you truly understand what your current motives are, you may be surprised. To start manipulating effectively, it's time to clearly and consciously define your goals.

If you have already done this, that's great. Make sure you have something with a clearly defined ending point.

Strength Is the Capability to Aid Other People Prosper

It is an interesting definition because it seems to subvert the typical idea of power to exert force on others. However, breaking it down, the two are closely related. Having the ability to exert influence on others can mean not harming them, not invading their country, not throwing them in prison, not creating laws that have a negative impact on them; these are all forms of power. The power to help other people succeed is very similar to the ability to make other people fail, if not exercised.

What can you provide to people that will help other people achieve their goals? The most obvious are extraordinary skills. Talent is precious in every aspect of life, from sports competitions, business, and raising children. If you have talents that other people can use, that's a powerful thing. Another form of power is authority. The boss decides who gets promoted and who fired. A police officer can arrest you or let you go with a warning, thanks to his or her legally authorized authority.

A judge can decide your sentence, based on specific constraints and their opinion of your nature. However, there is a problem: you may have the same or more extraordinary talents as another person. Still, they may be more successful than you, be valued more, and enjoy more significant benefits. The other aspect of power is reputation. It refers to the belief, held by others, in your control. Reputation is often the key to manipulation—the judgment of others regarding your abilities and authority.

Hypnosis is also a necessary type that should be considered. For the most part, those familiar with hypnosis know this by watching theatrical performances of participants doing ridiculous acts. While this is a type of hypnosis, there is so much more to it. We will focus more on hypnosis as a form of mind control.

What is Hypnosis?

To begin with, is the definition of hypnosis. According to experts, hypnosis is considered a state of consciousness that involves focused attention and reduced peripheral awareness, characterized by the participant's more extraordinary ability to respond to suggestions given. It means that the participant will enter a different mental state and be much more susceptible to following the hypnotist's suggestions.

It is widely recognized that two theoretical groups help describe what is happening during the period of hypnosis. The first is known as the altered state theory. Those who follow this theory see that hypnosis is like a trance or state of mind altered if the participant sees that their awareness is somehow different from what they would notice in their ordinary conscious state. The other theory is non-state theories. Those who follow this theory do not think that those undergoing hypnosis are entering different states of consciousness. Instead, the participant is working with the hypnotist to enter a type of imaginative role play.

During hypnosis, the participant is thought to have more focus and focus, coupled with a new ability to focus intensely on a specific memory or thought. During this process, the participant is also able to block other sources that could distract him. Hypnotized individuals are thought to show an increased ability to respond to them, especially when these suggestions come from the hypnotist. The process used to put the participant into hypnosis is known as hypnotic induction and will involve a series of tips and instructions used as a type of warm-up.

Some many different views and statements have been made about hypnosis. Some people believe hypnosis is genuine and is paranoid that the government and others will control their minds. Others don't believe in hypnosis at all and think it's just a sleight of hand. Most likely, the idea of hypnosis as mind control falls somewhere in between.

There are three stages of hypnosis recognized by the psychological community. These three phases include induction, suggestion, and susceptibility. Each of them is important to the hypnosis process and will be discussed later.

Induction

The first stage of hypnosis is induction. Before the participant undergoes full hypnosis, they will be introduced to the hypnotic induction technique. For many years, this was the method used to put the subject into his hypnotic trance, but this definition has changed in modern times. Some of the non-state theorists have seen this phase slightly differently. Instead, they see this phase as the method of increasing the

participants' expectations of what will happen, defining their role, getting their attention to focus in the right direction, and any other steps needed to lead the participant in the right direction for hypnosis.

Several induction techniques can be used during hypnosis. The best known and most effective method is Braid's "eye-fixation" or "Braidism" technique. There are some variations of this approach, including the Stanford Hypnotic Susceptibility Scale (SHSS). This scale is the most used tool for research in the field of hypnosis.

To use Braid induction techniques, you will need to follow a couple of steps. The first is to take any bright object, such as a watch case, and hold it between the left hand's middle, front, and thumb. You will need to hold this object approximately 8-15 inches from the participant's eyes. Hold the object somewhere above the forehead. It produces tension on the eyelids and eyes during the process so that the participant can keep a fixed gaze on the object at all times.

The hypnotist must then explain to the participant that they should hold their eyes always fixed on the object. The patient will also have to fully concentrate the mind on the idea of that particular object. They shouldn't be allowed to think about other things or let their mind and eyes wander, or else the process will fail.

After a short time, the participant's eyes will begin to dilate. With a little more time, the participant will begin to assume a wave motion. If the participant involuntarily closes the eyelids when the middle and index fingers of the right hand are brought from the object's eyes, they are in a trance. If not, the participant will have to start over and let the participant know that they must allow their eyes to close once the fingers are brought back towards the eyes in a similar motion. This way, the patient will enter an altered mental state known as hypnosis.

Although Braid supported his technique, he recognized that using the hypnosis induction technique is not always necessary for every case. Indeed, modern-day researchers have generally found that the induction technique is not as crucial to the effects of hypnotic suggestion as previously thought. Over time, other alternatives and variations of the original hypnotic induction technique have been developed, although the Braid method is still considered the best.

Suggestion

The next stage of hypnosis is known as the suggestion stage. When James Braid first described hypnosis, the term suggestion was not used. Instead, Braid referred to this phase as having the participant's conscious mind focused on a central and dominant idea. Braid's way of doing this was to stimulate or reduce the physiological functioning of the different regions of the participant's body. Subsequently, Braid began to place more and more emphasis on using different forms of non-verbal and verbal suggestions to bring the participant into a hypnotic state of mind. These include the use of "waking tips" and self-hypnosis.

Modern hypnotism uses many different forms of suggestion to be successful. These include metaphors, innuendo, indirect or non-verbal suggestions, direct verbal suggestions, and other rhetorical figures and suggestions that are not verbal. Some of the hint phase's non-verbal cues include physical manipulation, voice pitch, and mental imagery.

One of the distinctions made in the types of suggestions that can be offered to the participant includes those suggestions given with permission and more authoritarian. One of the things that need to be considered regarding hypnosis is the difference between the unconscious and conscious minds. Many hypnotists view the suggestion stage to communicate mostly directed to the subject's conscious mind. Others on the field will see him in the opposite direction; they see the agent's communication and the subconscious or unconscious mind.

Susceptibility

Over time, it has been observed that people will react differently to hypnosis. Some people find that they can fall into a hypnotic trance quickly and not commit to the process. Others may find that they can enter the hypnotic trance, but only after an extended period and with some effort. Still, others will find that they cannot enter the file

hypnotic trance, and even after continuous efforts, they will not achieve their goals. One thing the researchers found interesting about the different participants' susceptibility is that this factor remains constant. If you've been able to quickly get into a hypnotic state of mind, chances are you will be the same for the rest of your life. On the other hand, if you've always had a hard time achieving a hypnotic state and have never been hypnotized, chances are you never will.

There have been several different models developed overtime to try to determine the susceptibility of participants to hypnosis. Some of the older depth scales worked on inferring the participant's trance level through the available observable signs. These would include things like spontaneous amnesia. Some of the more modern scales work to measure the degree of self-rated or observed responsiveness to specific hint tests provided, such as direct arm stiffness cues.

Applications

Hypnosis, as a field and as an idea, has been around for a long time. Due to this, various applications have emerged that help put the hypnosis process to fair use. The various hypnosis applications span many entertainments, self-improvement, military uses, and medical uses. Other areas that have recently started using hypnosis include rehabilitation, physical therapy, education, sport, and forensics. Even artists have begun to use hypnosis to achieve specific creative purposes.

Different fields of hypnosis

We will discuss a few different fields in which hypnosis has grown and how the hypnosis process works in those fields.

Hypnotherapy

Hypnotherapy is the use of hypnosis as a form of psychotherapy. It helps the patient or person overcome troubling problems afflicting them, especially when other self-control methods are not sufficient. Licensed psychologists and doctors could perform a form of hypnotherapy on willing patients to help them treat post-traumatic stress, compulsive gambling, sleep disorders, eating disorders, anxiety, and depression.

It is also possible to visit a certified hypnotherapist to help you treat weight management and smoking cessation problems. If you go to a certified hypnotherapist, this is important to remember that they are not psychologists or doctors, so they will only help you achieve the hypnotic state and not cure your more severe ailments. You should make sure that the person you work with has been certified to provide you with these services, whether you choose a hypnotherapist or a doctor.

The hypnotherapy process has been viewed in many different forms in modern history. All have had varying degrees of success, depending on the problem faced and the participants. Some of the modules that have been used include:

- Cognitive Behavioral Hypnotherapy is a combination of clinical hypnosis along with several elements of cognitive-behavioral therapy

- Hypnoanalysis is also known as age regression hypnotherapy

- Hypnosis to help cope with phobias and fears

- Ericksonian hypnotherapy.

- Hypnotherapy to help with addictions

- Hypnotherapy to help with the control of habits

- Hypnotherapy to assist in pain management in those suffering from chronic pain

- Hypnotherapy to support the psychological therapy that the patient is already facing

- Hypnotherapy to help with relaxation

- Hypnotherapy to help with skin diseases

- Hypnotherapy to help soothing patients who are anxious to undergo surgery

- Hypnotherapy to assist athletes' performance before a competition. Hypnotherapy to help with weight loss.

Self-Hypnosis

In some cases, such as when a certified hypnotherapist or other professional is unavailable, you may decide to use the self-hypnosis process. This process occurs when a person can hypnotize themselves, often using the tactic of autosuggestion. The primary use of this technique is for self-improvement, and many people will perform it to reduce their stress levels, quit smoking, or get the motivation they need to go on a diet. While some people may be able to self-hypnotize, many find that they need assistance to achieve the altered state. It could include hypnotic recordings or even mental machine devices to help them achieve that state. Other areas you might use self-hypnosis to include your overall physical well-being, relaxation, and overcoming stage fright.

Hypnotic Phase

When most people think of hypnosis, they think of stage hypnosis. It is a form of entertainment that will take place in a theater or club in front of an audience. The hypnotist is often shown as a great showman, which encourages the idea that hypnosis is all about mind control. At the start of the act, the hypnotist will attempt to put the entire audience in an altered state before selecting specific individuals who meet the criteria to take the stage and perform several awkward acts. At the same time, the rest of the group watches.

It is unknown why stage hypnosis is so effective, although it is commonly thought to be a combination of deception, stage art, physical manipulation, suggestibility, participant selection, and psychological factors. For the most part, experts believe the participant is just playing one way with the hypnotist and providing a good show. These individuals may be willing to do this because they want to be the center of all attention, the pressure to please others, and the excuse to go against their fear repressors make it easy to get attendees to perform. The books that have been written by former stage hypnotists reinforce the idea of deception and deceit, and some are entirely composed of false hypnosis where private whispers were used all the time.

Types of Hypnosis

There are many different types of hypnosis that the subject will be able to undergo. Each of them will work in slightly different ways, and some of them work to help with various problems. Some may be better suited to help the person relax while others may be more suitable for weight loss or pain management. This section will talk in more detail about the different types of hypnosis available.

Traditional Hypnosis

The most common type of hypnosis used is known as traditional hypnosis. During this process, the agent is merely making suggestions directly to the subject's unconscious mind. This type of hypnosis will work best on a subject known to accept things said to them and don't ask many questions. If you visit a certified hypnotist or purchase a tape to perform the self-hypnosis process, you will go through the traditional hypnosis process. This type of hypnosis is so popular because it doesn't take a lot of experience or training to learn how to do it. The hypnotist will have to write a simple script and tell the subject what to do. While this technique will work very well on those who accept what is happening around them, it is ineffective for those who think critically and analytically.

Ericksonian Hypnosis

The next type of hypnosis to discuss is Ericksonian hypnosis. It is a bit more in-depth because it will require the use of metaphors and little stories. These are used to present the ideas and suggestions that are required of the unconscious mind. While this method will require a little more experience and training, it is a very effective and powerful method. The reason it works so well is that it can eliminate the resistance and block the subject may have to suggestions.

Two main types of metaphors will often be used in this type of hypnosis; isomorphic and interspersal. The metaphor of an intercalary nature, the command explained, was incorporated into the story and would not easily have been discovered by the subject outside his unconscious mind. The other type, the isomorphic metaphor, is a little more familiar and offers clues to the unconscious mind by merely presenting a story to the subject that will ultimately offer a moral. The unconscious mind will be able draw a one-to-one relationship by linking the elements from the story and the elements that arise from the behavior or problematic situation.

Built-in Technique

Another type of hypnosis is called an embedded technique. During this process, the hypnotist will tell the subject an exciting story. This story is intended to distract and engage the subject's conscious mind. It will also contain indirect suggestions hidden within the story, but that will be accepted in the subject's unconscious mind. Through this story, the hypnotist will use the process's instructions to direct the subject's unconscious mind to find the necessary memory. This memory is usually about the appropriate learning experience from the past. The hypnotist will then be able to apply that learning experience to help them change their present.

Hypnosis Video

While other hypnosis forms have been prevalent in helping individuals overcome obstacles and change how they think to live a better life, new forms of hypnosis are always being developed. One of the newer forms of hypnotherapy that has been developed is video hypnosis. This module is offered through commercial means so that people can purchase and use them as they please. The techniques used in some of the brands of video hypnosis are also based on the neuro-linguistic programming technology discussed above. It means that the video hypnosis technique will work based on using the subject's existing thought processes rather than using hypnotic suggestions like traditional methods.

Video hypnosis has overgrown that over 70% of people have found that they learn things easier and faster when they see things than when they listen to information. The subject's mind will learn to automatically change the sensations he is experiencing and his visual associations on a conscious level as he watches the presented visual films.

While there are many different types of video hypnosis programs available, Neuro-VISION is one of the most popular because it was developed using some of the business's best techniques. This type of video method works to train the subject's unconscious mind through digital optics, a high-tech simulation process on the computer. It will free the subject of their tensions, drives, and compulsions. Through this process, the smoker will find that quitting smoking is easy, dieters will lose their appetite, and those who feel stressed will begin to relax more. It often takes at least a few video hypnosis sessions to see results, although some believe that a single view will begin to show some of the desired results.

Subliminal Hypnosis

The last type of hypnosis that will be discussed in this chapter is subliminal hypnosis. Often the subliminal hypnosis messages will be inserted into a recording for the subject to hear. The recording will have two tracks, and each will speak to a different part of the mind. A track will contain a cover sound that will be heard through the subject's conscious mind. The cover sound is often easy for the brain to hear, like nature or music. The other track will contain direct suggestions that will be heard through the subject's unconscious mind. These tips on the second track will be repeated over and over again throughout the entire session.

Subliminal programs can be reproduced at any time and in any place. You may hear these messages while you work or even while watching TV. The best part is that you won't have to stop the task you are doing and sit back and relax as is required with traditional NLP or hypnosis. In some cases, subliminal programs will be added to regular hypnotic programs.

The use of subliminal programming is not that widespread. Most people will not choose this method to change their habits and behaviors. Research has shown that subliminal programs aren't really that effective and, therefore, won't replace NLP or hypnosis. According to some accounts, it may take more than 80 hours of listening to the subliminal message before it affects, and many times even that won't be enough for most people. According to Joel Weinberger, a professor at Adelphi University and a psychologist, ordinary subliminal audiotapes can be bought in stores, or online don't work.

Subliminal psychodynamics can work as long as some form of imagery is present. The popular options available contain only auditory components. Hearing is not enough to make this method work alone. The subliminal suggestion will have to be combined with other forms of hypnotherapy to have the desired effect.

Despite the media portrayal of hypnosis, it is not an evil plot that aims to take over reluctant subjects' minds. If the subject is unwilling to undergo hypnosis, it is practically impossible to convince him to enter the altered state. Often the use of hypnosis is to help others improve their lives. It could be in weight management, quitting smoking, improving other health conditions, and assisting in chronic pain management. Each of the techniques is also important in helping the subject achieve his or her overall goal. While all of them can be effective, the professional you choose to work with and the problem in question will be used to determine which of these methods best suits your needs and helps you improve your life.

CHAPTER 5: NEURO-LINGUISTIC PROGRAMMING (NLP)

NLP is brief for Neuro-Linguistic Programming and is the most modern mind control system available to the public. NLP was born of therapists who could achieve their therapeutic goals in a brief time. Not only has NLP proven to be a useful therapeutic tool, but it is also a powerful hidden instrument of persuasion and inspiration. If an analyst can delicately encourage a client to accept a new solution to their problem, similar methods can be worked to sell a product or even infuse a new list of principles. Considerably NLP is a science. It is also an art and requires a good understanding of the NLP model and techniques and the time to practice it.

To understand the NLP model, one must first accept that people are both the same and different in many ways. We are the same in that we only have an inadequate numeral way to comprehend our knowledge. We are distinctive in that each person has a particular form of creating the logic of their learning. For the person who distinguishes how someone else makes the logic of their world, they can customize their message to be accepted. With the power implicit in NLP, it has been picked up and tapped into the realm of sales, advertising, and helping men to stay courageous.

Sensual Insight

Sensory acuity is NLP jargon for "pay attention!" it means that when you work with somebody, you have to pay more responsiveness to how they respond than whether you are doing things right or not. When you do this, "pay attention!" You will observe that people reply to you in very subtle ways.

Connection

For mind control and NLP, the best place to start is the beginning. All NLP teaching begins with the topic of the relationship. The relationship is more than just having someone like you. It is probable to have a connection with someone who doesn't like you. What's essential in the relationship is that the other person perceives that you are very similar to her deep. It allows the person to feel comfortable and willing to respond to you with a certain recognition feeling. (yes, even if they don't accept you, they can be sensitive to you. Think of this as respecting enemies.) It has been told, and correctly so that without the affiliation, nothing is possible. Everything is possible with relationships. "mirroring and matching" are the first techniques to create a relationship. Mirroring means moving and talking like the other person and doing it in a way that doesn't seem to mimic. It makes an unconscious influence on the other person that you are like them.
You can see people subconsciously mirroring each other among those who are already in a relationship. They sit in a similar way. When one varies his position, the other person will change his position to

match the other person. It is a very typical result of having a relationship. Many NLP courses spend long hours doing mirroring and matching exercises to help attendees learn how to quickly get into a relationship. The activities are beneficial, but there is an easier way.

The simplest way to achieve a relationship is to think that you are mirroring yourself due to the relationship rather than its cause. When you like someone and feel like this person, you are in a relationship, and you will do all the reflecting and equaling without believing concerning it. Suppose the relationship is already there and that you both are deeply familiar with other people's thoughts and habits. At first, this can take some mental gymnastics, but it's a lot easier than paying close attention to people's movements and then moving your body to match theirs.

Encouragement and Supervision

Stimulation and guidance can be used in any situation in many different ways. Inspiration and guidance consist of the first stimulation, which essentially means that the controller does what the other person is doing, followed by the guide, doing something that takes the initiative to follow. Using rhythm and guidance is an essential part of traditional rapport exercises, as mentioned above. In the case of intercourse, the controller will follow the follower's movements and then lead him. Stimulation and guidance can also be used in almost any situation to take the initiative. Linguistically, stimulation, and guidance take the form of rhythm that is true and verifiable by the follower. A clue is a statement on which the controller wants the follower to agree.

Stimulus and Amusement

It refers to something a little more intense than pacing and driving. It requires strong sensory understanding and the ability to force the follower to follow your lead much sooner than generally with rhythm and guidance. Stimulation and entrainment need several things from the operator.

Attention

Attention means that the operator is wholly focused on the follower and intentionally ignores any personal concerns, whatever they may be. As a controller, this means that bills, mortgage payments, quarrels with spouses are put aside wholly when you are with your dependent.

Concern

As a controller, Concern means making the dependent the most critical individual in your world as you are with him. It can only be done using your focus and sense of care, even if you have to pretend.

Enthusiasm and Rule

Excitement and principle is the expertise that what you are fixing it right. To rekindle this influence, consider all the benefits of what you're doing that involves the topic. These benefits include reasons why it matters and also consists of the values or things it gives you. By combining these qualities, rhythm and dragging are made more accessible. Sensory acuity will be heightened by concentration and worry and can be used to see if the follower is somehow resisting the drag. When resistance is detected, the controller can make instant improvements to their performance.

The Effects of Operational

Functioning in NLP terms means how the body is used to create and lead emotional and mental states. By changing the physiology, it is much easier to access individual emotional states. An excellent example of this is the act of simply sitting with your back straight and looking up. It is complicated for anyone to maintain a depressed state while doing so. On the other hand, one will find that collapsing, looking down, and taking very short and shallow breaths are easy to achieve. It is a fantastic wonder that more people have not applied it.

But suitable Mind Controllers do. Consider how churches can have very high and ornate ceilings. It forces people to look up and access pleasant emotional states more easily. Another way to use physiology is for the controller to simply tell the follower what to do and how to get into position. Rites, contemplations, and breathing exercises are all designed to secretly influence the followers' physiology to aid in a consequence. By solely asking, "Can I show you something about how your body affects your mind?" a controller may then ask the follower to change posture or movements to prove the fact.

The critical factors of physiology under conscious control are posture, breathing, eye movement, and activity. Thus, by making any combination of these, a change in emotions can occur.

Sensory Modalities and Sub-Modalities

In NLP, the reality is interpreted through the feelings, and commonly, one of the emotions is domineering. Graphic/sight, auditory/hearing, and kinesthetic / sense are the primary modalities (or modalities) that people use. These are the preferred ways of thinking that people use, and in the NLP literature, it is referred to as VAK for visual, auditory, kinesthetic. People who think predominantly in visual terms will refer to something as to how they "see" things and use phrases like "It seems right," "it's clear to me." "I have a good picture of what you say."

An individual who thinks in auditory terms will say things like, "Sounds like a good idea." "Let me intervene." "

All you have to do to determine someone's dominant sensory modality is to listen to them speak. Therefore, sensory understanding is critical. When you use a person's predominant sensory modality, you increase the ratio and gain a more significant foothold to guide them.

Study Additional About Sensual Modality

Ask somebody how they determined to make their latest buying and hear what they say. In making choices, people will go through a mental process that they mention to the sensory modalities they use. For example, if you show someone a coat to buy and ask them how they got their latest skin and say, "I saw (visually) the coat at the window, and I said (audibly) to myself, 'It looks good.' Then I had this (kinesthetic) feeling that I had to have it. " To maintain a relationship, all you have to do is use the same process. For example, "Take a look (visually) at this coat, and when you do, listen (audibly) for" Looks good "and tell me how good you feel (kinesthetic)."

Sub-Mode

Sub-modes are more specific distinctions than various sensory modalities. When these sub-modes are changed, the impact of the message is also altered. Of the visual mode, some sub-modes are image distance, size, position, whether it is color or black and white, image position is the most prominent and common and sufficient for most to use effectively. Auditory sub-modes include volume, whether it is a voice that is heard or said (usually it is), the gender of the voice, emotional tone, direction position, whisper, speed of the voice. Kinesthetic sub-modalities include heat, heaviness, position in the body, tingling.

To comprehend how sub-modalities are used therapeutically, consider how someone might describe being depressed. Their head drops, and their physiology collapses (kinesthetic). They listen to a rambling, oppressive voice in their mind saying, "you are useless!" then hear your voice say, "I'm nothing." Then see a picture of yourself standing two feet tall and staring at them with contempt by all who see them (visual).

The NLP therapist should elicit this information, which the follower is not consciously aware of, and then intentionally alter these sub-modalities. The follower would start by imagining themselves, standing very tall, and seeing people seeing them and smiling (visually). Internal voices would turn into laughing murmurs with noisier, more optimistic voices saying, "you are the finest!" added. It will immediately affect the follower, but may only be temporary unless practiced as an ongoing project. Sub-modes can be used as a mind-control tool in stealth using some general rules about sub-modalities that affect most people.

Visual sub-modes tend to significantly impact people when pictured in the foreground, large, and color. So, describing your product or service as "great" and seeing it "up close and colorful" will tend to have a more significant impact. For example, note the difference between these two rental apartment listings: two bedrooms and one bathroom. Dining room with kitchenette. "Or" Spacious apartment with two colorful bedrooms and sunlit dining area. "Notice how the second description makes the apartment seem more real.

It can be used for Mind Control by adding more visual sub-modes to your product or service description. TV commercials and print ads often use this by showing their work the greatest and most colorful as possible and comparing their competitor in smaller black and white images. Describing auditory sub-modes as loud and echoing will tend to have a substantial impact. Still, you have to be cautious with this as some people will not respond positively to a "strong description" The kinesthetic sub-modalities of "warm," "soft," "comforting," and "enveloping" tend to be considered favorable for most people. To be considered negative.

To add effect to any message, a Mind Control practitioner can use a beneficial process to incorporate visual, auditory, and kinesthetic sub-modes into all of their communications. It will ensure that people will see, hear, and feel the message's impact regardless of their dominant sensory modality.

Ethics Evocation

Values are at the heart of our decision-making process. They are profound and oblivious until they are satisfied or dared. Standards are strong enough that when someone tells you that your values will be met by purchasing their product or service, it's nearly impossible to resist. For a seller, finding someone's deals is the same as finding the buy button and pressing it again. Using values as a mind-control tool is powerful enough that if you don't keep them as you promise, you will become a sinister enemy, so use this tool wisely. The process of using values as a mind-control tool is to discover a person's deals and then link them to your achievement. Both steps are surprisingly simple and straightforward.

The Enthusiasm

First, understand that everyone has criteria that must be met before accepting anything. If it's a new car, it may need to be fast, or a new model or color, or within a specific price range. Once these criteria are met, the person feels their value. Most individuals try to persuade by striving to meet all requirements. The elicitation of values bypasses it and goes straight to that motivating value. Achieving value is achieved simply by asking the question, "What is important." For instance, if you attempt to enroll someone in a communication seminar, you would ask, "What is important in connecting with individuals?" From that, you will acquire their first answer. Then ask them, "What's important in this (their first answer)?" giving you their second answer. Then ask, "What's important in this (their second answer)?" You will usually have reached their highest value by then. Don't be astonished if they show some strong emotion.

Let me give you some assistance on how to ask these questions. Keep in mind that you don't want to learn because only what's essential about "it" matters. The reason is that "why?" it causes people to get defensive. To keep it simple, don't ask, "Why is _ important?"! While asking these questions, it is essential not to craft it sound like an examination. You can do this by combining your questions with conversations about life and relevant issues. You will notice that people become interested when you show genuine curiosity about what is essential to people. To put it another way, asking these questions builds rapport because people like to talk about what they think is necessary.

Another way to get a recall of values is to listen. Many people will quickly start talking about what they like. If you simply give it to them and ask them to elaborate, you will find that they "turn on,"; a strong indication that you've come to something they appreciate.

Conveyance of Evocation Ethics

Once you have their principles, the rest is pretty simple. All you require to do is reference these values as you describe your service or product. Saying, "Do you think having X, Y and Z are important enough to take part in this seminar?" Or, even though this may be crude, you can say, "This seminar shows you how to have more X, Y and Z. Sounds like something you'd like to take part in?"

This process is so robust that you have to try it to test its efficiency. You should also notice that if your product or service doesn't meet that value as you implied, you may have a very ready person. In reality, enemies are made by deceiving them in this way. Be careful.

To uncover people's values on a large scale, some people will employ a survey asking various questions about certain aspects of their lives. From this information, you can customize your responses and presentations before individual meetings.

Emotive Elicitation

Emotional elicitation is NLP's process of fetching out the emotions you need a person to sense. It will be of enormous worth in the next section on anchoring. To begin, determine what your follower's emotions might aid tip to your result. These emotions could be eagerness, joy, fear, worry, frustration, despair, love, certainty, curiosity, etc.

There are several ways to arouse emotions. The simplest and most direct way is to ask, "What is it like when you hear X?" or "Do you remember a time when you felt?" Keep in mind that the relationship is vital to this process because these are pretty weird questions to ask a stranger. So, earn a report! As you ask these questions, observe how they respond. You should be able to witness the emergence of emotion. Another way to do this is to talk about the feeling of telling a story that describes the emotion.

Use your sensual insight when doing this as it doesn't promise your description will match your followers, so pay attention to how they react. By successfully performing emotional elicitation, the follower becomes a little more flexible. If they can provoke emotions to which you lead them, it is an indication that you have a great relationship and make them even more responsive to your driving. It is often done on TV shows and what makes watching particular series so compelling. Yes, the media know the power of mind control.

Emotive Elicitation in Inscribing

Emotional processing always occurs in writing and is more common in fiction because it allows the reader to identify with a character and be emotionally involved. You will also see emotional stimuli in the best advertisement.

Anchoring

Anchoring is the next step once you have learned how to arouse emotions. Anchoring is a very Pavlovian practice that links emotion to a gesture, a touch, an object or setting, or whatever. It is a very natural process that we humans have anchors. We adore our beloved restaurant because they treated us well and left us feeling warm every time, we think about it. Commercials use the anchoring process by eliciting emotion and then connecting the sensation to a product. By using anchor, your sensory acuity must be sharp enough to notice when someone is experiencing the feeling you are trying to elicit. As the emotion rises to its peak, you "fix" the anchor, meaning you bring what you want to associate with the sensation. Think about how anchoring happens in a romantic setting. The relationship is built, and warm, confused feelings begin to develop as you look at the person. It alone connects those feelings to the person so that all you have to do is think about the people they are dealing with and have those feelings.

But you can use it to speed up those thoughts by using the anchoring method with an aware purpose. It can be achieved by eliciting the sensation by asking how it feels to feel "a connection" with someone or describe the connection (or both). When you notice the feelings inside the person grow, you uniquely touch them. Here is a literal example of a romantic anchor that is often used in romantic contexts.

The solar plexus touch will anchor that feeling of connection (called "fixing the anchor"). So, whenever you want to bring that feeling back, all you have to do is touch the solar plexus, and the feeling will come back. You can fix anchor without contacting physically. Create a unique gesture, and it will work. In NLP jargon, that second touch that brings about the emotion is called "firing the anchor."

Built-In Commands

The built-in commands are incredibly useful as a mind-control tool because they send messages to the unconscious mind without the conscious mind being aware of them. You can consider them almost subliminal except that they become quite apparent when you are trained to listen to them. Thankfully, hardly anyone spends enough time learning how to use or listen to the built-in commands. To learn how to use built-in controls, first consider how we talk. We tend to say things in a specific voice or tone of voice. We usually get excited or get anguish, and our voice pattern changes by intensity or in volume. Still, mostly our voice pattern does not get significant changes in our modulation and rhythm.

The built-in commands work by using our voice to highlight certain words and phrases in our speech to send Messages conscious and unconscious. The conscious message is the necessary content of what we are saying. It would be the information conveyed to write our words and read them from a script. Oblivious messages are the brief words and expressions you mark as commands by changing your words' delivery.

There are several ways to pronounce sentences differently from the rest of the paragraph so that the unconscious mind begins to recognize the tapping. The simplest way is to pause before the built-in command, lower your voice, and then pause after the command ends and resume speaking typically. Try re-reading it this time and notice that the signs indicate a pause and when you read the command, read it as if you were giving a command and let the pitch go down as if you were giving an order.

Using built-in commands will seem awkward and unnatural at first. Get over it. It is a tool that people have paid a lot to learn for good judgment; It works. If you understand the steps below, you will become very good with the built-in commands, and you will see people respond to your commands without even knowing what is going on.

- State results not only in terms of actions but also in terms of the emotions that motivate the action.

- Write a short 2 to 4-word commands that lead to your result. The more, the better.

- Write a maximum of these commands as probable.

- Make sure they are in the command form.

- Start writing commands in a monologue about anything you would usually talk about.

- Read it aloud.

- Practice, practice, practice.

Using a single built-in command will not be effective because the follower's unconscious mind will not have enough samples of the commands to distinguish it as different from the rest of the speech and

271

determine that they are instructions. So, the instruction is to use a lot of them. Since the built-in commands are hidden, you can send them to one person in a group by marking the commands with a candid look at the follower.

Meta Programs

A Meta Program is an NLP text that describes the possible ways in which individuals order the information they perceive. Thus, they can bring about an appropriate reaction. It has been claimed by some that there are over 30 different Meta Programs that people use unconsciously. The NLP Model Meta Programs demonstrate that we will best interact with (and control) people if we treat them as they're rather than forcing them to be what we expect they ought to be.

Keep in mind that each one Meta Programs are context-dependent and not necessarily universal to the individual. So, someone could use a meta program towards (see later) to settle on a romantic partner but could use a foreign meta program to shop for tuna. So, people aren't considered "types" of meta-programs. Meta programs depend upon the context, not the person.

The key to using Mind Control Meta Programs is straightforward and easy. You employ the meta program your follower is using for the context you're discussing. Period.

When someone says "I want/don't want to try to to it because " what follows will tell you whether or not they are motivated by getting something (a meta program towards) or avoiding something (a distant meta program). Consider this, counting on the context and, therefore, the situation, and each folk is motivated either by eager to avoid something we do not like or by getting something we would like.

When given the selection of the way to do something, people will have two ways of responding. They're going to prefer to respond by choosing a predetermined procedure or deciding from a spread of options. People that tend to procedures will tend to possess a group way of doing things. They do not need much for motivation, just a process they will ask and believe. Those who tend towards options will always be looking for a better way to do things and will love to respond creatively with new ideas.

For example, when you ask, "How did you choose your current job?" an Options response will sound like "I wanted to be in a position that gave me the ability to travel. I went through my choices, started at the top of my favorite possible jobs list, and went down until I got one. "A response to the procedures will be very systematic and procedural! Something like this: "I went to a friend of mine, and he told me about the work the flight attendants do, so I researched and talked to some people. One of them worked as an assistant and told me where to apply, so I looked at some training courses, and "This kind of story can last for a while.

Meta Program: Affiliation

This Meta Program helps determine how many similarities and differences contribute to people's choices. When asked, "What is the relationship between the (service or product) you want and what you have now?" the follower will respond by saying that it is similar or different. There is a standard test that NLP professionals use in which they show three coins, two heads, and across.

When this question is asked about what the controller is trying to offer, the controller will adapt it to the meta-program of the relationship between followers. In other words, if the follower were asked about the ratio of his current car to an ideal car and he replied that it had to be completely different, the controller would emphasize the difference in the car he offers, even if he offers a very similar car.

You will notice that the follower is underlining an exception to "all the same" and "all different." In this case, the controller would also give an exception, thus matching the Meta Program followers.

Procedures of Fluctuating Inspirations

NLP is an incredibly valuable therapeutic tool to help people re-evaluate the influences that have held them back from achieving their goals. Since NLP is often used as a secret tool of persuasion, it can secretly change people's beliefs for mind control purposes. To understand the process of belief change, it is easier to see how it is used in an overt therapeutic context. In a therapeutic example, the follower reports that he is reluctant to go back to school because he believes he is too old to resume his education. Here the sub-modalities are used, and four different images are elicited and followed by the NLP process that will create the change they needed.

1. The person is asked to create an image of the idea, "I am too old to learn." Then, the sub-modalities of that image are asked; location, distance, black and white color, moving or still, etc. The NLP practitioner/controller takes note of these.

2. The person is then asked to imagine a new positive idea that could benefit him, such as "I

can learn at any age, " and the same sub-modalities are raised.

3. The same is done for "something true but is no longer true." It should be something mundane that has no emotional content.

4. The last image that is elicited is something the follower knows to be true.

5. The person is then asked to move the image of the idea quickly "I am too old to learn." in the position of "something true but is no longer true." and make sure it assumes all related sub-modalities of "something true but is no longer true."

6. The image of the idea "I can learn at any age." it is then moved very quickly into the position of "something true."

7. The person is then asked to try to see these changes. If done right, the influence is permanent.

Secret Alteration of Notions

Changing an idea on the sly is a little more complicated because it requires many relationships and becomes very adept with anchoring. To do this in a converted way, the controller will perform the same procedure mentioned above but embed hidden anchors. The controller's first step is to get the thing that was true or could be something they know as "wrong." Then drop anchor when the discussion moves to their current idea that the controller wants to remove. The next anchor is for something they know to be accurate and for shooting that when the discussion turns into the idea that the controller wants to be accepted. This process is performed regularly in many TV commercials.

Simple operant conditioning will also work (see Behavioral Conditioning). Reward any movement that is indicative of the new idea and give a hard look to opposing ideas. Using the light mouth is also useful in fighting an existing idea (see Gaslighting). Another method is to use the voice where any reference to the old idea is referred to with a whimpering tone, sarcasm, or contempt. A healthy relationship is significant as a warning because it can quickly be taken as an insult.

Timeline and Time Manipulation

Chronology refers to how people perceive time as a linear series of events from the past, leading to present events and being followed by future events. It can be drawn as a line in two dimensions.

To understand this, tell someone to assume they are on a timeline and ask them where they perceive the past and ask them to point it out. Then invite them to indicate their future. With this information, you will understand how they perceive the past and future.

A controller can elicit a history of people, or simple use of gestures can suggest it; the right hand extended to the side can represent the future, and the left hand extended can represent the past. The center is present, and it can be kept secret by talking about the past while extending the left hand and the future while extending the right hand. To suggest a future answer, the controller can simply point to the future and suggest the feeling of being there.

Time manipulation refers to the process of secretly suggesting that a response or feeling from the follower will occur in the future. It can also help the follower imagine that a sensation or event has happened in the past. An example would be to elicit a feeling and use linguistic patterns (mentioned below) to suggest it in the future.

Language Patterns

Linguistic patterns are phrases, stories, and metaphors combined with other NLP practices (such as anchoring and built-in commands) to secretly elicit a response from the listener. The desired response is usually something emotional so that it can be anchored in some way. Linguistic patterns are a unique form of secret hypnotic suggestion. In old-fashioned hypnosis, the hypnotist will give direct suggestions, tell the follower what to do, and respond. Linguistic patterns differ from traditional hypnotic suggestions in that they are not direct. Instead, the operator often describes a process. For the follower who is listening to the pattern to understand the process, he must go through it in his mind, doing it to himself.

The popularity of hidden language models evolved from NLP professionals who wanted to fuck. Then they were packed into "fucked" NLP products and seminars designed for consumption by the horny male masses too busy to take an NLP class and figure it out for themselves. If you can control the emotions of others, they are very likely to follow the suggestions. It is because people almost universally make their decisions based on emotion rather than reason.

Using emotions, a nation can be pushed into war or the construction of giant monuments. Individuals in a one-to-one are no different, and because a controller can get instant feedback, control is often more straightforward. When using linguistic models, the relationship is essential. Most people who learn language patterns first start memorizing existing patterns and, if they are intelligent, practice them. After some practice, most people understand the theory behind language models and start generating language models independently.

The Model of Unhappiness

This model is very advanced because it employs Elicitation and Anchoring of Values. The beginning of the model is to arouse the life values of the follower. In other words, the process begins with the relationship, and the practitioner asks, "What is important to you in life?". It will lead the follower to reveal what those values are finally, and, for this example, let's say the follower replies, "Family, Faith and Work" in that order of importance. The operator will then ask the query, "What are you not considering?" This question will cause a deep state of confusion in the follower. At that time, the operator will secretly anchor the misunderstanding with touching or gesturing.

The operator would talk about the followers' values of "Family, religion, and work" and shoot the anchor of confusion that links the confusion to these values, effectively canceling them. The most damaging use of this or any "Dark" model would be to have the follower practice this response and predetermine it as a result. Now consider why this type of pattern is so harmful. If done effectively, every time the follower thinks about what it had value in; Family, religion, and work now feel confused.

Essentials of Dark NLP Patterns

Some obscure NLP patterns are not bad and are often used to help in a therapeutic NLP situation. It is forming an anchor for "things that were real." The hypnotic type of this would be to have the follower create a place or even a box in his mind in which he puts things that are no longer true to him. They can put habits, compulsions, and cravings in the box to no longer be valid. The result is very significant and positive for the follower.

The Language Scheme as Storytelling

When someone tells a story, especially a vivid and compelling story, they use metaphors to influence and hypnotize covertly. Since a story is not about the people it is told to, they can listen without feeling preached. But to truly understand the story, they must, at some level, experience the emotions of the characters. It is where storytelling is an excellent tool for mind control. Many good examples of this can help a beginner understand the mind control process. The first example is quite common and happens every time someone reads a story or watches a movie and gets involved in the plot that they forget that they are getting involved in fiction. Although they may be sitting on the sofa reading or watching a TV show, they react as if they were in the story. In other words, they are influenced by what they are reading/watching.

If It Was True

Mind Controllers have used it throughout history, and many shamanic cultures place the narrator as the central person in their rituals. To learn this skill, the controller should enter their story first and remember the moments when they were reading or watching a show and got involved so intensely that they lost track of time and started taking care of the characters in the story. What made it so enjoyable? How did you forget where you were and "make history"? What emotions did the tale involve? By relying on these queries, the controller can understand what kinds of stories move them and create stories they can tell equally engaging.

How do you create a story that conveys a hidden message? There are a few influences that you need to understand and try to incorporate.

- Tell a story with a listener-like character. The main character must have something that the listener can relate to regardless of whether the main character is a turtle or a human.

- If you tell the story orally (aloud), get involved. The more desire, energy, and enthusiasm you can put into the story, the more the audience will react.

- Discuss the topic sometimes. The more convoluted a story becomes, the harder the listener has to strive to follow.

- Design a message in the story. The message in the story can be a moral of the story like Aesop's fables. The message can also be much more hidden. The hidden message is one of emotion, which means that there is an emotion that the main character feels that motivates him. This emotion must be justified in history. In this way, the follower who listens to the story can relate to the emotion.

As an insight into the purpose and power of emotions, this exemplary act of parental heroism testifies to the role of selfless love and every other emotion we feel in human life. It suggests that our deepest feelings, passions, and desires are essential guides and that our species owes much of its existence to power in human affairs. That power is extraordinary: only powerful love, the urge to save a beloved child, could lead a parent to ignore the urge for personal survival. It is viewed from the intellect, their self-sacrifice was arguably irrational, and seen from the heart, it was the only choice to make.

Sociobiology emphasizes the heart's prominence over the top at such pivotal moments once they speculate why evolution has given emotions such a central role within the human psyche. Our emotions, they say, guide us in dealing with difficult situations and too important tasks to go away the intellect alone with danger, painful loss, persevering towards a goal despite frustrations, bonding with a partner, building a family. Each emotion offers a particular readiness to act; each point us during a way that has functioned well to handle human life's recurring challenges. As these eternal situations are repeated and repeated throughout our evolutionary history, our emotional repertoire's survival value has been attested by the very fact that it's imprinted on our nerves as the human heart's innate and automatic tendencies.

A view of the attribute that ignores the facility of emotions is, unfortunately, short-sighted. The actual name humans, the thinking species, is misleading in light of the new appreciation and new view of the place of emotions in our lives that science now offers. As we all know from experience, when it involves shaping our decisions and actions, feeling matters the maximum amount and sometimes quite thought. We've gone too far in emphasizing the worth and Desire's importance of the purely rational of what measures IQ in human life. Intelligence cannot achieve anything when emotions dominate.

Passions Beyond Causes

When our emotions are wise guides within the long evolutionary period, the new realities that civilization presents have arisen with such rapidity that evolution's slow march cannot continue. As Freud pronounced in Civilization and Its Discontents, society has had to use rules from the surface to subdue emotional excess tides that run too freely within.

Despite these social constraints, passions overwhelm reason over and once again. This fact of attribute arises from the essential architecture of mental life. In terms of biological design for the essential neural circuits of sentiment, what we are born with is what has operated best for the last 50,000 human generations, not the last 500 generations, and positively not the last five. The slow and deliberate evolutionary forces that have shaped our emotions have done their beat in the last 10,000 years. Regardless of having witnessed the rapid rise of human civilization and the explosion of the human population from five million to 5 billion, we've left a touch footprint on our biological models for emotional life.

For better or worse, our assessment of every personal encounter and our responses to that are shaped not only by our rational judgments or personal history but also by our distant ancestral past. It leaves us with sometimes tragic propensities. In short, we are confronted with postmodern dilemmas with an emotional repertoire adapted to the Pleistocene urgencies. This example is at the guts of my topic.

Impetuses to Act

All emotions are, in spirit, instincts to act, the moment plans for managing life that progress has inculcated in us. The very origin of the word emotion is "motere," the Latin verb "to move," plus the prefix "e-" to connote "to move away," suggesting that a bent to act is inherent in every emotion. Emotions cause more alleged actions when observing animals or children; it's only in "civilized" adults that we frequently find the many anomalies within the Animalia, emotions - radical impulses to act - separated from the apparent reaction.

285

Each emotion plays a unique role in our emotional repertoire, as revealed by their distinctive biological signatures. With new methods of peering into the body and brain, researchers are uncovering more biological facts of how each emotion makes the body for a different sort of response:

- In anger, blood flows to the hands, making it easier to grab a weapon or hit an enemy; pulse increases, and a rush of hormones like adrenaline generates a surge of energy strong enough for vigorous action.

- With fear, the blood goes to the massive skeletal muscles, like the legs, making it easier to flee and turning the face pale when the blood is diverted (creating the feeling that the blood is "running cold"). Simultaneously, the body freezes, albeit just for a flash, perhaps allowing time to measure whether hiding could be a far better reaction. The brain's emotional centers' circuits trigger a flood of hormones that put the body on general alert, making it nervous and prepared for action. The eye is fixed on the threat in situ to gauge better which response to offer.

- Among the many biological changes in happiness is increased activity during a brain center that inhibits negative feelings, promotes a rise in available energy, and quiets people who generate troubling thoughts. But there's no particular change in physiology except inactivity, which causes the body to recover sooner from the natural arousal of upsetting emotions. This configuration gives the body general rest, and therefore the readiness and enthusiasm for whatever task is at hand and to strive towards the right sort of goals.

- Love, tender feelings, and sexual satisfaction involve parasympathetic arousal, the physiological opposite of the "fight or flight" mobilization shared by fear and anger. The parasympathetic pattern, nicknamed the "relaxation response," maybe a set of whole-body reactions that generate a common state of calm and contentment, facilitating cooperation.

- Surprise brow lift allows for a broader range of vision and allows more light to hit the retina. It offers more information about the unexpected event, making it easier to know what's happening and develop the best plan of action precisely.

All over the planet, an expression of disgust looks an equivalent and sends an equivalent message. The countenance of disgust - the upper lip curled to the side while the nose curls slightly - suggests an early attempt, as Darwin observed, to shut the nostrils against a noxious odor or to spit out a toxic food.

One of the sadness's primary functions is to assist adapt to a significant loss, like someone's death close or a perfect dissatisfaction. Grief brings a drop in vigor and eagerness for life's activities, mostly leisure and pleasure, and because it deepens and approaches depression, it slows down the body's metabolism. This introspective withdrawal creates the chance to mourn a loss or frustrated hope, grasp the results for your life, and plan for brand spanking new beginnings when the energy returns. This loss of energy may have kept the first humans saddened and vulnerable closer to family, where they were securer.

These biological propensities to act are shaped further by our life experience and our culture. For example, universally, the loss of a beloved elicits sadness and grief. But how we show our grieving—how emotions are displayed or held back for personal moments—is molded by culture, as are which particular people in our lives fall under the category of "loved ones" to be mourned.

When these emotional replies were beaten into shape, evolution's protracted period was undoubtedly a stricter certainty than most humans tolerated as a species after the dawn of recorded history. It had been a time when few infants survived to childhood and a couple of grownups to thirty years when hunters could attack at any moment when the whims of scarcities and floods meant the transformation between hunger and existence. But with the approaching of agriculture and even the foremost primitive human societies, the chances for survival began to vary dramatically. Within the last ten thousand years, when these advances took hold throughout the planet, the aggressive anxieties held the human population in restraint relieved gradually.

Two Minds

We've two minds, one that thinks and one that feels—these two fundamentally alternative ways of knowing to interact to construct our mental life. The lucid mind is the mode of understanding. We are typically aware of more prominent in awareness, thoughtful ready to ponder, and reflect. Nevertheless, there's another system of knowing: impulsive and powerful, if sometimes illogical, the emotional mind.

The emotional/rational dichotomy approximates the folks (the distinction between "heart" and "head"; knowing something is right "in your heart" may be a different order of conviction, somehow a more profound quite certainty than thinking so together with your rational mind. There's a gentle gradient within the ratio of rational-to-emotional control over the mind; the more intense the sensation, the more dominant the emotional mind becomes. Therefore, the more ineffectual the rational. It's an appointment that seems to stem from eons of evolutionary advantage to having emotions and intuitions guide our instantaneous response in situations where our lives are in peril and were pausing to chew over what costs us our lives.

Therefore, the emotional and rational, these two minds operate in tight harmony, for the significant part, intertwining their very alternative ways of knowing to guide us through the planet. Ordinarily, there's a balance between emotional and rational minds, emotion feeding, and informing the rational mind's operations. Therefore, the lucid mind is filtering and sometimes refusing the efforts of the sentiments. Still, the emotional and lucid minds are semi-independent capabilities, each, as we shall see, reflecting the operation of distinct, but interconnected, circuitry within the brain. These minds are exquisitely coordinated; feelings are essential to thought, thought, and feeling. But when passions surge the balance tips, the emotional mind captures the whip hand, swamping the rational mind.

How Did the Brain Nurture?

To better grasp the powerful hold of the emotions on the thinking mind—and why feeling and reason are so readily at war, consider how the brain evolved. With their three-pound approximately of cells and the human heart's natural juices, human brains are tensions of these in our nearest cousins in evolution, the nonhuman primates. Over many years of evolution, the brain has grown from rock bottom-up, with its better centers evolving as amplification of lower, more primeval parts.

The oldest root of our emotional life is the sense of smell or, more precisely, the cells that absorb and analyze the smell's sense in the olfactory lobe. Every living entity, be it nourishing, poisonous, sexual partner, predator or prey, has a distinctive molecular signature that can be carried by the wind. In those primitive times, the sense of smell was praised as a fundamental sense for survival.

The ancient emotion centers began to evolve from the olfactory lobe, eventually becoming large enough to surround the brain stem's upper part. In its primitive stages, the olfactory center was composed of little more than thin layers of neurons collected to analyze the sense of smell. A layer of cells absorbed the odor and divided it into relevant categories: edible or toxic, sexually available, enemy, or meal. The second layer of cells sent reflexive messages throughout the nervous system, telling the body what to do: bite, spit, approach, run away, chase.

As the limbic system has evolved, it has perfected two powerful tools: learning and memory. These revolutionary advances have allowed an animal to be much more intelligent in its survival choices and fine-tune its responses to adapt to changing needs rather than having invariable, automatic reactions. If a food causes illness, it could be avoided next time. Decisions such as knowing what to eat and what to refuse were still determined mainly by smell. The correlations between the olfactory bulb and the limbic system now took on making distinctions between smells and recognizing them, comparing a present odor with past ones, and distinguishing good from the bad. It was done by the "rhinencephalon," literally, the "brain of the nose," a part of the limbic wiring and the neocortex's rudimentary base, the thinking brain.

This new addition to the brain allowed for the addition of nuances to emotional life. Get love. Limbic structures produce feelings of desire and sexual desire, the emotions that fuel sexual desire. But the add-on of the neocortex and its correlations to the limbic system has allowed for the mother-child bond that underlies the family nucleus and the long-term commitment to child-rearing that makes human development possible. (Species with no neocortex, such as reptiles, lack maternal affection; when their young hatch, babies must hide to avoid being cannibalized.) In humans, the protective bond between parent and child allows much of the maturation continues throughout an extended childhood, during which the brain continues to develop.

Emotional Intellect and Fate

IQ offers little to explain people's different fates with more or less equal promises, education, and opportunities. When ninety-five Harvard students from the 1940s classroom - a time when people with a broader IQ prevalence attended Ivy League schools than they currently do - were followed into middle age. The men with the highest scores senior in college were not incredibly successful then their peers with lower scores in terms of salary, productivity, or status in their field. Neither have they had the most excellent life satisfaction or pleasure with companionships and passionate relations.

A related follow-up in middle age was done with 450 boys, most immigrants, two-thirds from assisted families, who grew up in Somerville, Massachusetts, and a "slum" a few blocks from Harvard. A third had an IQ below 90. But again, the IQ had little bearing on how well they had done at work; for example, 7% of men with IQs below 80 were unemployed for ten or more years, but so were 7% of men with IQs above 100. There was a usual link (as always) between IQ and socioeconomic level at forty-seven. But childhood skills, such as the ability to manage frustrations, control emotions, and get along with other people, made the most significant difference.

It also considers data from an ongoing study of eighty-one valedictorians and salutatorians of 1981 in Illinois's high schools. All had the top-grade point average in their schools. Nevertheless, while they continued to perform well in college and achieved excellent grades, they had only achieved average success levels by their late twenties.

And this is the problem: academic intelligence offers virtually no preparation for the turmoil or opportunities that life's vicissitudes bring. However, even if a high IQ is no guarantee of prosperity, prestige, or happiness in life, our schools and culture fixate on academic skills, ignoring emotional intelligence. Some might call it a character that is also immensely important to our destiny. Emotional life is a field. And how proficient a person is at these things is vital to accepting why one person prospers in life while another, of equal intellect, dead ends: emotional aptitude is a meta-skill, which determines how well we can use any other skill. We have, including raw intellect.

There are great ways to thrive in life, and many domains where other abilities are remunerated. In our progressively experience-based society, technical skill is undoubtedly one of them. There's a children's joke: "What do you call a nerd in fifteen years?" The answer: "Chief." But even among "nerds," emotional intelligence offers an added advantage in the workplace, as we will see in the third part. Much evidence shows that emotionally adept people. Who know and manage their feelings well and who read and cope effectively with others' feelings - have an advantage in any domain of life, whether romantic and intimate relationships or grasping the unspoken rules that govern success in organizational politics? People with well-developed emotional abilities are also more likely to be content and effective in their lives. Mastering the mental habits that promote their productivity, people who cannot exert some rule over their vibrant life fight internal battles that disrupt their work's attention and think clearly.

Many of us may have spent a long time in our life without even realizing that we have been persuaded and manipulated often. The damage from this manipulation can last forever and can be challenging to improve. Once you become conscious of how others might subliminally convince you, you can better protect yourself from these tactics in the future to maintain your independence and stay out of the influence of others. It is imperative to recall that you are better equipped to identify and defend yourself against them by understanding these concepts. Your new knowledge should not be about how you can use the same strategies to influence other individuals.

There is a variance among evil manipulation and trying to persuade someone of something. You don't want to get someone to do things for you when they're not going to benefit from it. You only need to use these tactics when you need to persuade someone about something and not openly ask for help. Some people are more challenging to convince than others, so you may need to use persuasion strategies. Who might need to convince? You definitely do not want to take the benefit of someone who doesn't already have much to give. The ones you should try to persuade our people who hold power. You may want to learn how to get your boss to get a raise. Maybe you want to try to get your girlfriend to move in with you. Maybe you need to borrow from your parents. You don't want to "punch," but instead, "reach out."

Body Language

One of the easiest ways to analyze other people is to look at their body language. The way a person holds himself moves, and even talks can tell you a lot about him. Everyone has many variations in their ways, and there is no exact way to tell what constitutes a person. There are still many similar clues between groups of people that can give your insight into how someone works. It's not easy because it begins with becoming aware of your body language. To understand and attempt to overcome the riddle of body language, you need to be hyper-aware.

Now is the time to work on becoming aware of your body. To learn what makes a person different from others based on their body language, you first need to look at yourself and analyze how you hold your body. Some people may be more aware of their movements than their thoughts are. Women will likely be more aware of their bodies and their space, mostly due to the patriarchal society we grew up in. Everyone may still find it challenging to cope with the way they hold their body. You can lose focus while maintaining awareness and becoming too insecure about your body and your movements. Once you get to know another person's body movements better, you can also understand what makes them unique. The more you know about a person, the better you can conclude the best persuasion strategy.

Social Variances

Each person is different, and sometimes the way a person holds their body has a different meaning than someone who is the same way. There are many ways that a person's body language is different, so it's important to remember that not everything about a particular body movement is 100% true for every person. It is especially important to remember when talking to people from different cultural backgrounds.

There are some cultures that practice modesty, so touching could be forbidden entirely. Other cultures may be more open to expressing their feelings through their bodies, so the culture is vital to remember when thinking about how they might use their bodies.

Acquire Other's Movements

Once you become more aware of body movements and what they might represent, you can start studying them when interacting with different people. Anyone who comes into contact uses their body to represent different things. Some people are closed, and others may be more open. These are some small differences you might notice just by looking at someone's body language. When you study other people and yourself, it is essential to try to act naturally as well. It can be comfortable to befit hyper-aware of your movements but know that you don't have to hold your body a certain way. Not everyone is aware of body movements as others might be, so don't look too much at your movements at the end of the day.

However, once you start studying others' body movements, you will begin to realize just how much you can learn about them. Some things may start to make sense after meeting a variety of people. You may notice that one of your friends is quite pretentious in how he holds himself or talks. Other friends may show how insecure they are with themselves, even if you thought they had been incredibly confident since you've known them.

Knowing a person's body language and getting an idea of why they might move a certain way can allow you to understand them deeply. It gives you better influence when it comes to persuading them. You may want to match your boss's confidence when you make a deal for a raise. You may have noticed that you need to be more relaxed with certain friends who seem shy or nervous. Becoming aware of your body language can be scary at first, but you will eventually feel comfortable with the way you move.

To start practicing being comfortable with your body, try spending time in front of a mirror. When you dine, watch TV, or even relax in bed, set up a mirror so you can see how you hold yourself back. Once you get a stranger's point of view on how you move, you will be able to see how others move as well.

Visual Communication

Eye contact is one of the most significant clues you can use to determine how someone is. It is also essential to become aware of your use of eye contact, as it gives others clues about your personality and true nature. Maintaining eye contact is vital in letting a person know that you are interested in what they are saying and that they have your full attention.

However, it can also be abused, and you let people know that you are trying too hard to convince them that you are listening. Too much eye contact can sometimes be intimidating to others too, so if you notice that a person is getting nervous due to the amount of eye contact you have with them, change it up every so often.

Pupil dilation can be a direct indication that a person is interested in what you are saying. Studies have shown that when a person's pupils begin to dilate with the person, you're making eye contact with, they're more interested in what you have to say. They are listening to you with their full attention and are thinking deeply about what you are saying. When a person's pupils are dilated while talking to you, you know that they are legitimately interested in the conversation.

The receding eyes will indicate otherwise. Someone who looks your eyes back and forth is probably trying to convince you that they are listening. They are aware that they need to make eye contact, but they are entirely excluded from what you say. Those with shifty eyes may also lie to you or try to deceive you in some way. They may have a hard time maintaining eye contact with you because they know they are deceiving.

Movements of The Mouth

What someone does with their mouth is very crucial to understanding their personality as well. Someone with pursed or pursed lips may be trying to focus, or they may even be trying to hide a sour face. You can also analyze a person's smile. If the corners of their eyes aren't bent, they could force you to smile.

Someone faking a smile isn't necessarily evil. May be thinking of something else and too distracted to pay full attention to what you're saying. Sometimes, smiles are also reactions to uncomfortable situations.

When monkeys smile, it is not because they are happy, but mostly because they show their teeth to threaten them. When they feel frightened and nervous, they open their mouths, showing that they have teeth that they could use to hurt. The same goes for dogs. They only show their teeth when they feel threatened. For humans, this can be true at times too, but on a subconscious level. Laughing nervously and smiling are just one way for a person to relieve their tension. You can tell someone is smiling sincerely when they have creases in the corners of their eyes.

A healthy person who covers his mouth all the time is also usually nervous. They might bite their lip, finger, or punch their mouth. Knowing when a person is uncomfortable or nervous can sometimes be helpful when trying to persuade them.

Nodding

The way a person turns and tilts their head can be a subtle movement. Most of the time, others are not so aware when they move their heads. The movements of the neck and head of the person you are talking to can give you an insight into what they might be thinking on a deeper level. Someone who nods their head rather quickly while listening to you may be anxious, trying to get the conversation going as quickly as possible. They are trying to set a pace for you so that you can speak faster. They want you to know that they listen to you, but you don't speak fast enough. If someone is doing this to you, try speeding up your words to get their attention.

Someone who tilts their head to the side may have a legitimate interest in what you are saying. They are trying to turn an ear towards you so that they can hear you better, whether they are aware of their movements or not. They are also indicating that they are listening to you and want you to keep talking. It's a way to get closer to you in conversation without having to do any interjection or interruption. If someone nods too artificially, they may just be trying to convince you that they are interested in what you say. They may be aware that they should be paying attention, but they may have lost interest.

In an attempt to keep up, they pretend to nod their heads. They may not even understand what you are saying, so they nod to make you think they are keeping up. If you notice that others around you are artificially nodding their heads, it might be worth changing the follower to regain attention or better explain why they may be confused. Imitating someone's head movements can be beneficial in using persuasion. A slight tilt of the head while listening to them can show that you understand what they say. It can also display that you are empathetic with them, especially if they seem to be talking about difficult things.

Hands and Arms

The way someone uses their hands and arms is another way that body language can be interpreted to understand better the people you interact with. Our hands represent so much of ourselves. They are a way to express stories, placing a different emphasis on various parts. If someone tells a story, they will use hand gestures to keep people interested. Think of someone engaged in conversation as someone conducting an orchestra. They will raise their hands to maintain the rhythm and pace of the listener. Someone's hands and arms can also express how open or closed they are. They can be like the door in someone's body. If they are crisscrossed tightly in front of someone's chest, that person maybe a little more withdrawn, not wanting to engage too much in conversation. Having your arms crossed doesn't always mean someone is necessarily closed. They may also want to rest their arms, so if they're hanging loosely in front of your chest, they're probably listening to you casually.

Someone who has their arms outstretched, perhaps above their head, will likely be very open and perhaps even seek to exert power over a situation. Someone with their hands on their hips might even try to assert their power.

Indicators

Everyone has different body language questions that they use as indicators. Across cultures, genders, and ages, the different movements someone makes with their body can be conscious or unconscious signals they are giving to the people around them. Signals allow other people to know bits of information without having to say anything. Someone with their arms crossed, eyes fading on a sofa at a party gives the signal that they are probably ready to go home for the night. Someone else on that sofa may be sitting on the edge of the seat, laughing loudly, signaling that they won't be going to bed soon. The signals help people around the beacon know things that they may not easily express with their bodies. Some are very good at picking up other people's signals, and some people struggle to understand those around them.

When it comes to persuading someone, there are some crucial signs a person will need to lead a conversation correctly.

Opening A Dialogue

The next time you're sitting quietly in a room with another person, wait for the conversation to start to talk. It will allow you to study how they might start a conversation. Most people will give some sort of signal with their body that they are about to start speaking. They may clear their throats, turn their heads, adjust their shirts, or move to the seat. No matter how small it may be, there is usually something that a person does right before starting a conversation.

When it's your turn to start a conversation, notice what you do before you start talking. Don't start with an "um" or "uh." It lets the other person know right away that you aren't very sure what you will say. Try starting a conversation without doing anything. See if you can start talking without clearing your throat, moving your head, or doing anything else. Study how the other person reacts. They might be surprised or surprised that one of you has started talking.

Starting a conversation, especially one meant to persuade another person, is vital in laying your discussion foundation. Nobody will want to give their full attention to someone who is struggling to get started. If you are nervous and jump straight at the words, it will be much harder to keep up.

Lead the Dialogue

Once the discussion has started, it can be challenging to maintain the right amount of back and forth. You don't want to be too pushy, but you also don't want to let them talk too much, not allowing yourself to make your points at any time. If you feel that the other person won't let you talk enough, there are apparent phrases you can use to express your opinion. You might try saying something like, "can I just say," "can I talk for a minute?" or "I'm listening, but can I say something fast?" These can be hard to say in some situations, and some people may even perceive you as rude if you make a big interjection. Your best choice may be to aid your body to redirect focus. Put your hands on your hips or tilt your head to let the other person know you have something to say. Try approaching to let him know that you want to take on the leader of your current conversation.

Leading the conversation can be tricky because no one wants to hear someone interrupt them. However, it is vital that you also have your turn to speak. There are ways you can practice conducting conversations to conduct it correctly when it comes time to have a critical persuasion. The later you want to say something, don't. Instead, let the other person keep talking and intervene later. Sometimes we are so eager to say our side that we distract ourselves from the real conversation, invalidating any discussion we have with the person we interrupted. An alternative way to practice leading the conversation is to talk the next time you want to say something. If you want to say but prefer to be silent, make an effort to say what you want. These two practice methods will give you two alternative perspectives for conducting a conversation that you may not otherwise obtain.

How Your Body Language Influences You

Believe it or not, the way you use your body can directly influence your functioning as well. Conclusion: there are ways to improve the way you think and your memory capacity by merely using your hands and arms. Not only are there physical differences in terms of how you use your body, but you will also be influenced by how others perceive you.

If you are closed continuously, always crossing your arms, there are probably many people who may not open up or talk to you because they assume you have no interest in the conversation. If you are always very open with your body, exercising confidence and holding yourself high, others may end up being intimidated by you. You may not intend to exclude others or to intimidate, but your body can demonstrate this in ways your mouth does.

It can be challenging to become aware of your body movements, but you can change what someone thinks about you once you do. Some people might have a robust conscious mind, but maybe they hate their bodies. So, they might shut others down by trying to hide their bodies, making others think they are judging. Sometimes, a person is just trying to cover their body and not themselves. You'd be surprised how much confidence you can feel just by changing the way you hold your body. People can still see what you look like, even if you keep your arms crossed. You may think you alter others' perceptions of you, but you are just closed in reality.

There are other ways your body language can affect you mentally.

Open Your Mind

Someone who starts to open their arms when they speak will begin to let others know that they are much more open-minded. If you stand with your arms outstretched or just relax by your side, let the people around you know that you are confident and willing to talk to them about different things. While having your arms outstretched is a signal to others, it is also a signal to your brain. Studies show that standing with open arms with crisscross verses can signal your brain to be more open. You will start thinking of new ideas that you would not have if you kept your arms crossed. The same goes for the rest of your body. The more open you are with your movements, the more you allow your brain to have different ideas.

Develop Your Memory

Those who speak with their hands also tend to have a better memory than those who do not speak. Using your hands can put physical reminders into your brain for ideas and thoughts you might be discussing. Suppose you imitate numbers or shapes when talking about different ideas, especially in a business context. In that case, you will not only remember what you are discussing better, but those around you will also find your story more memorable. Using your hands to talk while telling a story will also help you remember things you've been through. You're encouraging your brain to keep thinking and keeping your arms open, just like we alluded to in the last section, it will open your brain to new thoughts and feelings that you might not have if you talked with your arms folded and closed off.

Verbal Cues

While many things a person can say with their body, they can say many other things with their mouth. There is a seemingly limitless amount of languages out there, as each specific language has many sub-parts. Think about how many different accents there could be in New York City alone. As we continue to develop and blend different cultures and languages, we will only develop more. It's hard enough to keep up with what we already know, but there are ways to still grasp others' meaning without having to memorize every word in the dictionary.

Just because a person says, a specific word doesn't mean that they mean what they say. How many times have you told you were "fine" when you wanted to explode with thoughts in reality? We always say what we don't mean because it's not always easy to give words to our thoughts and feelings. Many people take their frustration or sadness out on others when they don't mean anything they say.

Knowing why people say they do can be one of the most complicated codes to try and crack. You don't always have to know what a person means to understand what they are trying to say. You can tell what a person's intention is by listening to how they speak and mixing it with their body language. It's crucial to read someone's mood, so you don't say the wrong thing or something that could potentially change the conversation's direction.

The next time you find something on TV in a language other than the one you can speak, try watching without subtitles. You will be surprised to see that you understand part of the plot. Don't look at what they say, but how they say it. Is there pain in their eyes? Do they look happy or sad? Sometimes, if you can't understand what a person is saying, perhaps because the room is noisy or talking in a low voice, try making eye contact. You may have a better gist of what they are saying than looking at the words their mouth is trying to put together.

There are some specific signals someone can give when they are trying to direct a conversation. When you're trying to persuade someone, you might want to try using different keywords to help lead the conversation. Some people get too stuck on the words someone says when they try to hear the message they are conveying. It may seem challenging to try to decipher what someone else means, but it can be done. Think about your pets. You can tell if your dog is sad, sleepy, hungry, or in a playful mood, but you have no real conversations with him. Sometimes you can analyze what a person is saying best by finding out the noises they are making rather than dissecting every word they say.

Signs of Prominence

When trying to persuade someone, you will want to have already prepared a good enough argument to build your case. You may want to include some cues of emphasis when speaking. It can be challenging to incorporate these phrases naturally, but it's good to practice so you can become a better persuader. "This is important," "you must know," "let me explain," are all phrases that catch the attention of the person you are talking to. You may begin to notice the emphasis of others better even after reading this section. You should listen to and use phrases in your speech that appear to emphasize an essential part of a conversation.

Sometimes, these emphasis cues aren't even real sentences. They could be verbal indications that something is essential, such as someone raising their voice when discussing an essential part of their argument. They may also repeat the word multiple times or pause for a break so the listener can understand what they just said. Emphasis cues are essential to understand better what may be necessary to an individual. If you listen to what they are stressing, you will also formulate your thoughts and arguments about the essential things.

Structural Ideas

"First, second, third," "summarize," "the topic is," are all phrases that could be considered Structural ideas. These cues help a person indicate that they are trying to organize their thoughts, perhaps by emphasizing the most important things.

Structural cues are vital for you to use in your arguments in persuasions to get people to your side. You want them to know that you are listening to what they have to say and that they should listen to you. You are trying to formulate a plan based on your thoughts and opinions, not just a specific individual's words. Organizational suggestions allow the speaker to emphasize what is essential while maintaining clear thinking and direct focus. Organizational signals may not be phrases either. It could just be someone clearing their throat, redirecting the conversation to a previous topic, or pausing so everyone can collect their thoughts.

Watch Your Presentation

The tone is an important key when trying to steer your conversation in their favor. Pitch is the level of your voice and the overall sound quality. Someone with a deep tone might have a more relaxing tone, while someone with a high-pitched voice might make their listeners more alert. Not everyone can help their natural tone of voice. Some people have extremely low voices that are hard to hear, and some people just have naturally high-pitched voices that seem to disturb everyone around them!

Even if your natural tone can't always be controlled, you can at least help direct that tone towards a more productive tone to keep your listeners engaged with what you have to say. Many of us let our tone get too loud and whiny when in professional settings, trying to keep our dictation sharp. If you feel that your voice is getting high and shrill, don't be afraid to stop, clear your throat, and start over. People around you will likely be grateful that you are adjusting your tone for their listening pleasure.

Be careful not to raise the end of your voice when you speak. Many people, especially when talking on the phone, tend to let the end of their words come up as if they ask a question. This type of speech is also common among those who might be giving a speech. They will say a sentence very clearly with dictation, but they will also sharply end the sentence as if they ask a question. It should be avoided to keep the attention of your listeners.

It is crucial to find your optimal presentation. Some people have very soft voices, which can be challenging to hear. It is significant to practice speaking when necessary. Someone who tends to speak loudly should try to speak softly as often as possible to balance the tone. The best way to practice is on your own and if you record what you are saying. You don't want to thoroughly analyze how you talk too much, but practice always helps, especially for those who have difficulty pronouncing their voice. It's also essential to have a confident tone to let others know they should listen to you. Someone who always speaks shyly or asks questions will let others around them know that what they have to say is not impressive. If you are so unsure of what you are saying, why would anyone else listen to you? The best way to make sure others pay attention is to make sure you speak confidently.

Listen to Others

Talking about yourself can elicit the same good feelings that money and food do. Individuals appreciate talking about themselves more than they enjoy listening to other people talking about themselves for the most part. While it may sound selfish, indeed, most people would rather talk about themselves. It means that when conversing with other people, you should avoid talking too much about yourself.

You don't want to make the conversation about other people altogether, but no one will pay attention if the only thing you talk about is yourself. Giving advice can also be helpful, but people generally don't engage with those who offer too much advice as often, especially when it's not in demand.

Significant people can be difficult for some. They may have a hard time not letting their mind wander, especially if the other person is talking too much about themselves. Some people will find that they are usually forming their next thought while the other person is talking instead of listening to them. If you find your mind wandering when someone else is talking, redirect your thoughts to their words. Don't just listen to what they say. See how they say it. Listen to their voice and look them in the eye. People will notice if you are listening to them or not. Even if they are not experts in body language, they will still be able to sense at least that you may not be fully involved.

Don't just emphasize listening to others. Talk about them too. Ask questions about the person, trying to get to know them better. You will find that people usually like to answer questions about themselves. It is often a technique you will see in many sellers. They will ask you where you got the shirt or if you had a good day. It is to make the person think about themselves and usually open up a little more to the seller. People don't like being fair. While it can be hard to avoid, most people don't want to be interrupted by being told they're wrong. Most people will respect you a lot more if you let them talk instead of trying to prove them wrong. It is imperative to remember, especially when trying to persuade and analyze others.

Talk about "us," not "you." If you are looking to make suggestions, perhaps to a spouse or friend, about improving their lifestyle, use "us" instead. Don't say, "you should try to wake up early on weekends," say, "we should get up early on Sunday and go for a walk together!" People will respond much better to suggestions if you include yourself.

To Apologize

It can be challenging to apologize, especially for someone with a high level of pride, but it's vital to win the respect of the people around you. If you apologize for being late rather than giving all possible explanations, most will respond much better than if you tried to make yourself look better with an apology. They also like to see humility and that maybe you're not afraid to express yourself. If you can open up to someone and say, "I'm sorry I didn't respond to your message, I was just having a bad day," they will usually be very forgiving rather than if you would have just brushed them off.

However, don't apologize too much. It can cause others not to trust you. Sometimes we need to apologize for things that were out of our control to make us look better. We'll say, "I'm sorry the movie was so bad!" after going out for a movie night, even though we didn't have control over the production. It is nice now and then and certainly shows humility and vulnerability to those around you. But too much can also make you seem unreliable to others.

If you have to apologize after every little thing you say, why would anyone listen to you in the first place? The next time you get the need to apologize for something out of your control, try saying thank you. After having a long conversation with a friend, don't say, "Sorry, you had to hear me rant!" Instead, try something like, "Thank you for being such a great listener. I'm happy I have a companion like you!" People generally respond much more positively to a grateful person than someone who is always disabled. You'll find that you start treating yourself a lot better if you stick to this method of apology as well.

The Power of Your Body

Our bodies have so much power, and not just as much as we can lift or carry. Physical strength is essential, but even the weakest people can control a room with just body movements. It would help if you had a basic understanding of what a person's body language might mean by this point. We can't go into every specific detail of what someone's physical actions might try to convey, but the framework for analyzing those movements is there. Once you understand how someone else might use their body to persuade others, you can start working on your persuasion skills.

There are many ways someone can use their body to get others to do what they want, but it won't always work for everyone. Some people respond to sexual persuasion while the thought rejects others. Some people respond to a physical threat from those who seem healthier than they are, but others may be ready for the fight. There are many ways you can use your body to persuade others without being sexual or physically intimidating. Keeping your body open and visible is key to letting others know they can trust you. Try to remove physical barriers that could keep you separate from the person you are talking to. Move around a chair or table that prevents you from making a complete connection with the person you are trying to talk to.

It also shows that you are confident and interested in expressing your opinion while also listening to others. When you analyze other people's movements, you can also figure out what things you can do on your own to be more confident. Study some celebrities and see how they perform in various scenarios. Everyone has their movements, but imitating others can still help you find your position in having persuasive behavior overall.

Smiling Is Important

Our smiles are one of the most powerful tools we have been given. You can turn any situation from wrong to the right by merely raising the corners of your mouth. Some people feel like they don't have straight teeth or bright white smiles. They're worth nothing. Even those who don't have all their teeth can have much nicer smiles than someone who has spent thousands of dollars on dental work. A smile isn't just about the teeth you're showing.

It is a way to involve another person. Studies have shown that most people will smile if someone else smiles first. If they smile, they will end up having a better overall mood. It may sound strange, but merely smiling can lift someone's spirits. The next time you're feeling significantly down, smile. It sounds so silly, but it might work. Smile repeatedly, and while it may not change your mood, it will definitely help lift your spirits at least temporarily.

Subliminal Encouragement

The idea of subliminal persuasion involves convincing someone to do something below their conscious level. You won't openly persuade someone if you are subliminal about it. Instead, you would try to get to do what you want without even realizing what you are doing. The idea of subliminal persuasion is primarily thought of in advertising. Many companies will do everything possible to persuade us to buy something, even at the cost of partially brainwashing us.

The idea of subliminal persuasion doesn't have to be that insidious for those who wish to use these tactics to convince another person. There are many vital parts to subliminally persuading someone. First, make sure you do it for the right reasons. You don't want to become someone who brainwashes others. It's not about getting inside their head and getting them to think about something. Instead, you should look at what you know about them and use them in your persuasion plan.

It's Not About Manipulation

You certainly do not crave to make a person feel crazy. You don't want to make sneaky suggestions that lead them to question their sanity. Subliminal persuasion should only be used as an excellent way to tell someone how you feel when you might be too scared to tell the blatant truth. Some people have a more challenging time accepting the truth, persuasion, or reality than others. These types of people cannot be openly told what someone else wants. Sometimes, people like to disagree with others just for the sake of being controversial. There are ways you can ask someone something. Subliminal persuasion should never be about manipulation. You shouldn't "fool" someone into something that will only benefit you. You should use this method to try to prevent better being subliminally persuaded. It is also useful for stubborn, intimidating, or other people who cannot be conversed easily.

Trusting Is the Key

The trick to subliminally persuading someone is to exude as much confidence as possible. Some people will see open trust as delusional, so you don't want to go too far. However, no one will be persuaded, no matter how subliminal you may get, by someone who can't even defend their thoughts and opinions. Trust is also vital to distract the person from realizing that you may be trying to persuade them of something. Imagine talking to your mom or dad, hoping to get a car loan again when you were a teenager. You would like to use some trust, but not so much that it makes them think you don't care about their permission. To subliminally convince them, you might raise the fact that no one else can safely take you to a party. Instead of asking brazenly and giving them a chance to say no, instead, you are more able to influence them how you think. It may therefore become their idea to get you to borrow your car for the weekend.

A persuasion is an additional form of mind control that will be discussed. While there may not be as much media hype about this form of mind control as there is with brainwashing and hypnosis, it can be just as effective when done correctly. The problem with this module is that there are so many different forms of persuasion present in daily life that it can be difficult for any source to reach the topic and make a difference.

While persuasion works to change the follower's thoughts and beliefs like other forms of mind control, it looks like everyone is trying to persuade you of something, so it becomes easier to ignore the follower's persuasion. For example, in commercials on television, when there is an argument going on or when a conversation is going on, there is some form of persuasion. People will often use persuasion to their advantage without realizing.

What is Persuading?

To begin with, is the definition of persuasion. When people think about persuasion, they often come up with many different answers. Some may think of the commercials and advertisements they see around them that prompt them to purchase one particular product over another. Others might think about persuasion in terms of politics and how candidates can try to sway voters' opinions to get another vote. Both are examples of persuasion because the message is trying to change the way the follower is thinking. Persuasion can be found in everyday life and is a compelling force and a significant influence on followers and society. Advertising, mass media, legal and political decisions will be influenced by how persuasion works and, in turn, will also work to persuade the argument.

As you can see, there are some key differences between persuasion and the other forms of mind control that have been discussed so far in this guide. Brainwashing and hypnosis require the individual to be in isolation to change their mind and identity. Manipulation will work even on one person to achieve the ultimate goal. While persuasion can be done on one subject to change your mind, it is also possible to use persuasion on a larger scale to persuade an entire group or even society to change the way they think. It can make it even more effective and possibly dangerous because it can change many people's minds all at once rather than the mind of just one follower.

Many people have the false impression that they are immune to the effects of persuasion. They consider they would be able to see any sales pitch launched in their way, whether the agent is selling a product or some new idea, and then understand the situation and find the conclusion. It will be true; no one falls in love with everything they hear as often as they use logic, especially if it goes entirely against their beliefs, no matter how intense the argument may be. Most people will also avoid messages about buying TVs and luxury cars or about the latest product on the market. Often, the act of persuasion will be much more subtle, and it may be more difficult for the person to form their own opinions on what is being said.

When it comes to the act of persuasion, most people will see it in a negative light. They will think of a salesperson or scammer trying to get them to change all their beliefs and push and annoy them until the change occurs. While this is undoubtedly a way to think about persuasion, this process can often be used positively rather than just a negative way. For example, public service campaigns can encourage people to quit smoking or recycle can be forms of persuasion that can improve a person's life. It's all about the way the persuasion process is used.

Elements of Persuading

As with other forms of mind control, there are a few things to look out for when it comes to persuasion. These elements help define what persuasion is so that it is more recognizable. According to Perloff in 2003, persuasion is defined as "A symbolic process in which communications seek to convince other people to alter their outlooks or behaviors about a problem by transmitting a message in an atmosphere of free choice."

It is one thing that makes persuasion different from other forms of mind control. The follower is often allowed to make his or her own free choices on the matter. However, the persuasion tactic will work to shift the follower's mind in a particular direction. The follower can choose which way he wants to think, whether he wants to buy a product or not, or whether he thinks the evidence behind the persuasion is strong enough to change his mind.

- There are some elements present in the persuasion that help define it further. These elements include:

- Persuasion is symbolic, which means it uses sounds, images, and words to make the point.

- Persuasion will involve the agent deliberately trying to influence the follower or group.

- Self-persuasion is a vital part of this process. The follower is usually not forced and instead is given the freedom to choose its own decision.

- There are many ways that persuasive messages can be conveyed, including face-to-face, the Internet, radio, and television. Communication can also take place non-verbal or verbal.

Let's take a look at each of these points in a little more detail. The first element of persuasion is that it must be symbolic. To get somebody to think or act a certain way, you need to show them why they should change their thoughts. It will include the use of words, sounds, and images to make the new point understood. You can use words to start a debate or discussion to show your point. Images are an eminent way to show the evidence needed to persuade someone to go one way or another. Some non-verbal cues are possible, but will not be as effective as using words and images.

The second key is that persuasion will be used deliberately to influence how others act or think. It is pretty apparent, and if you're not intentionally trying to influence others, you're not using persuasion to get them to change. The persuader will try different tactics to get the follower to think the same way he does. It could be somewhat as modest as having a debate with them or presenting evidence to support their perspective.

The unique thing about persuasion is that it allows the follower to have some form of free will. The follower is allowed to make his own choice in the way. For the most part, no matter how hard someone tries to persuade him of something, he doesn't have to. The follower might hear a thousand commercials about the best car to buy, but if they don't like that make or don't need a new vehicle right now, they won't go out and buy it. If the follower is against abortion, no matter how many people come out and say how big the abortion is, the follower is unlikely to change his mind. It allows for much more freedom of choice than is found in other forms of mind control, which could explain why many people don't see it as a type of mind control when asked.

A persuasion is a form of mind control that can happen in many different ways. While brainwashing, hypnosis and manipulation have to happen face to face, and in some cases in complete isolation, persuasion can happen in other ways. You can find examples of persuasion everywhere, including talking to people you know, on the Internet, and through radio and television. It can also deliver persuasive messages through non-verbal and verbal means, although it is much more effective when verbal techniques are used.

Prevailing Persuading

Over time, the persuasion has been able to evolve and change from its original origins. The persuasion has been around for many years; in fact, it has existed since ancient Greece. It does not mean that the art and persuasion processes are the same as they were then. Indeed, some changes have been made to the art of persuasion and how it is used in modern times. Some of the critical elements of modern persuasion will be discussed in this section.

The use of modern persuasion is different from how it was used in the past. These five ways include:

- The number of messages considered persuasive has grown by leaps and bounds: in ancient Greek times, persuasion was only used in writing and debates among elites. The occurrence of persuasion wasn't a significant thing, and you wouldn't see it very often. In modern times, it's hard to get anywhere without a persuasive message following you. Think about the diverse types and sources of advertisements available; the average adult in the United States will encounter up to 3,000 of them every day. In addition to that, there are always people knocking on your door trying to get you to buy something, believe their ideas, or try something new. Persuasion is much more a part of modern life than it has been at any other time in history.

- Persuasion travels very fast: in ancient Greek times, it could take weeks or more for a persuasive message to arrive from one point to another. It limited the impact of persuasion because most people would not be able to get the message. Most of the persuasion had to be done in the context of face-to-face communication. In modern times, persuasive messages can cover a great distance in no time thanks to the Internet, radio, and television. Political candidates can reach voters all at once in seconds, and any message can be spread easily. Persuasion takes on a much more critical role when it can be spread so quickly.

- Persuasion can mean a lot of money: Now that companies have discovered the power of persuasion, they are doing all they can to make it work for them. The more effective they are at persuading consumers to buy their products, the more money they will make. Some companies are pure because of the persuasive process, such as public relations firms, marketing firms, and advertising agencies. Other companies will use these companies' persuasive techniques to reach and exceed the sales goals they have set for themselves.

- The persuasion has become more subtle than in the past. At the beginning of the persuasion, the agent announced his opinions aloud for the whole group to hear them in hopes of changing everyone's mind. Those days are over, and the persuasion process has become much more discreet. While it is possible to find persuasions that are still very loud and, in the face, many others follow a more subtle path in some forms of advertising.

An instance of this is when businesses create a specific image of themselves, such as being family-friendly, to achieve consumers to buy their products. You may also notice that instead of getting into a debate with your friend about going to a party, they will use peer pressure or just list some facts to get you to come with them. Despite being more subtle, persuasion is even more significant today than ever.

The persuasion process has become more complex: Along with persuasion, which is more subtle and sometimes more challenging to point out, it is also going to become more complex. The topics target more diverse than in the past, and they have many more choices to make. If an individual went to a store in town to buy everything they needed, they could now choose from different stores for their needs, from the hardware store to the grocery store and the convenience store. Clothing. Additionally, there is often more than one option available for each shopping category in the area. These choices make it harder for the agent to develop an excellent persuasive message for the consumer or any other topic.

Approaches of Persuading

Persuasion methods can often go by other names and be referred to as persuasion strategies and persuasion tactics. Resultantly, there is no specific approach that can persuade someone to think or act in a certain way. The agent may be able to speak to the follower while presenting evidence to change the follower's mind, may be able to use some sort of force or pull at the follower, and may perform some sort of service for the follower or use another tactic. This section will detail the different persuasion methods available and how they could be useful in persuasion.

Usefulness of Strength

Depending on the situation, the agent may decide that it is good to use some force to persuade the follower to think his way. It can happen if ideas don't match up correctly, if regular talking doesn't work, or if the agent feels frustrated or upset with the conversation's turn. Force is often used as a scare tactic because it gives the follower less time to think logically about what is happening than when a normal conversation occurs. Force is usually used when the agent has been less successful using the other means of persuasion available, although it is sometimes initiated using force. Other times, the force can be used if the agent feels that he is losing control or when the follower can present contradictory evidence to the agent, and the agent becomes angry.

It is regularly not the best idea to use force when it comes to the persuasion process. Many people will see the use of force as a threat due to the agent giving no other options to the request they are making. The whole appeal of persuasion gives the follower choice of paths, but the force has entered the mix, freedom of choice is gone, and the follower is more likely to feel threatened. Once the follower feels threatened, they are less likely to listen and take into account everything the agent is saying, and therefore, the process will not go further. Because of these causes, the use of force is generally discouraged and avoided in the art of persuasion, unlike the other forms of mind control discussed.

To Inspiration

Another method that can persuade the follower to lean in a specific way is to use the available influence points. We discuss persuasion's art and define the six points of influence that can make the agent succeed in his goals. The six influence points are reciprocity, commitment and consistency, social proof, sympathy, authority, and scarcity. These six points of influence are critical to the agent as they are part of their subjects' change. Each of these six points will be discussed below:

Exchange

The first point of influence is the principle of exchange. This principle states that when a person, the agent, provides the other person, the follower will attempt to repay the agent in kind with something of value. It means that when the agent performs some service to the follower, the follower will feel that he should perform a similar service to the agent sooner or later. Although the two services may not be identical, they have the same kind of value so that the obligation of each is equaled. The act of exchange ends up producing a sense of obligation in the follower, which the agent can then use as a powerful tool when he wants to use persuasion. The exchange rule is very significant because it helps the agent bring the follower into the right frame of mind for the act of persuasion by instilling and overwhelming the follower with a sense of obligation. The agent may be more likely to persuade the follower to act somehow because it will have that sense of obligation hanging over him.

Another added benefit to the agent in using an exchange is that it is not just a moral position that will put the follower but also a position supported by social codes. The agent will not worry if the follower has the right moral code to return the favor. If the follower does not feel the need to do so, the agent has some tools to spur him to action.

As a society, people don't like negligent people about returning a favor or payment when offered a gift or service. If the agent has not considered that the follower will exchange it with them, they will hand it over to their social group. They can do this by telling other friends or colleagues how they did the follower a favor, but the follower never returned it when needed. Now the agent has imposed social standards on the matter by declaring favor, making it even more likely to persuade the follower to do something.

For the most part, the follower will be happy to exchange with the agent without external forces. When the favor is granted, the follower will begin looking for ways to repay the agent so that the score is even and does not seem greedy or selfish. The agent will then provide an easy solution to repay this debt; the follower will be grateful for this easy solution and will be more likely to go the way the agent wants.

Commitment and Consistency

The next weapon of influence that needs to be discussed is that of commitment and consistency. The agent will need to use both if they want to persuade someone to change their perspective. When things are consistent, they are easier to understand and help individuals make their own better decisions. It is not suitable for the agent to always change the facts he uses or change other information necessary to help the follower process the information. Rather than helping with the persuasion process, consistently staying out of consistency will make the agent seem like a liar and cannot be trusted, failing the persuasion process.

Dependability is one of the significant features of the persuasion process. It is why:

- Consistency is highly valued in society: People like things to stay a certain way most of the time. People feel safe knowing that things will remain fairly consistent overall. It allows them to remember what happened, know what to expect, and be prepared should changes occur. If consistency weren't available, things would be complicated to plan, and there would always be chaos issues around. If you want to persuade a follower of a particular thing, you need to ensure that your facts are consistent and make sense to them.

- Consistency benefits most people's approach to daily life. Have you thought of trying to plan a day out when something unexpected happens? It can make things nearly impossible to do, and it will end up looking like a disaster. People like consistency because it lets them know what to expect and what to do. They know when it's time to eat when it's time to work, and when other things will happen throughout the day.

- Consistency provides a very valuable shortcut through the complications present in modern existence. Life has been hard enough without having to add other things they haven't done since. When people can have a coherent life, it makes things a lot easier.

Consistency is a great tool because it allows the individual to make the right decisions and process information. If the agent is to persuade the follower successfully, he must ensure that his message is consistent. There is no room for false evidence that can reveal itself later and ruin the whole process. Keep the facts truthful and concise, and it is much better to persuade the argument.

Something that binds to consistency is the act of commitment. It is good to know that the follower is persuaded and that the effort has paid off. It is essential to have some commitment. In advertising, this can mean that the follower will buy the product or politics; it can mean that the follower will vote for a particular candidate. The commitment made will vary according to the nature of the persuasion. According to the consistency concept, if a person undertakes, in writing orally, he is much more likely to honor his commitment.

It has been found that this is even more true in terms of written commitments as the topic will be psychologically more concrete, and there is some hard evidence that they have accepted the commitment. It makes much sense; many people will promise that they will fix something or do something, to turn around and not do it. Sure, some people will do what they said, and they are more likely to do it if they promise orally. They don't promise, but it is often difficult to achieve the desired results this way. Plus, there's no way to back it up as an oral agreement will just become a disagreement, she said, and no one will win. On the other hand, if the mediator can produce a written commitment from the follower, he has the proof he needs that the thing has been done.

The reason it is so essential for the agent to get the follower to accept a commitment is that once the follower has committed to the new position, they have more of a disposition to act in a way that fits that commitment. After that point, the follower will continue and begin to engage in self-persuasion for the cause. Various justifications and reasons for supporting the commitment will be provided to avoid any problems with the agent. If the agent can bring the follower to that point, they will have much less work to tackle.

Societal Proof

Persuasion is a method of a standard interface and will have to follow social rules where it occurs. The people around it will influence the topic; they will be more likely to want to do what others do rather than do their own thing. The follower will base their beliefs and actions on what others are doing around them, how they act, and how they believe. For example, if the person grows up in a city, he is more likely to behave like others who come from that area. On the other hand, those who grow up in a very religious community can spend much of their time praying, learning, and helping others.

Under this influence, the saying "crowd power" can be beneficial. The follower will want to know what other people around them are doing at all times. It has become almost an obsession in this country to do what others do to fit in, even though people will say how they want to be different and be individuals.

An example of how people will do something because others can be found on the phone. If the host says something like "Operators are waiting, call now," the follower may assume that operators sit with nothing to do because no one calls them. It will make the follower less likely to call because they imagine that if someone else isn't calling, then they shouldn't either. If the host changes only a few words and instead says, "If the operators are busy, call again," the result can be very different. The follower now assumes that operators are busy with many other followers' calls, so the organization must be reasonable and legitimate. The follower is much more likely to call if they can get through right away or have to be put on hold.

The social proof persuasion technique is most effective in situations where the follower is unsure of what he will do or when there seem to be many similarities in the situations. In ambiguous or uncertain situations that require multiple choices or possibilities, the follower will often choose to conform to what others around him are doing. The choices are so similar that each one will work, but they will assume that the choice others are making is the right one. The other way social proof can be used is when some similarities occur. For example, the follower is much more likely to conform and change around those similar to them somehow. If someone is similar to the follower responsible, the follower is likely to listen and follow him more than if the response is very different from the follower.

The mediator will be able to use the idea of social proof to help with their persuasion process. The first way they can do this is to look at the words they are saying. With the given an example from the game show, both quotes said the same thing, but they got two different meanings by changing the wording. Neither was a lie; they were only useful in eliciting a different kind of response. If the agent can observe the way things are expressed, he can get the right answer from the followers and persuade the follower to follow the same ideas and beliefs.

Additionally, the agent will find that there is more successful if he can persuade those like them to share ideas. It is why politicians will try to campaign against like-minded groups. If they need to reach a larger group, they will modify their ideas to make them more attractive to these new groups.

Likeness

There is a straightforward reason or this; if the follower likes the agent, he is much more likely to say yes. Two main factors will contribute to how well the follower likes the agent. The first is physical attractiveness, and the second is similarity.

First, if the agent is physically more attractive to the follower, they will feel more persuasive since they can get what they want more quickly, also changing others' attitudes. This pull factor has proven effective in sending encouraging messages and impressions of other traits the agent may have, including intelligence, kindness, and talent. These work together to make it more likely that an attractive person will more easily persuade the follower.

The second factor, the similarity, is a little more straightforward. The idea states that if the follower is similar to the agent, they are more likely to respond in the affirmation to what the agent is asking. This process is quite natural, and most of the time, the follower won't have to think about whether it's the real thing to do when they like and are similar to the agent.

Authoritative

One of the ways the agent will be able to persuade the follower is to become an authority. Resultantly, there is an inclination for most people to believe that something an expert says about a topic is correct. The follower is more likely to enjoy listening to a reliable and competent agent; if the agent can bring these two things to the table, he is already well on his way to getting the follower to listen and believe them.

Studies have been conducted to show how this authority technique can persuade the follower to listen to what the agent says. Of course, when it comes to persuasion, pain isn't always needed to change the way people think. Conclusion This study illustrates how the follower will react to the agent if the agent can prove that he is authoritarian. Keeping this in mind can help the agent reach their agenda.

Shortage

The shortage is another form of persuasion that people may be familiar with but is often underestimated. When a product or idea has limited availability, it is more likely to be assigned a higher value. People want more of what they can't have. While it might sound like it describes a child trying to get into the cookie jar when said no, it could also describe how normal adults will act. When there is a question of scarcity to consider, the context will also matter. It merely means that, within specific contexts, the idea of scarcity could be an advantage.

The agent of persuasion will be able to use the idea of a shortage to his advantage. A way is needed to be defined to make the follower believe that the object is scarce by explaining why that object is so unique and what it does that nothing else can do. The agent will have to work on the topic right. The agent can also choose to go to the other side; instead of explaining what the customer will gain from the item or idea, they can explain what they will lose by not having the item.

There are two reasons why this principle of shortage works. First of all, when items or products are challenging to obtain, they usually gain more value. The more value an item has, the better the quality it will appear to have, even if this is not true. The second thing is that when something is not as available as it once was, the follower will realize that it will lose the ability to acquire it in the future. Once this begins to occur, the follower will begin assigning the service or item in short supply a higher value only because it will become more challenging to acquire.

A significant deal behind this principle is that the follower will want things out of their reach. If something is easy, sometimes, he'll want it as much as when the object is more complicated. If the agent can plant the idea that his thoughts, beliefs, or objects are scarce and hard to find, he will have a much greater chance of seeing success in his persuasion efforts.

Appeal to Societal Needs

After that, the agent could appeal to the follower's social needs. Although social needs are not as significant to use as primary needs, they are still an important tool that can be used. People like to be wanted and to be part of the crowd. They like the prestige that some objects can give them and feel like they belong to a higher social position. The idea of appealing to the follower's social needs can be found in most television commercials on the air; in these commercials, the viewer will be encouraged to purchase an item so that it can become famous or be just like everyone else. When the agent appeals to the follower's social needs, he can reach a new area that might interest the follower.

Use of Uploaded Imageries and Expressions

When it comes to persuasion, the choice of expressions that are made can make all the difference. There are several diverse ways to say the same thing, but one way might push the follower into action while others don't. Telling the correct words in the right way will make all the difference when using persuasion. The example on the telephone at the beginning of this chapter is an excellent example of how words can persuade followers to take action.

Persuasion is a powerful mind-control tool that is often underestimated and overlooked. Perhaps this is because it offers more choice to the follower than other forms of mind control. In the other options, the follower is forced into submission, sometimes in isolation, by the agent, and does not have much choice about what is going on in the process. In terms of persuasion, the facts presented so that the follower can decide, even if the facts are posed in a certain way, show them in the best light.

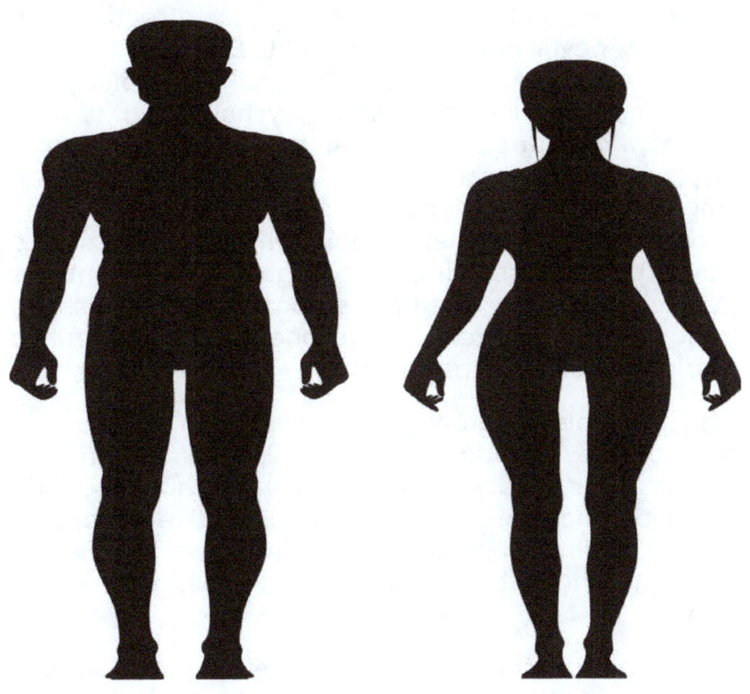

Subliminal psychology is just the tactic of influencing others using subliminal means. Subliminal means your follower isn't in the least conscious of what you're doing. They do not notice the pictures, sounds, or other stimuli you employ to condition their minds. However, the subconscious is conscious of this stuff and strongly influenced by them. The subconscious will then direct the follower's thoughts, feelings, and actions, creating an enduring and meaningful change in their life.

Subliminal psychology isn't as bad because it suggests. Subliminal psychology is just the technique of influencing someone secretly. You employ images, sounds, and conditioning to urge someone to think a particular way or do something you would like. You do not need to influence anyone directly. You certainly never need to get caught. But that does not mean you've got to use subliminal psychology for evil. You can use subliminal psychology in a wide variety of contexts. When you use subliminal psychology, you can connect with anyone. You can improve your relationships and make people pay attention to you, even people who feel superior to you. It makes subliminal psychology excellent for relationships with loved ones, romantic relationships, seduction, and parenting. No one is too powerful to work on subliminal psychology.

This psychology can also save you if you are stuck in an abusive situation. It can help you soften and soften your attacker so you can escape the dire situation and protect yourself. Abusers like to control, so use subliminal psychology to give them the illusion of submitting to them and then flee when their guard is off.

Subliminal psychology is also something you can use on yourself. What if you have trouble losing weight and engaging in a healthier lifestyle or breaking down bad habits? What if you can't stop a habit, like gambling or compulsive lying? What if you have a terrible memory that you want to forget, or want to help yourself memorize lists and remind yourself to perform specific tasks? You have the most acceptable objectives in your heart, but you do not get what you want despite your best efforts. When you feel stuck in a version of yourself that you are not satisfied with, it's time to use subliminal psychology on yourself. You can reach the depths of your mind and train your subconscious to do what you want. Then you will notice genuine changes manifesting in yourself and your life. It works so well because the subconscious mind is the only part of your mind with real power. What happens in the subconscious mind will manifest in your conscious thoughts, feelings, and behavior.

Subliminal psychology is not evil. This book will not teach you how to become an evil mind, plotting world domination in an underground lair while you rub your hands, giggling. Instead, it will teach you how to influence others for the better subtly. People hate being influenced, so you will benefit more if you can influence them in secret. Plus, the power of subliminal psychology is mind-boggling, so these methods are fail-proof. You will enjoy immense success with them. Just make sure you use these methods for good because they give you a lot of power to go wrong if you use them for evil. Learn to control your urge to dominate the world and simply use subliminal psychology to improve and promote the lives of the people you love, as well as yourself. Of course, if you use these methods for evil, it is at your own risk. You will enjoy success regardless of how you apply subliminal psychology to your life and the people you know.

Secrets of Subliminal Psychology

To employ subliminal psychology, you must first learn to understand it extremely well. The basic principle of subliminal psychology is mind-affecting or conditioning that passes below ordinary human perception limits. It means that a follower will neither notice nor realize that they are exposed to a subliminal stimulus. However, the stimulus is still present and still acting on his brain.

A person's senses are not necessarily reliable. The brain registers individual senses perceived when those senses fall within a specific range or spectrum. The brain may also register certain stimuli that are always present, but then choose to ignore them and prefer new stimuli. For example, you can see your nose 24/7. But your brain chooses not to process the image, as it's always there. So you are blind to your nose, even if your eyes perceive it a lot. You may be able to give someone a subliminal message using a constant, repetitive stimulus that the person comes to ignore. The brain still perceives it, however, and this allows the stimulus to act on the subconscious.

Something can pass below human perception if it is inaudible and falls above or below the human hearing range. Using a low tone can make a person feel depressed, even if that tone is too low for the person actually to hear. Using a high pitch can increase someone's anxiety, even though that pitch is inaudible.

It is believed that images in ultraviolet light or in other shades of the light spectrum that fall just below or above the reach of human sight can affect someone. Just because the eyes don't see the light doesn't mean they can't understand it at some level in the brain. The brain can perceive things far beyond the scope that our conscious mind perceives.

It is believed that we only use ten percent of our brains. So, imagine what the other ninety percent is capable of? You may be able to see colors or hear sounds far beyond human reach. You may be able to discern things that are not visible or audible to the naked eye or ear. It is the beauty of subliminal psychology: it penetrates the hidden side of our mind and activates responses that we don't even know we have. But the unknown aspect of subliminal psychology and how the subconscious works can make it a bit of a guessing game.

Perfume is a powerful way to condition someone, and the perfume evokes powerful feelings or memories. A person who has been abused might go crazy when he smells the cologne his attacker was wearing. A person can suddenly develop a craving for Chinese food after releasing the smell of takeout food into the room. Or he could get defensive after being exposed to the cologne scent his high school bully always carried. Perfume works so well because it instantly connects to the human brain and appeals to our primary ability to defend ourselves from ourselves by interpreting the world around us through perfume. We can't always see or hear things, but we can smell much better than we think. Our olfactory ability is incredibly strong, but most of the things we smell never become evident to our conscious brain. It is believed that a man can smell when a woman is ovulating, for example, but he won't immediately or consciously understand why he is so attracted to her.

Speed can make a stimulus subliminal. If a message or sound is fast enough, a person may not notice it. It is the technique behind subliminal advertising. The image of a Big Mac is shown on TV so quickly that people don't notice. However, part of their brains did, and now they crave McDonald's fast food.

You can use subliminal cues to unlock repressed memories in a person. These memories will then trigger a torrent of emotions and do their work on a person's behavior. A person who represses a memory has compelling reasons for doing so. The memory probably causes him considerable discomfort. Reminding him of the memory with a small hint or stimulus can throw him into a state of intense upset, terror, anger, or even confusion.

Use this information to monitor the person's behavior and perhaps even sabotage their reputation. You can also use it to help someone unlock and start healing painful repressed memories that won't go away. Remember that just because a memory is repressed doesn't mean it does not affect someone's behavior and feelings. A repressed memory can be responsible for anger, depression, drug use, and emotional feeding, even if they don't know it.

Subliminal signals or triggers are useful in hypnosis or hypnosis. When you hypnotize someone, you put them in a trance state where they are incredibly emotional. Then you can access his mind and train him to associate a trigger with a specific thought or action. For example, you could teach someone to punch a bell. When the person has returned to a conscious state, the association remains.

Then, when a trigger is presented, the person will act with the desired action. He can act with fear if he is reminded of a terrifying memory or acts with joy if he is reminded of a beautiful memory or a warm and happy memory from childhood. Her emotional response to memory can affect her mood and the decision she makes right now. It can help form associations for him even within his brain, making him harsh towards certain people or things and making him make decisions based on memories.

You can also use subliminal cues to influence your emotions without bringing out a memory. Memories are powerful emotional tools, but you can still inflict a mood on someone with no memory. Instead, flash an image or play a soft sound that is sure to affect someone's mood. A person who is terrified of spiders can become terrified for seemingly no reason if you flash a subliminal image of a spider around.

Use of Subliminal Psychology

Subliminal psychology is useful in a variety of skills. Primarily, it's used to train people to do what you want without their knowledge. It means that you can use it to persuade people to do what you want, especially if they don't initially want to.

Subliminal psychology is excellent for children. Children love to be stubborn. As a parent, you've probably learned that if you tell your child not to do something, he or she is obligated to do it. But subliminal psychology allows you to tell your child to do or not to do something, without actually saying it. He or she is less likely to resist if you step into his subconscious and plant an idea instead of telling him what to do or what not to do. She is beautiful.

It also works with other stubborn people in your life. It allows you to train family members, colleagues, roommates, and partners to do what you want when you want it. Instead of asking and fighting for what you want, make it happen. It almost works like magic.

When you work under someone, you may feel that you have no power over him or her. You are not allowed to make requests or give orders to this person. He may feel this way with the bosses, the superiors in the military, or the individuals they control in your life. But with subliminal psychology, you can make them follow your orders without them even knowing that you ordered them to go around. It will feel like his or her idea so that they will be more open to it.

You may not have a lot of relationships with a stranger. Someone as a new customer is new to you and unfamiliar to you. Since he has no reason to trust you or like you, he may be reluctant to do what you want. It may resist buying your brand or doing you a favor. You can inspire confidence and make this person want to buy your product or do you a favor by using subliminal techniques. Create a relationship that is not there and make this person want to please you, without him or her knowing why. Subliminal cues can work great for advertising or sales. It can also work when meeting new people, and relating to strangers, gaining more connections and friends.

Subliminal methods can be employed in seduction. To make someone fall in love with you or want to sleep with you, you can plant the idea of romance in their brain. Inspire him to associate with romance. This association will make him want you. You can bypass the hard work of getting to know someone and charm someone and probably fail with subliminal seduction. Instantly become attractive to others by using just a few hidden psychological tricks.

You can hypnotize yourself to train your brain to think differently. It allows you to overcome evil thoughts and problems like addictions or bad habits. You can train yourself to become the person you want to be. Get rid of bad habits, intrusive thoughts, or problems like depression and anxiety.

You can see that subliminal psychology is beneficial in many areas of life. You know that it is a beneficial skill. You can make life easier by bypassing the power struggles and efforts required to make people like you and do what you want. People will bow to your will and won't know why. They will magically feel inspired to do something, and they will not realize that it is what you want. Benefits in many ways. The best part of all is that you can avoid many failures, and the word "no." Subliminal psychology works like magic.

How Subliminal Psychology Works

Subliminal psychology works by acting on the subconscious brain. The subconscious brain is the part of your mind that works in the background, just like code works on a computer. It is the part of your mind that controls complex algorithms, telling you how to behave and think without any conscious concentration or effort on your part. You save a lot of time when processes like breathing, how to deal with strangers, and how to talk are automated in the back of your mind, instead of being frontline things in your mind that you have to think about. Imagine how distracted and overwhelmed you would be if you had to think about every little thing you do, how to manage your organs, and determine how to behave in each situation.

There are probably often situations where your behavior is automatic. Don't even think about it. You just have to do something and then wonder how you knew what to do. When this happens, your subconscious brain takes over and helps you make quick decisions. There is no need to think about why your subconscious brain is intervening.

The subconscious brain also handles a lot of memories and the way you think. It is why you may have intrusive thoughts or memories that surface randomly throughout the day. Nobody understands how or why the subconscious mind will bring out a thought or memory, but this is thought to result from conditioning. For years your mind has been trained to create an association between a stimulus and a thought or memory. So, when you are exposed to this stimulus, you think a certain way or remember something. A repressed memory can even come back, causing you considerable discomfort. You may not even be aware of what this stimulus is. It could be a perfume, an image, or a sound. Anything from your environment can cause your subconscious to remember something, even if it doesn't make sense to you.

For years your mind has been trained and conditioned in ways you don't fully understand. You have learned things without realizing that you have learned them. For example, you may have experienced fourth-grade rejection that made you nervous with the opposite sex and now believes you are a loser when it comes to romance. Or you may have learned that blue-eyed people are terrible because someone with blue eyes has abused you, so now you don't automatically like certain people based on your eye color. The great thing about this is that it means that the subconscious mind can also be retrained. You can bypass the analytical and reflective part of your brain with no control over you and slip into the subconscious. You can perform a powerful workout that will change the way someone thinks and responds to the world. You can perform this workout on yourself or others.

The subconscious mind is incredibly susceptible to influence. It's just that the subconscious mind is buried beneath our conscious thoughts, so no one is aware of it or its processes. Many individuals had no idea when they were influenced or influenced by something. All they know is that they begin to think or feel a certain way, or they start doing things differently.

Who influences a topic? Well, anyone can, in the end. Even a stranger or an advertisement managed by a multimedia platform can have an intense and significant influence on any topic. But usually, a person who has a lot of contact with the follower has the most significant influence. A romantic partner or parent is the type of person who exerts the most influence. These people can actively train and influence the follower without the follower questioning it. Getting to know someone helps because you begin to understand how to connect with this person for training purposes. But repeated exposure to the follower is the main factor that helps you achieve training. You have to have repeated contact with the person to cement the training.

People may not realize they are training others, but when you try to correct a behavior or teach your follower new behaviors, training is precisely what you are doing. It is natural and even ethical to train those around you. Often these training methods fail because you are merely projecting them into the follower's conscious mind. The follower can think about it and choose to discard them. Alternatively, they may want to undergo training, but their subconscious is trained differently and has a different acting idea. For Instance, you may need your partner to stop drinking, and he too wants to stop to please you and put his life in order. However, he drinks to deal with the pain of personal ideas and hidden memories lurking in his subconscious. Therefore, telling him not to drink and pointing out why his drinking is wrong won't do much good. You have to get his subconscious to rely on different methods or heal his wounds to banish alcoholism.

Subliminal training works by getting into the subconscious mind and doing its job there. So, it works from memory. It is why military or torturers can alter someone's personality because they repeatedly perform individual training. To achieve subliminal training, you must first find a stimulus and perform discreet training to induce the subconscious to form a definite association between the stimulus and a thought or action. Therefore, it is necessary to repeat the exposure to this stimulus several times to make it adhere.

Is Subliminal Psychology Dark?

The unfortunate fact is that the worst people and dictatorships have used this type of psychology, giving subliminal psychology a very dark and negative connotation. When you hear "subliminal psychology," you probably think of the CIA conducting mind control experiments on people or McDonald's facing a class-action lawsuit regarding subliminal advertising.

In reality, subliminal psychology is not bad unless it is used for evil purposes. Subliminal psychology is what you make it be. You can use it for evil, of course. You can train people to hate themselves or to kill themselves or to kill others. But that's not why you should use it. Use it forever. Use it to improve your life and that of others. The power of subliminal psychology isn't a joke, so don't abuse it. Instead, turn to it as a last resort to make positive changes in your life. Influence yourself and others on a deep and intimate level that allows everyone to work together peacefully and do what's best.

Subliminal psychology could allow you to save a relationship while retraining your partner to abandon relationship-destructive behaviors. It can enable you to steer your business in the right direction and avoid business catastrophes by making your business partners rethink the harmful strategy they are determined on. It can allow you to train your children to love themselves and stay away from harmful people or bad decisions they will naturally want to make as children or teens. Finally, it can even allow you to save the world. Imagine yourself in a scenario where you meet a serial killer or a manic dictator. It may sound like a fantastic scenario, but it could very well happen in today's crazy world with its vast array of mentally unstable maniacs. If you can successfully retrain a psychopath's brain from not wanting to do the wrong, he set out to do, you can save many lives, including yourself.

The ethics of subliminal psychology is undoubtedly a subject of debate. Mainly individuals will agree that it's not okay to train someone's mind against their will and without their permission. Psychologists and psychiatrists will surely agree that mind control is never ethically acceptable; the American Psychological Association bans it. Experiments with mind control and subliminal psychology are severely limited due to the ethical problems they pose. But this ethical dilemma has a vast gray area. Is it so wrong to train someone if you are improving their life and situation? If you can positively influence someone through subliminal training, then what's wrong with it? Using it forever may not be ethical, according to most people. But that doesn't mean you shouldn't do it. It's not okay to violate others or harm others with subliminal psychology, but you should certainly use it in self-defense. In situations where subliminal psychology seems acceptable to you, be your moral judge and do so if you wish.

However, subliminal psychology is not generally accepted as an ethical means of treating others. Most people are vehemently opposed to having their brains rewired by others and want to control themselves. The fundamental problem is trust. Nobody trusts you to know what's best, so they oppose your redevelopment. It is why subliminal psychology should be kept as discreet and stealthy as possible. There is nothing erroneous or dishonorable about doing this workout yourself. Subliminal psychology about yourself implies your full consent and knowledge. But it's probably best to avoid telling others what you're doing, as people tend to misunderstand what subliminal psychology is. In reality, what you are trying to do is nobody's business. So, keep using this type of psychology under wraps and only bring it out when you need it. Don't go around telling people that you are using subliminal psychology on yourself, or people will think that you are trying to hurt yourself and that you are crazy.

How Effective Is Subliminal Psychology?

The short answer to the question "How effective is subliminal psychology?" is: very useful. The long answer is that subliminal psychology is incredibly powerful but only when done correctly. Unfortunately, it is not commonly understood how to properly perform this form of psychological training, as it is not well researched due to ethical complications with such research.

When you use the appropriate methods of subliminal psychology, you will achieve great results. Some similarities tie most people together. Therefore, you must understand how human being's work. What could motivate a person? What could scare a person? All people are driven by desire or fear. They will act to get a reward or avoid something that scares them. However, you also understand that all people are different, so what might scare one person may not scare another. You need to understand what rewards and threats push different people for subliminal psychology to work. Therefore, it may take some time and research, but you should also rely on your instincts. Look for clues about how a person operates and what matters to them based on what they say to you, their photos on their desk, or the things they do in their free time.

You also need to understand that training can sometimes require several exposures. Just because a stimulus doesn't lead to an association with first exposure doesn't mean this form of psychology is crap. Some people are more resistant to training than others. Getting someone's full concentration and exposing them repeatedly to the stimulus can help form the association over time. A more violent and vivid stimulus may adhere better than a softer stimulus. Be patient, and keep working on it until it takes effect.

Finally, understand that some factors can get in the way of your subliminal mental training. A person with deep self-belief can be particularly resistant to your training because they hold on to their ideas more firmly. Meanwhile, distractions can interrupt your training, and rendering is less effective. Make sure your environment is peaceful. Try to develop trust with the person you are training. It will make training easier. Also, learn this person and their deep convictions. So, find ways to get around those ideas and replace them with better ideas. You may need to become very persistent with your training to stay, especially if other factors stand in the way. It's best to make sure no one else is working on this person and try to make your workout the most attractive and rewarding to get the person to choose to follow you if you have any competition in training.

How to Use Subliminal Psychology?

Subliminal psychology works by entering someone's subconscious mind and planting an idea or concept in it that can work in your favor. So, to use it, you want to give someone a series of undetectable signals or clues. These could be in the form of pictures, memories, or a choice of words. How you talk to someone and how you touch them can also convey ideas and plant ideas in their minds. Subliminal psychology is a sleight of hand. You are using little tricks to make someone's thinking change without their awareness. So being prominent or energetic is not what subliminal psychology is about. You will use tricks like subliminal imagery and classic conditioning to train people. You will use words, hidden signals, and physical touch. No verbal force or work is involved.

Control of Your Usage

Avoid using subliminal psychology for evil. Sure, you could use it for all kinds of bad intentions. It can certainly be used for obscure means. But do you want to be such a person? It is bad enough in the world. You can use subliminal psychology forever. Here are some tips on how to control how you use this kind of forbidden psychology to stay on the side of the light.

When you want to control or coerce someone, stop. It isn't excellent. You have no right to control another's mind. You can influence and persuade people, but don't try to control them or change who they are. Never try to get them to go against their morals and values.

When you want to use subliminal psychology to hurt someone emotionally or bring down their self-esteem, that's bad. Stop immediately. You have no right to make someone hate themselves. You can push someone to commit suicide by doing so, and then death will be in your hands.

When you want to use this psychology to get someone to do something horrible, like a crime, stop. It should never be used for crimes or illegal activities. You shouldn't get people to do evil through subliminal psychology, or you are just as guilty. You're not using it to train murderers or bank robbers to do your dirty work for you. You are merely using it to make your life easier, so leave out the legal complications.

To use it on yourself, you don't want to hurt yourself. Use self-hypnosis only forever. Don't use it to change yourself too much or to break your morals or to make you behave unnaturally. You can do a lot of harm if you start trying to change the very elements of who you are.

Leak Detection

The whole secret of this type of psychology is to avoid detection at all costs. You have to be discreet and stealthy. Use methods that help you escape detection by disassociating yourself from the source. Don't reveal you're the one showing subliminal images, for example, and don't pretend it was an unintentional accident. Always play like you're not doing this kind of psychology. When using subliminal methods, you shouldn't be detected anyway because word choice and other small gestures are hard for others to detect as it is. This type of psychology is already stealthy by nature.

Protect Yourself from Attacks

What if someone uses it on you? Now that you know its power, the idea of someone performing this type of psychology on you can be terrifying. You have every right to want to protect your mind from potential invasion and control by someone else. Also, you are wise. You'd be a fool to blab into thinking that people aren't already trying to tap into your mind. It always happens with advertising and manipulative individuals in your life. Protecting your mind is a beneficial skill to learn and develop. The first key to protecting your mind is to read people. When someone appears to have malicious intent, be very cautious. Don't let them show you the pictures and turn off the phone or TV around them. Preclude speaking to them for a long time.

Muting the TV during ads can help you avoid the subliminal effects of advertisers. You can also get up and do something instead of watching the commercial. Be aware that you are probably a subliminal psychology victim if you suddenly develop a craving for something. So, turn off the desire and don't force it. If you've prepared your mind about something and suddenly feel differently, you could be a victim of subliminal psychology as well. Stick to your visceral choice. Avoid talking to people about it. Notice how people make you feel. If you feel different than usual with a specific person, pay attention to that person. He or she can manipulate your emotions, probably subliminally. That person is toxic and not right for you.

Subliminal Psychology to Win People

Domination is a big deal at work. Everyone is fighting for power over each other. There is always a hierarchy at work, and sometimes that hierarchy doesn't obey titles. For example, if your boss is a weak leader, someone else who is not in the boss's position will likely take control and leadership and act as your superior. No matter what the hierarchy is, you probably have people you need to respond to. These people can block your way up the corporate hierarchy and can put an end to your bright and creative ideas or new policies.

Even if you're the boss, you probably have to deal with disobedient people and don't care what you want. It can frequently seem like everyone is working against you at work, and you are nobody to whom no one listens or cares. Subliminal psychology at work can offer you a position of subtle domination. Being dominant will allow you to get rid of the problem of control and allow you to gain power over everyone, even your superiors. The best part? Nobody will realize that you are dominant or have power over them, and nobody will be able to resist your control. You will rule the office, and no one will know why. No one can tell you no, harass you, or make you do what you don't want to do.

The Chair Tricks

Where and how you sit, you can portray a lot without anyone noticing. Why do you think bosses like to sit in tall chairs behind desks, while others have to sit across from them in shorter chairs? Why do you think bosses like to sit at the head of the table or choose reclining swivel chairs that allow them to rest their feet on their desks? There is a reason for this. And that reason is control. To gain dominance over people, you need to position yourself powerfully. The way you sit down can convey your power and dominance subliminally. When someone walks into your workspace, ask them to sit down. Give them a lower chair than yours, so that they look down on them. You can stand or sit on a higher chair. This height gives you an immediate advantage because it makes you look more imposing and dominant.

Add Height to Your Stature

Being taller than others and looking down on them as you speak helps get people upset. They feel immediate and natural submission and submission when you look taller. Your imposing height may not feel natural, so wear high heels or shoes that increase your height at work. And remember the chair trick described above to add height to your appearance too.

Wasting People's Time

One way to subliminally enter someone's mind and gain dominance is to dominate that person's time. Calling pointless meetings, bombarding people with small talk, and sending constant messages may not earn you much favor with your colleagues. But guess what? It continually puts you on your head and gives you a monopoly on your time. Micromanaging also makes it possible to achieve this result. By always being there, you make others think of you and assert dominance that can help you immensely in the workplace. People will look at you more when you are dominant.

Excessive Planning

When you plan too much, you subliminally send the message that you are actually in control. The moment you start meddling with plans and injecting your ideas, you tell others you are taking over. You can gain a lot of control at work by actually taking control. Regularly plan and assert your domain in all situations. Join planning committees and become one hundred percent involved in business lunches, happy hours, meetings, office parties, and work trips.

First Session

It can be rude if you sit down first in a meeting or interview. But that's just because you say you're the boss. When you sit down first, you send the message that you are in control. You are not postponing for somebody to give you directions or to sit first. Choose your seat and take it without any doubt.

Posture

Have you ever wondered why your boss likes to sit in his seat, legs on the desk? This posture of power sends the subconscious message that his time is his to spend. You can adopt this position yourself. Having an overly casual and dominant power posture at work, whether sitting or standing, makes people seem to like you're in control. You are not troubled by the stress because you are totally in control of the situation. Being overly casual and confident in how you talk, walk, and sit at your desk causes others to subconsciously associate you with being the boss, even if you're not in the boss position.

Deepen Your Voice

A more resonant, more masculine voice lends you an incredible dose of dominance, even as a woman. People will think twice before challenging you or disobeying you when you go with Barry White. Doing this can give you a lot of credibility and respect, even with your superiors. People may not notice that you have deepened your voice, but you know your little secret. Put it to work and see what happens.

The Firm Handshake and Eye Contact

Send a precise meaning that you are not afraid of anyone by maintaining clear and constant eye contact and offering a firm handshake. Offer your hand first and overwhelm the other person with your grip. People will subconsciously associate you with trust, power, and security when you do this. The handshake and eye contact are not something to sneeze at. There is a reason why it is so emphasized in the business and professional world.

Be Quiet

Silence can make you seem like you're holding back a lot of thoughts. You watch everyone calmly, making them nervous and making them a little nervous about what you think. When you hold back your judgment and sit quietly or create uncomfortable pauses, you are subliminally sending the message to others that they are doing something wrong. They will take a moment and wonder what they are doing wrong, which gives you effortless control over their thoughts and actions. You can also talk when you choose, which adds dominance to your stance. People will be surprised when you talk and listen more. They will give more importance to your words since you are so thrifty with them. Be very careful with silence, though, because if you come across as a rat, no one will pay attention to you. You want to insert dominance in your posture when you use stillness as a subliminal weapon.

Establish Dominance and Submission

All relationships have some sort of unspoken balance between domination and submission. A partner is increasingly dominant and always makes decisions.

When you establish dominance and submission, you end the need to fight because of one person delegates all decisions to the other. However, the problem in most relationships is that there is no division of power, and both partners want dominance, so they fight. You can eliminate this problem by assuming dominance using subliminal techniques. In this way, you are the leader, and your way is the law. Your partner obeys you and doesn't fight with you. Your partner is more likely to sacrifice things for you, and you don't have to anymore.

Take control of the relationship and put an end to all conflicts and power struggles. Does it seem like something your partner will never put up with? All right. Because your partner won't even guess what's going on, he or she will feel the sudden, inexplicable desire to submit to you and let you have your way. He or she won't even ask questions or put a strain on you. From one day to the following, the whole dynamic of your relationship will change in your favor. If you are a loving person, it means that they too change in favor of your partner as you gain control, because now you can take better care of your partner and provide more love.

The subliminal secret to gaining dominance is to make a power move that floods your partner's subconscious mind with respect and awe. The method to do this is to use guidance and rhythm. So, when you go out with someone, you already have some relationship. You already have a natural reflex that connects you like people in a relationship. But to strengthen your bond and set your driving mode and pace, you should start practicing mirroring regularly. Then you can start making a few small movements to see if your partner mirrors that. For example, after imitating the other person's gestures for a few minutes or even hours, flip your right hand over.

Ideally, the other person will also turn their right hand. Once someone from your partner starts following your lead, you know you've gained some control. Now you can start driving. You can guide them to do what you want just because they want to follow you. #You trained your partner. He starts using this control to start planting ideas in others' minds and guide them to new ways of thinking. They will be inclined to follow you as they already know they are following your subtle movements.

Using truly emotional language, start walking by stimulating some emotional response you desire in your partner. Playing on his hopes, doubts, fears, likes, and dislikes will increase his emotions as you wish. Summon the things that will make him think positively or negatively about something; then, you come up with another idea, and he'll associate it with his bad mood and won't want to, or he'll start thinking darker thoughts. Or vice versa to make him feel happy and more receptive to an idea.

Remember that people form strong memories and associations with their emotions. It means that while you are talking about a person, you can get someone to form a negative association by mentioning their fears concerning the person you are discussing. So you could raise your mother, an overbearing mother-in-law, to your partner to sadden him before asking him to make a decision. In his negative frame of mind, he will decide to help him avoid his mother-in-law. Bingo, you just influenced his thinking. The pace allows you to set the pace for what someone does while driving, which means that you lead someone to do what you want. Combine the two to get superpower over someone's mind.

Create A Good Vibe

The atmosphere you give off is probably the first thing people perceive when they meet you. If you show off a bad vibe, people automatically shut down and want to avoid you. It gives off a good vibe, and people will feel more attracted to you and appreciate your company. But how do you control the atmosphere you convey?

Nobody understands what makes up the vibrations that people perceive in others. Social scientists have studied it well and concluded that vibrations are likely a combination of body language, facial expression, appearance, and the associations they create between you and other people they know. But you can help the way you present yourself to others. Essentially, you want to make a great first impression and give off vibes that you are a warm and welcoming person that others can comfortably talk to.

The initial way to do this is to smile. Smile as if your life depended on it. Smile until your cheeks hurt, and you're tired of smiling. Be the first to look at someone and smile. A smile increases the good vibes you transmit to other people. Smiling and making eye contact make others think that you are the right person. They feel you like them; why else would you smile and keep eye contact? Expressing positivity with your facial expression is great for attracting others. A smile is a massive part of the good vibes you're trying to put off.

Another way to give off good vibes is to look your best. Being well-groomed, well dressed, and comfortable with your appearance increases the impression you make. People will have good vibes if you are pretty. They will feel more relaxed talking to you and appreciating you if it seems to you that you care about your appearance and that you have your stuff together. So, put in a little effort to look good and boost your confidence. Others will understand this very quickly. The more elegant or cute you are, the more confidence and warmth you will exude just because you feel good.

To increase your sense of well-being, you can try wearing charming underwear. Of course, other people may never see that underwear. But you know you're wearing them. You feel that you look great under your clothes and that gives you a nice little confidence boost. As a result, you naturally project more good vibes and safety vibes than yourself. A subliminal trick is to wear red lipstick like a woman. The red lips make you more seductive. It gives the idea that you are a warm and positive person. Find a shade that suits your skin tone and wear it when you go out to meet new people. As a man or woman who doesn't like lipstick, you could try a red tie, a red hat, or a red scarf. The splash of red can make others associate you with warmth, power, and even sex. The result will be good automatic vibrations.

Another subliminal trick for giving off good vibes is to warm your hands. When you offer your hand for a squeeze, a cold hand can make a wrong impression. A sweaty hand is also unpleasant. Then rub your hands into the pockets to create dry heat, so that when you shake someone's hand, you give them a warm and lasting impression. A trick to up the ante? Offer the person you meet a hot drink to give the idea that you are a loving person. When people hold hot drinks in their hands, they tend to associate you with that heat. Offering someone cold your coat is a courteous gesture that can charm people and give those good vibes you aim for.

Finally, you want to be positive. It could mean you have to pretend. But when you talk to someone, you don't want to sound down. You may complain a lot to new people you meet without even realizing it. When your first words to someone are, "This weather is hot, huh?" or "I'm so tired," you are projecting

negativity. It creates a hostile atmosphere, and people may feel sorry and may not make any positive association with you. Communication will most likely be reduced quickly. So, you want to minimize complaints and talk about good things instead. Offer positive comments or compliments. He looks optimistic and happy, even if you aren't. Try to say positive things to people and find ways to uplift them.

Also, you want to create similarities. People bond with similarities. You may subconsciously reject people with negativity when you say things like, "Oh, you watch films? I hate films. Not for me!" See how saying things that make you different from others can give off a bad vibe? You want to create a positive vibe by finding a similarity instead. So, going back to the previous example, maybe someone loves to watch films, and you hate it. Then say something like, "It's great that you enjoy films. I went to the theater and saw a great film." Alternatively, ask them questions to find out what else they like so that maybe you can find something to share in common and talk about. Stop rejecting people with unconscious negativity and attract them with positivity instead.

The use of psychological principles of influence and manipulation to undermine or limit the person's liberty and power is vital to understand. However, it's going to benefit the perpetrator. We call "dark psychologists" those that employ tools of influence and persuasion that harm the recipient. Dark psychology may be a tool for dark psychologists, manipulators, cheaters, or outright criminals and harassers. Of course, sometimes, the road between a standard person and a dark psychologist is often blurred. You'll also manipulate others to exact revenge or to make personal defenses. However, let's not stray within the sea of relativism. Let's be realistic. Some are "darker" than others; others are far more manipulative than others, and the other way around. Some people have more important values and ethics, and you'll more reliably expect them to be honest and fair.

Most folks have a desire to satisfy our needs and wants, and when these ideas are realized, the person is often analyzed better. The way an individual was raised and how they grew up is critical in determining what makes an individual unique. When analyzing another person, you begin by watching their visual communication. Do they hold high, or do they hide behind their bodies? How people use their eyes, face, and arms are essential for determining what they really could be like. You'll understand that their anxiety could debilitate someone who seems confident if you begin to note the way they hold themselves.

You may also find that somebody you thought you would trust is deceiving you. It is often challenging to pinpoint what a few people separate them from others and why they could behave that way. You'll never have an entire understanding of another person, but you'll a minimum of being ready to begin to know why they could act that way. Once you've got been prepared to analyze someone, you'll start persuading them. It's essential in some cases to urge what you would like or, at the very least, what you deserve. A bit like we discussed within the first book, you'll read it repeatedly, but nothing will change unless you're taking action. It is often stimulating to become conscious of yourself, but it's vital to become mindful of those around you. Once you analyze yourself, you'll persuade and convince them better. Once you do, you'll realize all the facility you've got over your own life.

instructions contained therein is the total and absolute obligation of the user addressed.

The author is not obliged, directly or indirectly, to assume civil liability for any restoration, damage, or loss resulting from the data collected here. The respective authors retain all copyrights not kept by the publisher.

The information contained herein is solely and universally available for information purposes. The data is presented without a warranty or promise of any kind.

The trademarks used are without approval, and the patent is issued without the trademark owner's permission or protection.

The logos and labels in this book are the property of the owners themselves and are not associated with this text.